Mainstream AIDS Theatre, and Gay Civil Rights

This book demonstrates the political potential of mainstream theatre in the U.S. at the end of the twentieth century, tracing ideological change over time in the reception of U.S. mainstream plays taking HIV/AIDS as their topic from 1985 to 2000. This is the first study to combine the topics of the politics of performance, LGBT theatre, and mainstream theatre's political potential, a juxtaposition that shows how radical ideas become mainstream, that is, how the dominant ideology changes. Using materialist semiotics and extensive archival research, Juntunen delineates the cultural history of four pivotal productions from that period—Larry Kramer's *The Normal Heart* (1985), Tony Kushner's *Angels in America* (1992), Jonathan Larson's *Rent* (1996), and Moises Kaufman's *The Laramie Project* (2000). Examining the connection of AIDS, mainstream theatre, and the media reveals key systems at work in ideological change over time during a deadly epidemic whose effects changed the nation forever. Employing media theory alongside nationalism studies and utilizing dozens of reviews for each case study, the volume demonstrates that reviews are valuable evidence of how a production was hailed by society's ideological gatekeepers. Mixing this new use of reviews alongside textual analysis and material study—such as the theaters' locations, architectures, merchandise, program notes, and advertising—creates an uncommonly rich description of these productions and their ideological effects. This book will be of interest to scholars and students of theatre, politics, media studies, queer theory, and U.S. history, and to those with an interest in gay civil rights, one of the most successful social movements of the late twentieth century.

Jacob Juntunen is Assistant Professor in the Department of Theater and in the Women's, Gender, and Sexuality Studies Program at Southern Illinois University, USA.

Routledge Advances in Theatre and Performance Studies

For a full list of titles in this series, please visit www.routledge.com.

13 **The Provocation of the Senses in Contemporary Theatre**
Stephen Di Benedetto

14 **Ecology and Environment in European Drama**
Downing Cless

15 **Global Ibsen**
Performing Multiple Modernities
Edited by Erika Fischer-Lichte, Barbara Gronau, and Christel Weiler

16 **The Theatre of the Bauhaus**
The Modern and Postmodern Stage of Oskar Schlemmer
Melissa Trimingham

17 **Feminist Visions and Queer Futures in Postcolonial Drama**
Community, Kinship, and Citizenship
Kanika Batra

18 **Nineteenth-Century Theatre and the Imperial Encounter**
Marty Gould

19 **The Theatre of Richard Maxwell and the New York City Players**
Sarah Gorman

20 **Shakespeare, Theatre and Time**
Matthew D. Wagner

21 **Political and Protest Theatre after 9/11**
Patriotic Dissent
Edited by Jenny Spencer

22 **Religion, Theatre, and Performance**
Acts of Faith
Edited by Lance Gharavi

23 **Adapting Chekhov**
The Text and its Mutations
Edited by J. Douglas Clayton & Yana Meerzon

24 **Performance and the Politics of Space**
Theatre and Topology
Edited by Erika Fischer-Lichte and Benjamin Wihstutz

25 **Music and Gender in English Renaissance Drama**
Katrine K. Wong

26 **The Unwritten Grotowski**
Theory and Practice of the Encounter
Kris Salata

27 **Dramas of the Past on the Twentieth-Century Stage**
In History's Wings
Alex Feldman

28 **Performance, Identity and the Neo-Political Subject**
Edited by Matthew Causey and Fintan Walsh

29 Theatre Translation in Performance
Edited by Silvia Bigliazzi, Peter Kofler, and Paola Ambrosi

30 Translation and Adaptation in Theatre and Film
Edited by Katja Krebs

31 Grotowski, Women, and Contemporary Performance
Meetings with Remarkable Women
Virginie Magnat

32 Art, Vision, and Nineteenth-Century Realist Drama
Acts of Seeing
Amy Holzapfel

33 The Politics of Interweaving Performance Cultures
Beyond Postcolonialism
Edited by Erika Fischer-Lichte, Torsten Jost and Saskya Iris Jain

34 Theatre and National Identity
Re-Imagining Conceptions of Nation
Edited by Nadine Holdsworth

35 Nationalism and Youth in Theatre and Performance
Edited by Angela Sweigart-Gallagher and Victoria Pettersen Lantz

36 Performing Asian Transnationalisms
Theatre, Identity and the Geographies of Performance
Amanda Rogers

37 The Politics and the Reception of Rabindranath Tagore's Drama
The Bard on the Stage
Edited by Arnab Bhattacharya and Mala Renganathan

38 Representing China on the Historical London Stage
From Orientalism to Intercultural Performance
Dongshin Chang

39 Play, Performance, and Identity
How Institutions Structure Ludic Spaces
Edited by Matt Omasta and Drew Chappell

40 Performance and Phenomenology
Traditions and Transformations
Edited by Maaike Bleeker, Jon Foley Sherman, and Eirini Nedelkopoulou

41 Historical Affects and the Early Modern Theater
Edited by Ronda Arab, Michelle M. Dowd, and Adam Zucker

42 Food and Theatre on the World Stage
Edited by Dorothy Chansky and Ann Folino White

43 Global Insights on Theatre Censorship
Edited by Catherine O'Leary, Diego Santos Sánchez & Michael Thompson

44 Mainstream AIDS Theatre, the Media, and Gay Civil Rights
Making the Radical Palatable
Jacob Juntunen

Mainstream AIDS Theatre, the Media, and Gay Civil Rights
Making the Radical Palatable

Jacob Juntunen

Routledge
Taylor & Francis Group
LONDON AND NEW YORK

First published 2016 by Routledge

2 Park Square, Milton Park, Abingdon, Oxon, OX14 4RN
605 Third Avenue, New York, NY 10017

Routledge is an imprint of the Taylor & Francis Group, an informa business

First issued in paperback 2020

Copyright © 2016 Taylor & Francis

The right of Jacob Juntunen to be identified as author of this work has been asserted by him in accordance with sections 77 and 78 of the Copyright, Designs and Patents Act 1988.

All rights reserved. No part of this book may be reprinted or reproduced or utilised in any form or by any electronic, mechanical, or other means, now known or hereafter invented, including photocopying and recording, or in any information storage or retrieval system, without permission in writing from the publishers.

Notice:
Product or corporate names may be trademarks or registered trademarks, and are used only for identification and explanation without intent to infringe.

Library of Congress Cataloging-in-Publication Data

Names: Juntunen, Jacob.
Title: Mainstream AIDS theatre, the media, and gay civil rights: making the radical palatable / by Jacob Juntunen.
Description: New York: Routledge, 2016. | Series: Routledge advances in theatre and performance studies; 44 | Includes bibliographical references and index.
Identifiers: LCCN 2015038257
Subjects: LCSH: Gays and the performing arts—United States. | Homosexuality in the theater—United States. | Theater—United States—History—20th century. | American drama—20th century—History and criticism. | Homosexuality in literature. | AIDS (Disease) in literature.
Classification: LCC PN1590.G39 J86 2016 | DDC 791.086/640973—dc23
LC record available at http://lccn.loc.gov/2015038257

ISBN: 978-1-138-94172-4 (hbk)
ISBN: 978-0-367-73732-0 (pbk)

Typeset in Sabon
by codeMantra

For the dead

Contents

Acknowledgments		xi
	Introduction	1
1	Repairing Reality	14
2	Resistance: *The Normal Heart*	32
3	Assimilation: *Angels in America*	60
4	Commercialization: *Rent*	97
5	Normalization: *The Laramie Project*	125
6	Conclusion: *Does It Get Better?*	163
	Index	177

Acknowledgments

This book developed over a period of 15 years, so any acknowledgment section is bound to be incomplete. But even before this project began, the faculty at Clackamas Community College (CCC) gave me a home when I needed one, particularly Sue Mach, Kay Davis, and Allen Widerburg. CCC's student writers' group offered me a place to hone my creative writing, which led to my becoming a playwright—something I could never have foreseen. Without that, I would never have even considered the questions of mainstream theatre's effect on society.

At Reed College, my professors demonstrated what an academic life could be, often generously opening their homes to me. Of these, I am especially grateful to Lisa Steinman, Gail Sherman, and Roger Porter for hospitality and patience. I still return to William Ray's literary theory course pack, without doubt one of the most significant seminars I ever experienced. I am also indebted to my fellow undergraduates, too many to name. At the time, I thought my peers and I engaged in scholarship, but I now see it was the serious play of youth that trained me for what is, I hope, more mature thought.

At Northwestern University there are again too many generous peers to thank, but I need to single out my doctoral cohort, Sheila Moeschen and Shelly Scott, for crucial moral and emotional support. I was also lucky to meet Jyoti Argade, Rashida Braggs, Suk-Young Kim, Christina McMahon, Lauren McConnell, Jeffrey McCune, Stefka Mihaylova, Jesse Njus, Natsu Onoda Power, Sam O'Connel, Coya Paz, Elaine Peña, Tamara Roberts, Emily Sahakian, Rashida Shaw, Jon Sherman, Ioana Szeman, Jennifer Tybursczy, Anne Folino White, and Katie Zien. However, without my most dedicated reader at Northwestern, Dan Smith, much of whatever insight this book contains would not exist.

As for faculty during my time at Northwestern, many made a lasting impression on me, but this book's ideas owe most to Jennifer Devere Brody, Scott Curtis, Susan Herbst, Craig Kinzer, Chuck Kleinhans, Lisa Merrill, Sandra Richards, Anna D. Shapiro, Harvey Young, and, of course, Tracy C. Davis, whose rigor still serves a constant, unattainable benchmark for me.

The University of Illinois, Chicago (UIC) provided me with crucial employment while I finished doctoral work. The entire theatre faculty acted kindly to their young colleague, and Yasen Peyankov deserves considerable credit for managing to get my adjunct contract renewed repeatedly. At UIC, Anthony Graham White provided early mentorship in what it means to be faculty. Southern Illinois University (SIU) presented me the stability to complete this project, finally, and everyone in the departments of Theater and Communication Studies have shown nothing but kindness during my initial years. In particular, Anne Fletcher's generous guidance and willingness to discuss at length the writing of this book delivered the crucial energy to cross the finish line.

The amazing, unique, collaborative theatre community of Chicago has influenced my art and scholarship in ways I am sure I do not begin to understand. The Chicago artists I met and worked with after my move from the West Coast offered me a generosity of spirit and an adventurous appetite to explore theatre. The MFA students at Northwestern were crucial for connecting my scholar and playwright halves. The Chicago theatres with which I have been fortunate enough to work as a playwright or dramaturg have never failed to inspire all my thinking on theatre, both scholarly and artistic. Most notably, the side project, Steep Theatre, Chicago Dramatists, TUTA, and the late-Caffeine, Mortar, and Infamous Commonwealth Theatres provided me vital proving grounds.

I was fortunate enough to have a second chance at graduate school when I better understood what I was doing. At Ohio University (OU), the professors and students greatly enhanced the ideas of this book; especially, William Condee. Charles Smith, Erik Ramsey, and Annie Howell changed how I think about dramatic writing forever. Similarly, the playwrights of Ohio University's MFA program have become generous collaborators. While they may be surprised to know it, our conversations about playwriting have deeply influenced some of the ideas in this scholarly book. Chief among my collaborators are Rebecca Abaffy, Greg Aldrich, Andrew Black, Sarah Bowden, Mark Chrisler, Anthony Ellison, Ira Gamerman, Chanel Glover, Bianca Sams, and Jeremy Sony. Greg has provided, and continues to provide, support for me and my family. This support has been instrumental in making SIU home.

At OU I also met Angela Ahlgren, who would later become my writing partner, providing crucial external "deadlines" when no official ones existed, and kindly reading drafts of chapters.

The students I have had the honor of teaching at Northwestern, UIC, and SIU have all honed the ideas of this book. I hope they see some of themselves in it.

James Fisher provided me with my first publication when he accepted an early version of Chapter Two in his edited volume, *We Will Be Citizens: New Essays on Gay and Lesbian Theatre*. That chapter has also had versions published in a special issue of *Peace and Change* edited by Heather Fryer and Robbie Lieberman and online at HowlRound.com, edited by Polly Carl. I appreciate all of their permissions to include revised material from these articles. Early versions of this book's thesis also gained strength at conferences, particularly ATHE, ASTR, ACLA, and the International Conference on American Theatre and Drama. There, I met many scholars whose conversations, however brief, shaped this book. Particularly helpful were Cheryl Black, Sarah Bay-Cheng, and Julia Walker, who provided valuable feedback on early conference papers about *Angels in America* and *The Laramie Project*.

My parents have been patient and generous. When I dropped out of high school, they encouraged me to enroll in community college. When I refused, they gave me space to explore the world, as I needed. When I finally attended CCC, they did not say they told me so but paid my way and graciously allowed me to move back in, wounded pride and all. I was also privileged enough, and had a lucky enough birth, for my parents to all but pay for Reed. Without their generosity, without their support, financial and emotional, I would never have the amazing privilege of thinking, writing, and teaching for a living.

Finally, Meghann Pytka has given me everything, and I hope I have returned as much. She has never known me without this book being in progress, though she has known me a decade. Many ideas in here are owed to our years of conversations. Luckily, I know there are many years' worth of topics left for us to discuss.

This book would not exist without all these people, and many more. Thank you.

Introduction

In 2015, the United States Supreme Court heard the case of Obergefell v. Hodges and legalized marriage between two people of the same sex. In the aftermath of the decision, most images in the national press pictured attractive pairs of men and women proudly holding wedding certificates, newly married same sex couples standing on court steps, or crowds of revelers outside the U.S. Supreme Court waving brightly colored rainbow flags. Some of the most moving pictures presented men and women late in life who were finally recognized as legal domestic partners by the nation, many after decades of cohabitation. These men and women tended to look as shocked as they did joyful, as if in a dream. And perhaps, in some respects, it was a dream, for a nation changing who is allowed new rights and responsibilities is a type of reimagining.

What changed literally overnight for these couples was their inclusion in the national legal code, and what is a legal code except for a set of shared beliefs, an embodiment of the dominant ideology? The Supreme Court decision of Obergefell v. Hodges legitimized an ideology that people of the same sex should be able to marry. While not universally hailed as a noble decision, and narrowly passed by a 5-4 majority, support for same-sex couples' right to marry had risen steadily from 2001 to 2015, changing from 57% of the U.S. population opposed to 55% in favor.[1] The court reflected this shifting ideology in its decision. Support was particularly robust among young Americans, those called Millennials and born loosely between 1983 and 2004, with 70% in favor of gay marriage in 2015.[2] In 2015, when the majority of these young people supported the state-legitimated union of two same sex individuals in love, many Millennials would have been shocked to know that a short 30 years earlier tens of thousands of gay men were dying in the U.S. because of a plague and social invisibility.

The ubiquity of gay characters in mainstream entertainment and profound achievements in gay civil rights in 2015 belie the complexity of how much changed in the representation of LGBT[3] citizens in the U.S. since the HIV/AIDS epidemic struck the U.S. in the early 1980s. In terms of legal representation, every U.S. state now has a queer representative at some level of government.[4] In mainstream entertainment, LGBT characters are now commonplace, and their sexuality so conventional that it need not be the focus of the narrative's plot. But in 1985, it was possible for a character in a play to state that he grew up believing he was the only gay person on earth, and offstage a similar social invisibility allowed the HIV/AIDS epidemic to strike dreadfully among U.S. citizens. What changes in culture allowed for the increased visibility of LGBT citizens in the United States? How did the emergent ideology that gay men and women were part of the U.S. nation become part of the dominant ideology? Did theatre, and, in particular, mainstream theatre, play any role in this transformation?

Without question, HIV/AIDS struck the gay community hard in the 1980s and 1990s, and a robust theatre movement rose up to address the massive loss of life. In his 1998 work *Acts of Intervention*, David Román assesses in the moment the accomplishments of late twentieth century HIV/AIDS theatre. This imminently hopeful book suggests that readers engage in the power of "AIDS theatre and performance [to] create new ways of imagining community in the face of crisis."[5] Román's wide-ranging book skillfully interprets early 1980s AIDS fundraisers, unheralded early AIDS plays, commercial successes, solo performance by white gay men, and ensembles of gay men of color. The heterogeneity of his book is part of Román's own intervention as he strives to point out the function and necessity of each type of performance, to reassign performances off the mainstream stage a place in theatre history. In fact, he sees the commercial success of mainstream AIDS plays such as *As Is* and *The Normal Heart* as obscuring earlier, equally important if not as heralded performances. Román writes that for the Broadway and off-Broadway productions of *As Is* and *The Normal Heart*, "The actual venue of the performance, along with its geographical location in the city, inscribes the performance into already marked (albeit veiled) ideologies based on the artistically conservative conventions and tastes of cultivated, mainstream, elite audiences."[6] What is striking about this description is the implicitly derogatory portrayal of mainstream theatre. The representation of mainstream theatre as a "veiled" deception of the "market" leading these AIDS plays into "conservative conventions." Román depicts mainstream plays like *As Is* and *The Normal Heart* writing over the history of "various plays and performances already in circulation throughout the early 1980s."[7] And to some degree he is right. Certainly contemporaneous critics reviewing *As Is* and *The Normal Heart* did not seem to be aware that these were not the first plays to deal with HIV/AIDS. But, by studying mainstream plays produced in privileged venues in New York City, *Making the Radical Palatable* reveals how these plays actually influenced the type of national reimagining that Román desires.

Mainstream theatre in the U.S. played an important part in assimilating emergent ideologies into the dominant ideology throughout the twentieth century. However, in the process, it often erased the more radical expressions that came before. While the African American civil rights movement is not analogous to the gay civil rights movement, superficial similarities in theatre production history are instructive. Langston Hughes' 1935 Broadway production of *Mulatto* set a record for the number of performances for a play by an African American, but overshadowed previous, more radical, Harlem Renaissance plays. In fact, Hughes' play came under attack from within the African American community because it portrayed undesirable stereotypical elements of African American characters, such as uneducated speech. Similarly Lorraine Hansberry's, *Raisin in the Sun*, taking its title from a Hughes' poem, gave Broadway its first female African American playwright, first African American director, and Sidney Poitier's first major role. But, in 1959, *Raisin in the Sun* was not as radical as the bourgeoning Black Arts Movement. Nevertheless, on the twenty-fifth anniversary of Hansberry's play, Frank Rich writing in *The New York Times*, stated that *Raisin in the Sun*, "changed American theatre forever."[8] These examples show the potential of mainstream theatre to shift what is acceptable on the U.S. stage, and, thus, within the dominant ideology of the national imagination.

Consequently, even as they erased more radical performances, mainstream plays taking HIV/AIDS as their topics participated in a tremendous ideological shift surrounding the representation of LGBT citizens. This moment of reform was both cultural and legal. Román reminds readers that HIV/AIDS was not just an illness, that it could not "be separated from the discourses that construct[ed] it and, in fact, sustain[ed] it."[9] The fifteen years following the 1985 opening of *The Normal Heart*—a play that cried out for recognition of gay men as "normal"—was a period of great national reorganization in the U.S. around the topic of LGBT citizens. In that short time, the dominant ideology shifted towards LGBT visibility within the culture industry and the body politic. The simultaneous normalization of LGBT citizens and commercialization of HIV/AIDS signaled a tension within the United States' dominant ideology that can be traced through onstage representation. The conflict between the emergent ideology of LGBT inclusion in the national imaginary and a residual ideology of LGBT social invisibility created a two steps forward, one step back pattern of LGBT civil rights change, and the chronological order of this book's case studies in no way advocates positivism. Setbacks plagued every victory of the LGBT community throughout the end of the twentieth century. But examining mainstream theatre's representation of HIV/AIDS and LGBT civil rights helps mark this movement and answer important questions. Why were HIV/AIDS plays so popular in New York City during those fifteen years? How did the representation of people with HIV/AIDS change? How did that relate to changes in representation of gay characters? And how did the reception of these plays shift over time?

Making the Radical Palatable investigates the importance of mainstream theatre's role in reforming and redefining the dominant ideology in the United States, demonstrating mainstream theatre's crucial place of activism within the culture industry. The book advocates for a rethinking of the supposedly conservative nature of mainstream theatre. It shows instead that while emergent ideologies develop from radical subject positions, only by incorporating emergent ideologies into a mainstream setting can they become part of a new national imaginary and thereby shift the dominant ideology. Mainstream theatre assimilates and capitalizes on emerging discourses, often to the dismay of the originators of the radical ideology. The distress comes during the assimilation process, when the radical is tamed and made palatable for a mainstream audience. While the radical ideology may in the process lose some of its teeth, the wide spread dissemination that occurs from inclusion in the culture industry is the only way to shift the dominant ideology. The plays examined in this book, then, were not only commercial successes within the elite, conservative culture industry. They were also complex sites of ideological transmission to audiences, to readers of media reviews, and even to those who simply knew of the plays' existences. After all, simply understanding that plays on Broadway dealt sympathetically with LGBT characters shifted the dominant ideology away from the social invisibility that helped lead to tens of thousands of HIV/AIDS deaths.

Matters of visibility and radical performance are at the heart of previous writing on the politics of performance. In 1999, only a year after Román's recovery of HIV/AIDS performance beyond mainstream theatre, the noted scholar of politics and performance, Baz Kershaw, articulated what he saw as a crisis in contemporary theatre: modern capitalism was bleeding theatre of its radical potential.[10] To overcome theatre's powerlessness, Kershaw proposed a turn to radical "performance beyond the theatre" to engage the tensions caused by "the conformity forced on cultural production by capitalist consumerism."[11] In other words, to produce representations of ideological positions onstage not bound by profit-motivated "conformity," Kershaw argued that one must utilize performance beyond the stages of mainstream theatre, such as parades, protest, and theatre taking place in non-typical environments. But do these radical performances produce the same type of visibility as a Broadway production with the attendant reviews, advertising, and merchandising? Building on Kershaw's insight that radical performance is the venue in which new political structures of feeling can be created, *Making the Radical Palatable* establishes that mainstream theatre can incorporate a tame version of these emergent ideologies and sell them to a large, heterogenous audience. In the process, mainstream theatre can integrate a palatable version of radical performance's politics into the dominant ideology.

A few years earlier, in 1997, the distinguished NYU theatre professor David Savran declared skepticism of mainstream theatre similar to Kershaw's, suggesting that in the U.S. "our 'classic texts' … [have] a way of conceptualizing utopia so that it may be adopted by 'the dominant culture … for its purposes … Utopianism has served … to diffuse or deflect dissent, or actually to transmute it into a vehicle of socialization.'"[12] Román's incredulity here related to *Angels in America*, one of the most mainstream AIDS plays of the 1990s. He feared that the culture industry's acceptance of the play's optimism and utopianism drained the production of social critique and, instead, made it one more way that the dominant ideology socialized U.S. citizens. But, in order to make a profit, *Angels in America* portrayed a gay male ensemble sympathetically, and audiences empathized with them. The question inherent in Savran's critique of the play's socialization, then, is whether this show harmed the gay rights movement through its commercialized portraits of gay men or helped by portraying gay people sympathetically in the mainstream. The answer hinges on one's feelings about assimilation. If one is looking for a radical restructuring of society, then assimilating gay men into the dominant ideology is counterproductive. However, if one looks to expand the rights and representation of gay men within the current legal system, then assimilation is worthwhile. *Making the Radical Palatable* takes the latter view as its premise, and thus holds that the type of integration via commercialization Savran describes may be a way to fruitfully expand the U.S. body politic.

If the mainstream stage was fenced in by profit-motivated conformity, what accounted for the dramatic changes in LGBT representation between 1985 and 2000? And if plays like *Angels in America* were simply vehicles of socialization for the dominant ideology, what exactly were the ideologies they promoted? What ideological changes can one trace in the conditions of production, production texts, and conditions of reception in mainstream AIDS theatre during these 15 years of rapid civil rights victories by the U.S. LGBT community?

To explore these questions, this book examines the New York City premieres of four of the most prominent plays to take HIV/AIDS as a topic in the U.S. at the end of the twentieth century: Larry Kramer's *The Normal Heart* (1985), Tony Kushner's *Angels in America* (1993), Jonathan Larson's *Rent* (1996), and Moisés Kaufman's *The Laramie Project* (2000). These plays each embody a turning point in the representation of LGBT characters and people with HIV/AIDS on mainstream stages in New York. *In toto*, this selection of case studies shows how gay men and HIV/AIDS were incorporated into the dominant ideology, going from social invisibility to normalization. Taken separately, each case study illuminates pressing concerns of the contemporaneous moment and allows one to see change over time, particularly in the plays' press receptions.

Theatre scholars have studied the politics of performance, and researchers in cultural studies have delineated systems that promote, maintain, and challenge ideologies, and, while these fields are often connected, the place of mainstream theatre and its surrounding discourses to date have not received major study.[13] *Making the Radical Palatable* reveals mainstream theatre's important place in creating a space in the U.S. national imaginary for LGBT citizens at the end of the twentieth century while also addressing the political potential of mainstream theatre more generally. In so doing, the book shows how radical ideas become mainstream, that is, how the dominant ideology changes. This knowledge is necessary for artists, activists, and academics to utilize and theorize theatre's power.

Most research on LGBT theatre focuses on reclaiming obscured performances or highlighting radical performances that dramatically challenged the dominant ideology. What these studies tend to overlook, however, is how those radical beliefs became palatable to a majority of Americans. Thus, LGBT theatre is the starting point that allows *Making the Radical Palatable* to explore how an emergent ideology became part of the dominant ideology, looking at a specific example in order to suggest a more general theory of political theatre. It does so using its case studies as a way of understanding political change in terms laid out by cultural theorist Raymond Williams: a model of society possessing simultaneous, competing types of ideology—emergent, dominant, and residual—alongside his understanding of where new ideologies come from, structures of feeling.

Furthermore, the majority of scholarship on gay theatre in the 1980s and 1990s does not trace ideological change over time. Examining four plays that take HIV/AIDS as topics from 1985 to 2000, this study is able to track the ideological change in the discourse that surrounds them using the media theories of James Carey, founder of Columbia University's Communications PhD program. Carey suggests that mass media, such as newspapers, engage in transmission of information but also in a ritualized act of representing shared beliefs.[14] Therefore, by tracking how newspapers incorporated—or, to use the philosopher Louis Althusser's term, *interpellated*—representations of LGBT characters and stage pictures of HIV/AIDS, one can see how the U.S. nation's shared set of beliefs shifted quickly towards an ideology that called for gay civil rights over this 15-year period.

Why do theatre scholars so rarely address mainstream theatre's ability to support emergent ideologies? Perhaps there is some subtle manifestation of antitheatrical prejudice at work in theatre scholarship itself,[15] but more likely the scholarly hesitation to comment on mainstream theatre's potential liberal effects dates back to the enmity towards the culture industry first expounded in 1944 by cultural critics Max Horkheimer and Theodor Adorno in *Dialectic of Enlightenment*.[16] Researchers often cite that work as evidence that entertainment produced in the mainstream culture houses of a society cannot critique said society. However, Horkheimer and Adorno rely almost solely on a transmission view of communication—that is, a piece of art has a message and relays it to the viewer—and do not note that different viewers may interpret the same art differently, as cultural critic Stuart Hall and the Birmingham School demonstrate in their writing focusing on how readers "decode" texts.

The work on politics and performance is riddled with this prejudice against the culture industry. There is a long-standing interest in the events of 1968, for instance, that makes the standard for political performance coterminous with street demonstrations and the takeover of public buildings. Perhaps as a Gen Xer who primarily teaches Millennials, it is difficult for me to find the violent and assassination-filled 1960s nostalgic. And for my students, 1968 is as far away historically as the First World War was to the students killed at Kent State. Instead of a radicalism based on a 1960s aesthetic, then, I am interested in a substantial change in who constituted a member of my nation's imagined community during my lifetime. In other words, I am excited at the change from my 1980s childhood in the San Francisco Bay Area during which gay people, even in my region, were largely absent from mainstream culture to a point in history where gay people may legally marry. Instead of applying cultural theory alongside material semiotics to understand this change and theatre's part in it, queer scholarship has tilted towards reconstruction and recuperation—valuable and important work, to be sure, but not the explanatory work necessary to understand the late twentieth century accomplishments of the gay civil rights movement.

Some prejudice against commercialism itself, particularly from scholars of a Marxist bent, is also at work in eliding mainstream theatre's liberal potential. While the plush, red velvet seats of mainstream theatre in New York City may not welcome everyone—a complaint leveled against mainstream theatre—the powerful elite of this country, those who aspire to that clout, and those who report for influential news outlets inhabit those seats. Changing what these elites believe may lead to corresponding change in the nation's imagined community, and, eventually rule of law. It did so in the case of LGBT civil rights in the U.S. at the end of the twentieth century, which is why HIV/AIDS theatre from 1985 to 2000 is such a rich case study to understand a changing nation.

Placing an emphasis on ideological change over time, the first chapter of *Making the Radical Palatable* explicates keywords. Since ideology is such a contested concept, it is important to align its use in this volume with the scholars that inform the book's understanding of the term. These are Althusser and Williams, primarily, taking from Althusser the idea that ideology is an unconscious lens through which people see the world, and from Williams a model of change through structures of feeling in a mix of emergent, dominant, and residual ideologies. However, since both Althusser and Williams were neo-Marxists, it is important to locate this book's use of their concepts *outside* the culture industry framework of the Frankfurt School. To that end, Chapter 1 contextualizes *Dialectic of Enlightenment* within European history, to show that, as a product of its time, it overestimates the power of propaganda and the dominant ideology. Nevertheless, the simultaneous use of materialist analysis and rejection of Marxist pessimism regarding the culture industry requires further explanation than mere historical contextualization of the Frankfurt School.

To this end, the first chapter provides an account of how mainstream theatre works in concert with the media to help create the national imaginary. Political theorist Benedict Anderson's interest in newspapers' expansion of ideology across a nation is part of this explanation of the national imaginary, but even more so are James Carey's thoughts on journalism since that was his specialty. Expanding beyond the news media, the first chapter also situates mainstream theatre spectatorship within the Birmingham School's reader response theories and suggests along with theatre scholar Susan Bennett that the peripherals of the production—the neighborhood, program notes, and advertising—are crucial to understanding the ideological transaction taking place when one attends the theatre. Examining the production text as a multifaceted object beyond what happens onstage communicates an actor network theory *á la* the sociologist Bruno Latour into which the four case studies may be placed and analyzed.

The remaining four chapters are each dedicated to a single case study, every one constituting a particular turning point in mainstream theatrical representation and reception of gay characters in plays from 1985 to 2000 that take HIV/AIDS as their topics. While some films during the period also represented similar themes, this study is primarily interested in the effects of mainstream theatre. Thus, it focuses on plays, and if it mentions films, does so to provide context. Besides, mainstream theatre more quickly took on the subjects of HIV/AIDS. The plays each mark a significant shift in how AIDS plays were received/interpellated, which means that they differ in significant ways. While all take HIV/AIDS as a topic and portray gay men on the mainstream New York stage, this book questions the assumption that all mainstream theatre must suffer a conformist straightjacket. Instead, by placing the productions firmly into their historical and material contexts, *Making the Radical Palatable* demonstrates the variety and volatility of mainstream theatre and its political potential. First and foremost, as the title suggests, this book demonstrates how some aspects of each case study were radical enough to usher in ideological change while other aspects were palatable enough to be produced in a mainstream venue.

This is, then, by no means a survey of LGBT theatre in the 1980s and 1990s. *Making the Radical Palatable* does not seek a breadth of case studies. Instead, it examines productions in depth, making use of a methodology suggested by Savran in which productions' "cultural and economic positions" are prized above authorial intention.[17] And whereas each spectator would have brought his or her own expectations, hopes, and desires to the productions under study, *Making the Radical Palatable* utilizes reviews as archival sources of representative responses. While not every spectator will be represented by reviews, understanding how a review by a liberal gay critic in the *The Advocate* differs from that of a conservative critic in *The Wall Street Journal* gives a sense of how the same production was incorporated into varying ideological standpoints. By concentrating on the material performance and reception of four premiers in New York City, *Making the Radical Palatable* shows how mainstream theatre helped change the dominant ideology over one 15-year period. It aims to encourage others to examine political aspects of mainstream theatre in different geographies and eras.

HIV was declared an epidemic in 1983, and performances ranging from benefits to vigils to theatrical works sprang up almost immediately. However, a play that is frequently heralded as the "first" play to address HIV/AIDS is the subject of the book's second chapter: Larry Kramer's *The Normal*

Heart produced off-Broadway at the Public Theatre in 1985. Regardless of claims to primacy, *The Normal Heart* was, as Román notes, "the most notorious AIDS play of the 1980s ... [because it] relentlessly castigated the various structures of power contributing to the AIDS crisis."[18] As such, it was one of the first HIV/AIDS plays to command a multiplicity of reviews in national papers, an important aspect of the production as AIDS was still relatively unknown at the time of the play's production. Further, because Kramer based the play on actual events, such as his role in forming the activist group Gay Men's Health Crisis, the play was received more as activist journalism than as theatre. This was reinforced by the Public's advertising campaign, the set design, and the lobby displays that held informative material and ways to get involved in the fight against HIV/AIDS. While many reviews found the artistry of the play lacking, nearly all found its subject matter compelling, making it an important beginning of making gay men and the disease visible in national discourse.

The third chapter centers on Tony Kushner's *Angels in America: A Gay Fantasia on National Themes*, produced on Broadway in 1993. Unlike *The Normal Heart*, critics received this play as art and almost immediately canonized it, from reviews comparing Kushner to classic U.S. playwrights to a landslide of academic writing about the production. Most important about this play, however, is the fact that reviewers frequently declared it "universal." That is, instead of being received as a propaganda play about a narrow segment of the population—as *The Normal Heart* was labeled—*Angels in America* was hailed as a play that, as its subtitle suggested, was about matters relevant to the entire nation. In part, its Broadway appeal depended on conservative aspects of the script, such as its lack of class or gender critique, but, in so doing, it reimagined middle-class, white, HIV-positive gay men as potential U.S. citizens. Its famous end, though, was in the future tense: "We will be citizens,"[19] suggesting that there was more work to be done even if this production was a major turning point in gay representation.

The fourth chapter's subject, the 1996 musical *Rent* by Jonathan Larson, may seem a step backward for LGBT civil rights because its dual protagonists are each straight, white, middle-class men. However, as already noted, there is no need to believe in a forward progression of gay civil rights. And, besides, *Rent*'s large ensemble included a host of ethnicities and sexualities, including *Making the Radical Palatable*'s first examples of onstage lesbians, bisexuals, and transgender characters, which provided support to the emergent ideology of LGBT representation. And, of all the plays examined here, *Rent* was the most commercially successful. While commercializing the HIV/AIDS epidemic and the gay civil rights movement may prove distasteful to some, it is also a sign that the dominant ideology in 1996 was willing to interpellate certain aspects of an emergent ideology in order to sell them. *Rent* was hardly a radical play, but its conservative aspects, which harken back to U.S. entertainment's melodramatic roots, made it possible to sell a production that included the spectrum of LGBT characters alongside relatively frank conversations about HIV/AIDS to adolescents from the suburbs, their parents, and tourists. Beyond the effects of the production onstage, the original cast album debuted at #19 on the Billboard charts, and the merchandising for the play included color spreads in popular magazines like *People* and *Rolling Stone,* putting the play's message out to a national audience that might not be able to see the Broadway production. The popularity of this national merchandising, again, hinged on the play's very conservative aspects, but without them its more progressive aspects—such as complete LGBT Broadway representation—would not have been possible.

Finally, in Chapter Five, the book investigates a play that through an appeal to emotion and Christian compassion successfully represents a gay, HIV-positive man as a U.S. citizen, just like *Angels in America* prophesied. That play is *The Laramie Project,* written by Moisés Kaufman and the Tectonic Theater Project, produced off-Broadway in 2000. A docudrama based on over 200 interviews with the citizens of Laramie, Wyoming, after the brutal murder of the openly gay University of Wyoming student Matthew Shepard, *The Laramie Project* successfully argues against the "gay panic defense" in a representation onstage of a gay man deserving full protection of U.S. law. This approach was particularly successful because the play was based on actual events, and the dialogue was based on verbatim lines from interviews, so spectators supposed that *The Laramie Project* was a more thorough examination of Shepard's murder than the sound bites heard throughout the crime's immense media coverage. And because of the play's context, coming as it did two years after a flood of journalism about Shepard's murder and during a campaign by the Bill Clinton Administration to create hate crimes legislation that protected LGBT citizens, the play was received as a synecdoche for the nation. That is, rather than simply representing Laramie, reviewers reported on the play as if it were a stand in for the United States. And, if that were so, then the play's rejection of the gay panic defense, and the normalization of Shepard as a gay man with HIV, represents a turn in stage representation to a more full citizenship for LGBT individuals.

Each chapter begins with a brief prologue and ends with a short epilogue. These do not assume an audience familiar with the historical context of the plays discussed. For instance, while Shepard's murder was major national news between 1998 and 2000, his name no longer resonates as it once did. Thus, each prologue serves as a quick contextualization that gives the necessary information to understand the circumstances that are expanded within the chapter itself. The epilogues suggest the importance of each particular case study before moving on to the next production in question. In this way, the prologues and epilogues serve as signposts along the way within the manuscript. The conclusion of the book brings the previous chapters together and goes beyond the confines of the case studies' periods and theatre as a medium.

Giving reign to the ability of media such as film, television, and the Internet to distribute representation beyond what live performance can do, the conclusion points to how ritual communication can also take place in the culture industry outside the theatre. Each of the case studies was made into a film between 2002 and 2014, and the conclusion posits how the screen versions of the films may have affected the dominant ideology of the U.S. and furthered the work begun by the plays' theatrical debuts. Further, the conclusion examines the popular "It Gets Better" videos initiated by gay journalist Dan Savage in which over 50,000 people ranging from celebrities to random teens with laptops assure LGBT citizens that, if they are experiencing bullying or prejudicial treatment, the future will be "better." This project boasts corporate sponsors, a video from U.S. President Barack Obama, social media sites, a staff, and merchandise. In one sense, the examination of the "It Gets Better" project is the book's most conjectural section because it relies almost exclusively on textual analysis instead of a more full examination of conditions of production and conditions of reception.

However, in another sense, the "It Gets Better" project is the book's most concrete evidence that invisibility of LGBT U.S. citizens is now an impossibility. While there is still much work to be done before true equality exists for LGBT citizens in the U.S., no LGBT youth can feel like the only gay person in the world with 50,000 "It Gets Better" videos accessible via any Internet connection. In fact, though only three decades ago LGBT youths might have thought they were alone in the world, that world is beyond the memory of those who grew up or were born after 2000. Therefore, demonstrating mainstream theatre's place in this ideological change is important both to understand how the dominant ideology changes in general, but also to specifically remember the pain of LGBT citizens who grew up and perhaps died of HIV/AIDS, violence, or despair and suicide due to social invisibility. This book is for them.

Notes

1. http://www.pewforum.org/2015/07/29/graphics-slideshow-changing-attitudes-on-gay-marriage/.
2. http://www.pewforum.org/2015/07/29/graphics-slideshow-changing-attitudes-on-gay-marriage/.
3. The case studies of *Making the Radical Palatable* primarily represent characters who are lesbian, gay, bi-sexual, or transgender, with gay men by far the most prominently represented group. Therefore, this book primarily makes use of the acronym LGBT instead of the more inclusive LGBTQ or LGBTQA acronyms.
4. Phil Reese, "2012 Proving a Busy Year for Victory Fund," *Washington Blade*, 26 April 2012.
5. David Román, *Acts of Intervention: Performance, Gay Culture, and Aids* (Bloomington: Indiana UP, 1998), 284.
6. Román, *Acts of Intervention*, 123.
7. Román, *Acts of Intervention*, 58.
8. Frank Rich, "*Raisin in the Sun* Anniversary in Chicago," *New York Times*, 5 October 1983.
9. Román, *Acts of Intervention*, xxiii.

12 *Introduction*

10. Baz Kershaw, *The Radical in Performance: Between Brecht and Baudrillard* (London: Routledge, 1999), 5.
11. Kershaw, *The Radical in Performance*, 16.
12. David Savran, "Ambivalence, Utopia, and a Queer Sort of Materialism: How *Angels in America* Reconstructs the Nation," in *Approaching the Millennium: Essays on Angels in America*, ed. Deborah R. Geis and Steven F. Kruger (Ann Arbor: U of Michigan P, 1997), 32.
13. The study of politics and performance is a deep and rich field, as is that of cultural studies, and many scholars' work deeply informs the arguments in this book. Those who have written on LGBT theatre and AIDS theatre, besides the aforementioned Román and Savran, and provided this book's foundation include David Bergman, Michael Cadden, John Clum, Kate Davy, Elin Diamond, Jill Dolan, James Fisher, Nicholas de Jongh, Allen J. Frantzen, Deborah Geis, Steven F. Kruger, D.S. Lawson, Thomas L. Long, Sally Munt, Emmanuel S. Nelson, Nick Salvato, Robert Schanke, Alisa Solomon, Sara Warner, and Stacy Wolf. A number of scholars beyond Kershaw have combined cultural studies and theatre research and informed the methodologies utilized in this book, such as Phillp Auslander, Susan Bennett, Herbert Blau, Jennifer Devere Brody, John Bull, Marvin Carlson, Dwight Conquergood, Tracy C. Davis (whose insistence on evidence of efficacy led to this book's main argument of ideological change over time in reviews), Lizbeth Goodman, Graham Holderness, Amy Hughes, Barbara Kirshenblatt-Gimblett, Ric Knowles, Anne McClintock, Lisa Merrill (who first suggested reviews of productions could be a worthwhile site for contemporaneous ideological evidence), Peggy Phelan, Janelle Reinelt, Rebecca Schneider, Eve Kosofsky Sedgwick, and Harvey Young. There are also many theorists of ideology dating back to the earlier half of the twentieth century whose notions are critical for this book's arguments: Theodore Adorno, Louis Althusser, Benedict Anderson, Walter Benjamin, Susan Buck-Morss, James Carey, Terry Eagleton, Erika Fischer-Lichte, Clifford Geertz, Stuart Hall, Susan Herbst (whose early guidance led to much of this book's use of political theory), Nadine Holdsworth, Max Horkheimer, Richard Johnson, Bruno Latour, Raymond Williams, and Lambert Zuidervaart. This book would not be possible without the strong foundations provided by these intellects.
14. James W. Carey, *Communication as Culture: Essays on Media and Society* (Boston: Unwin Hyman, 1989), xviii.
15. Jonas A. Barish, *The Antitheatrical Prejudice* (Berkeley: University of California Press, 1981).
16. Max Horkheimer and Theodor W. Adorno, *Dialectic of Enlightenment* (New York: Continuum, 1997).
17. Savran, "Ambivalence," 32.
18. Román, *Acts of Intervention*, 61.
19. Tony Kushner, *Angels in America: A Gay Fantasia on National Themes, Part Two: Perestroika* (New York: Theatre Communications Group, 1993), 147.

Bibliography

Barish, Jonas A. *The Antitheatrical Prejudice*. Berkeley: University of California Press, 1981.

Carey, James W. *Communication as Culture: Essays on Media and Society*. Boston: Unwin Hyman, 1989.

Horkheimer, Max, and Theodor W. Adorno. *Dialectic of Enlightenment*. New York: Continuum, 1997.

Kershaw, Baz. *The Radical in Performance: Between Brecht and Baudrillard*. London: Routledge, 1999.

Kushner, Tony. *Angels in America: A Gay Fantasia on National Themes, Part Two: Perestroika*. New York: Theatre Communications Group, 1993.

Reese, Phil. "2012 Proving a Busy Year for Victory Fund." *Washington Blade*, 26 April 2012.

Rich, Frank. "*Raisin in the Sun* Anniversary in Chicago." *New York Times*, 5 October 1983.

Román, David. *Acts of Intervention: Performance, Gay Culture, and Aids*. Bloomington: Indiana UP, 1998.

Savran, David. "Ambivalence, Utopia, and a Queer Sort of Materialism: How *Angels in America* Reconstructs the Nation." In *Approaching the Millennium: Essays on Angels in America*, edited by Deborah R. Geis and Steven F. Kruger, 13–39. Ann Arbor: U of Michigan P, 1997.

1 Repairing Reality

Prologue

This book began with an image of the legalization of gay marriage in the U.S. and its celebration, but this development, that some LGBT activists saw as a move towards a more perfect union, was not seen as a panacea by everyone in the gay civil rights movement. Rhodes Scholar Colin Walmsley, writing in the *Huffington Post*, describes two very different 2015 Gay Pride celebrations in New York City after the landmark Supreme Court decision. At one, $80 could afford one a ticket to an outdoor concert and megaparty billed as "one of the world's top tier LGBT events."[1] The other, just across the Hudson River, was an impromptu party by homeless LGBT youth. While recognizing that both groups celebrated the recent victories of the gay civil rights movement, Walmsley worried that, "Although marriage is a declaration of love, in many ways it is also an expression of interpersonal stability, economic security and social respectability—attributes that many marginalized LGBT people do not have."[2] Walmsley's concern was that the homeless LGBT youth, primarily lower-income and people of color, would not enjoy the benefits that came with marriage.

Nevertheless, Walmsley supported the movement to legalize gay marriage, understanding it as a tactic to win mainstream support for the LGBT movement more broadly. He writes, "The fight for gay marriage suggested that the gay community had grown up, left its radical past behind … replaced it with a more wholesome image that mainstream America found more palatable."[3] For Walmsley, then, the Supreme Court decision was a double-edged sword. On the one hand, it conferred new rights and status on LGBT citizens. On the other, these rights primarily went to the privileged class of LGBT citizens who had the wealth and stability to take advantage of them. Walmsley fretted that such a division could bifurcate the LGBT community into an advantaged, assimilated class and a more radical, uncared for "fringe" community of LGBT people.

This danger is well noted, but what Walmsley's argument inherently suggests is not that the gay marriage decision was a setback, or that assimilation is, in itself, problematic. Instead, he implicitly hopes in his article that *more* of the LGBT community will be assimilated and have the advantages of legal respect and protection. While some might see this type of assimilation as a radical shift in the U.S. national imaginary, it is more of a liberal shift. A useful, if simplistic, delineation between the two terms might be that a radical wants to fundamentally change the structure of society while a liberal, as a product of the Enlightenment, wants to include more people within the existing and expanding structures of legal protection. Walmsley's line of reasoning, and that of this book, is firmly in the liberal camp.

In order to be part of a liberal nation, one must be assimilated by it.[4] For good or for ill, that is the fundamental lesson of the Enlightenment, under the strictures of which we still live. If one is seen as property, chattel, or otherwise less than human, one will not be part of the nation's imagining of itself. In other words, if one wants the protections and the oppressions that come from the U.S. Constitution, Bill of Rights, and legal code, one must fulfill the current definition of citizen. That definition, thankfully, is malleable. Examining the mainstream theatre in which LGBT characters appeared between 1985 and 2000 helps show how.

Art is part of how a nation defines the imaginary boundaries that enclose some people and omit others. It is also a barometer of how a particular group is received in a nation. As the cultural anthropologist Clifford Geertz notes, art in a nation is "a story they tell themselves about themselves."[5] The self-definition that takes place in national art is part of a rich web of signification that helps define an acceptable citizen. But it is not a static classification. Not only does the national imaginary change, it must be constantly performed. Every day performances great and small, from national elections to newspaper headlines, are the tools with which nations "are created, maintained, and transformed."[6] It stands to reason that the most prominent art—that is, the art within the mainstream, or what others might call the culture industry—is the most determining art of a nation's daily constituency. Why, then, has the scholarship on politics and performance concentrated primarily on radical art outside mainstream theatres?

To some degree, theatre scholars focus on radical performance due to a prejudice against mainstream theatre that suggests a play produced in the culture industry cannot bite the hand that feeds it by critiquing the economic structure of which it is a part. This begins with the Frankfurt School of thought early in the twentieth century and is not wrong but overlooks the ideological complexity of an artistic transaction within the culture industry. For instance, in his foundational study on the politics of performance, Baz Kershaw writes of mainstream theatre that seems to have liberal content: "These plays *appear* to be attacking the injustices produced by late capitalist hierarchy and exploitation in modern democracies, but in the process of being staged in theatre buildings, in submitting to contemporary theatre as a disciplinary machine, they succumb to what they attack."[7] The insight here is that one cannot take a play's content at face value, and a conservative setting, such as the culture industry, affects the play's ideological message. But a play's ideological content is not black and white. That is, one should not assume a production is exclusively radical or conservative. Instead, looking at a specific production with as much nuanced analysis as possible often shows aspects of radical, liberal, and conservative politics simultaneously available to a spectator. And, besides what the production text encodes, each spectator will decode the production differently as well.

In order to examine productions with such specificity, materialist semiotics may be used. Kershaw points to the theatre building as a disciplinary system, and materialist semiotics includes an analysis of the theatre's architecture as well as all conditions of production, such as the neighborhood, advertising, historical context, and the text's development history. Beyond studying the conditions of production and the production text—including *mise-en-scène*—materialist semiotics likewise examines the conditions of reception. Thus, reviews, program notes, merchandizing, and other peripheral aspects of the production that would influence spectators' receptions are examined. Taking all these variables into account shows how mainstream AIDS theatre in the U.S. culture industry at the end of the twentieth century helped the emergent ideology of gay civil rights enter the dominant ideological discourse. But, beyond its oft-assigned negative definition opposing it to radical and alternative performance, what exactly is mainstream theatre?

Mainstream is a label ubiquitously applied to many cultural artifacts that are popular, commercial, and widely disseminated. Those are indeed aspects of mainstream theatre in the twentieth century, but a definition needs more precision. Popular with whom? Is the profit motive of a Broadway production the same as an off-Broadway theatre's non-profit attempt to make money to put back into the organization? And because theatre, by its location-specific nature, will never be as widely disseminated as film or television, what line must be crossed before a play is disseminated enough to be considered mainstream? In answering these questions, it is again useful to appeal to specificity and to the fact that mainstream theatre's definition must be *relational* rather than *essential*. That is, rather than claiming that a production is mainstream or not, there is a spectrum on which one can measure a production's mainstream status. For instance, Broadway and off-Broadway are the theatrical loci of U.S. theatre, and productions housed there are likely to have national press coverage, advertising campaigns spanning multiple states to cater to New York's tourist trade, and, if successful, national awards, that will carry their titles across the United States. By contrast, a production at a large Equity—that is, union contracted—theatre in Chicago will certainly be mainstream in Chicago, complete with local press coverage and advertising that reaches the many millions that live in Chicago and its suburbs, but it may not have the national reach of Broadway and off-Broadway. Moving down the spectrum, a small, 30-seat theatre in a remote Chicago neighborhood with advertising only consisting of posters hung in local coffee shops will not qualify as a radical performance as defined by scholars such as Kershaw, but is certainly not as mainstream as Broadway or Chicago's Equity theatres. However, even that 30-seat theatre in Chicago will receive reviews in the local press and be eligible for area awards.

And there are far more factors: is a movie star in a Chicago production? Is a production of a musical premiering in a town outside New York before transferring to Broadway? Is a regional production part of a national tour that originated on Broadway? These and other aspects may all add to a production's mainstream status.

Many of the qualities that made up the traits that led to a theatre production's mainstream status in the U.S. at the end of the twentieth century were economic connections to the culture industry. For instance, because sizeable ticket sales were a primary goal, an ideal audience for mainstream theatre was the largest and most inclusive group possible with varied backgrounds, political beliefs, and personal identities. Similarly, in the hope of promoting ticket sales, a production would likely have had an official, gala opening night, to which all major reviewers were invited, leading to reviews in high-subscription periodicals. A well-known venue also contributed to mainstream theatre's social visibility, and, hence, ticket sales. All these attempts to sell tickets also facilitated mainstream theatre's "registration into theatre history."[8] The mainstream review process—far larger than that of alternative theatre or radical performance—functions as history's first judgment of the production. And a popular or "landmark" production at a theatre may secure more spectators at following shows, in some case leading avant garde troupes, such as The Wooster Group, down a path from alternative to mainstream theatre complete with commercial touring shows.

Capitalism's ability to incorporate and sell radical performances as mainstream leads to the skepticism many scholars of politics and performance feel towards the liberal political potential of mainstream theatre. Elin Diamond, in her decisive text examining performance and cultural politics, assigns conservative disciplinary power to theatre and gives radical performance the ability for "dismantling textual authority, illusionism, and the canonical actor in favour of the polymorphous body of the performer."[9] Similarly, in the introduction to *Performance, Identity, and the Neo-Political Subject,* Matthew Causy and Finton Walsh write that "capitalism sees in the fracturing of identity a wonderfully lucrative commercial project" of which mainstream theatre is a part and that radical performance may resist.[10] But if mainstream theatre and, by extension mainstream culture, can only reflect the dominant ideology to which it sells its products, what accounts for shifts in mainstream entertainment? Is mainstream theatre merely reflective of political change that is accomplished elsewhere? Or, can mainstream theatre help to effect change?

Making the Radical Palatable demonstrates that mainstream theatre is able to simultaneously incorporate elements of an emergent ideology while reproducing enough of the dominant ideology to be palatable within the culture industry. Although the object of study in *Making the Radical Palatable* is the U.S. gay civil rights movement at the end of the twentieth century, to understand the book's position one must first understand that it has an atypical interpretation of the Frankfurt School's culture industry concept.

First proposed in 1944, the typical culture industry notion fuels the pessimism of much scholarship on politics and performance. But when the culture industry's largely ignored WWII context is invoked, one can see that the typical view gives too much power to the dominant ideology. Likewise, to understand this book's suggestion about how mainstream theatre functions in liberal political change, one must understand how *Making the Radical Palatable* specifically utilizes the term *ideology*. Like the culture industry, ideology is often employed in work on political performance in a particularly pessimistic Marxist fashion. *Making the Radical Palatable* understands ideology based on Marxist foundations but also utilizes the Birmingham School's insights to help account for change in the national imaginary. The concept of the nation in this book is heavily reliant on Benedict Anderson, but equally so on media studies, particularly James Carey's theories of mass communication and newspapers. Before moving on to the case studies, then, each of these concepts must be dealt with in turn.

The Culture Industry in Context

In 1938, soon after what would be their final meeting, Walter Benjamin wrote to Theodor Adorno of a great sadness. Benjamin wrote from Paris, and Adorno would soon sail for New York with his wife, all in exile from Nazi Germany. Benjamin told his great friend and collaborator, "as regards the sadness I referred to above, there were, apart from my presentiment, sufficient reasons for it. For one thing, it is the situation of the Jews in Germany, from which none of us can disassociate himself."[11] Indeed, the Nazis stripped Benjamin, a German Jew, of German citizenship, and he spent three months in a French prison camp as a stateless man. Though he was released, Benjamin would not survive the war, dying at his own hand after he was unable to escape Europe despite a visa to the U.S. that colleague Max Horkheimer had negotiated. It was in this environment that Horkheimer and Adorno wrote *Dialectic of Enlightenment* in which they coined the phrase, "the culture industry."

While the work's central tenets—that mainstream art has become a commodity and that it and twentieth century political slogans are similarly structured—are brilliantly argued, for 70 years the culture industry concept has been used primarily without contest or contextualization. All texts are products of their times and must be understood as such in order to properly utilize their insights. Ideas are not transportable from one time to another without some translation. The culture industry concept has often been taken wholesale, from 1944 to the present; thus it has continued an overestimation of the power of the culture industry to control the masses in writing on political theatre. The literary theorist Terry Eagleton writes that for Horkheimer and Adorno, "Capitalist society languishes in the grip of an all-pervasive reification, all the way from commodity fetishism and speech habits to political bureaucracy and technological thought. This seamless monolith of a dominant ideology is apparently devoid of contradictions."[12] This means that, according the Horkheimer and Adorno's use of the culture industry, no space exists within mainstream art for resistance to the dominant ideology. In this way, citing *Dialectic of Enlightenment* has been used to justify a distrust of mainstream theatre.

Given their concern with what they call the "hordes … of Hitler youth,"[13] it is not surprising that Horkheimer and Adorno view the masses as hot wax on which propaganda—such as *Triumph of the Will*—can imprint a hateful worldview. Their colleague, Siegfried Kracauer, also offers this explanation for ordinary Germans' behavior during World War II in his foundational work on German film *From Caligari to Hitler*, so blaming the culture industry for Nazi Germany's heinous crimes obviously held weight in the moment. But excusing Nazi soldiers' guilt due to media indoctrination is not born out by historical evidence that has since come to light.

In the quintessential work on the psychology of German soldiers who killed Polish Jews during World War II, Christopher Browning finds that the majority of his historical subjects were not particularly ideologically motivated. The Major who commanded the unit Browning studied in depth was not even "considered SS material" by his Nazi superiors.[14] What drove the men to murder unarmed civilians, including women, children, and infants, was not Nazi media inculcation, but simply a desire to conform and submit to authority, more in the vein of the psychology experiments of Phillip Zimbardo[15] and Stanley Milgram[16] than a particular susceptibility to propaganda.[17] And the major vulnerability that the European Jews—such as Benjamin—faced was their lack of state protection, their want of citizenship.[18] Which is why, though it is not an analogous situation, *Making the Radical Palatable* particularly notes the question of citizenship surrounding LGBT people in the United States, especially when threatened by HIV/AIDS in the 1980s and 1990s. Without full citizenship, a person is not protected by the mechanisms of the nation. But Horkheimer and Adorno wrote before historical work demonstrated the rationale used by ordinary men who became genocidal killers, and *Dialectic of Enlightenment* exhibits the belief that Nazi propaganda stood as a prime mover for the chaos of World War II.

This is in large part because Horkheimer and Adorno believe spectators to be blank slates on which the culture industry may write. But the work of Stuart Hall and the Birmingham School contradict this uncomplicated view of ideological transmission. Hall suggests that regardless of how a text is "encoded," it may be "decoded" in three distinct ways: the dominant-hegemonic position in which the viewer completely believes the text;[19] the negotiated position in which the viewer agrees with the "dominant definition of events while reserving the right to make a more negotiated application to 'local conditions';"[20] and, finally, the oppositional mode in which "events which are normally signified and decoded in a negotiated way begin to be given an oppositional reading."[21] Horkheimer and Adorno's view of spectators as *tabula rasa* on which media prints itself is defied by Hall's work and is, perhaps, partly a product of their formalist analysis.

Horkheimer and Adorno make the formalist mistake of giving priority to structure over context. Their formal analysis that "works of art, suitably packaged like political slogans, are pressed on a reluctant public at reduced prices by the culture industry" remains as relevant in 2015 as on the day they wrote it.[22] But their equivalence of Nazi propaganda and 1940s U.S. entertainment takes neither context nor content into account. This lack of contextual specificity leads to Horkheimer and Adorno's suggestion that the culture industry can only support the dominant ideology, one that, whether fascist or capitalist, must be conservative. One can see this in comparisons of Nazi propaganda and U.S. entertainment throughout *Dialectic of Enlightenment*. Take, for example, a discussion of the NBC Symphony Orchestra, created for U.S. radio in 1937 and directed by the exiled anti-fascist Italian Arturo Toscanini:

> Each note of the symphony is accompanied, as it were, by the sublime advertisement that the symphony is not being interrupted by advertisements—"This concert is brought to you as a public service." The deception takes place indirectly *via* the profit of all the united automobile and soap manufacturers, on whose payments the stations survive, and, of course, *via* the increased sales of the electrical industry as the producer of radio sets ... It thereby takes on the deceptive form of a disinterested, impartial authority, which fits fascism like a glove. In fascism radio becomes the universal mouthpiece of the *Führer*; in the loudspeakers on the street his voice merges with the howl of sirens proclaiming panic, from which modern propaganda is hard to distinguish in any case. ... The gigantic fact that the speech penetrates everywhere replaces its content, as the benevolent act of the Toscanini broadcast supplants its content, the symphony.[23]

In one paragraph, Horkheimer and Adorno proceed from a formal analysis of the economics of a U.S. radio broadcast by a man in exile for defying Mussolini, to a comparison of Hitler's voice ringing in German streets alongside sirens, and back to the Toscanini concert as if each false "benevolence" is equivalent. While the insight that seemingly free broadcasts in the U.S. are nevertheless advertisements *par excellance* is brilliant, the content of a symphony and that of Hitler's speeches are at great odds, as are the contexts of these broadcasts. But Horkheimer and Adorno's analysis suggests that content is replaced and supplanted by its medium: radio, a device that is part of the culture industry. But if one were to look at the conditions of production, the performance text, and the conditions of reception, one would find fundamental differences between the NBC symphony and Hitler's speech. This lack of specificity drives contemporary scholarship's mistrust of mainstream theatre, and largely motivates the suggestion that mainstream AIDS plays could not have swayed the public with the same liberal efficacy as alternative theatre or radical performance. Horkheimer and Adorno's work has, as Eagleton noted, too much confidence in the power of the "dominant ideology." But what exactly does that term mean? And how does mainstream theatre fit in the ideology of the nation that wields a particular culture industry?

Mainstream Theatre and Ideology

Between 1981 and 2000, the AIDS epidemic swept through the United States, infecting 774,467 U.S. citizens and killing 448,060 of them[24]—nearly eight times the U.S. military dead in Vietnam.[25] While this was a medical issue, it was also one of ideology. President Reagan did not mention the disease in public until 1987 when 36,058 U.S. citizens were diagnosed with the disease and 20,849 were dead from it.[26] By contrast, in 2000 President Clinton declared AIDS a national security threat.[27] This change constituted more than the difference between Republican and Democratic administrations. It represented a fundamental shift in how AIDS was *seen* by the U.S. government, that is, a change in the dominant ideology. The change in ideology surrounding AIDS in the 1980s and 1990s was not due to any one factor, but to a host of actors, including activists, politicians, media, the medical establishment, and cultural texts. Often thought a toothless part of the culture industry, mainstream theatre was one of the prime actors in this ideological fluctuation, incorporating emergent ideologies into the dominant ideology and, through marketing and reportage, disseminating these new beliefs.

Ideology is a polysemous word, with usage beginning in the French Revolution, and rather than try to define it, this chapter seeks to explain how it is used in this book. Such explanation is necessary because *Making the Radical Palatable* often hinges its arguments on evidence of ideological work. Eagleton's useful primer *Ideology: An Introduction* begins with a list of 16 potential definitions,[28] but for *Making the Radical Palatable*'s purposes, ideology "is a 'representation' of the imaginary relationship of individuals to their real conditions of existence."[29] In other words, ideology is a lens through which people see the world. No matter the society, or the organization of that society, there is always ideology providing meaning and interpretation to an individual's experience. This is, of course, Louis Althusser's view of ideology. He further suggests that "ideology 'acts' or 'functions' in such a way that it 'recruits' subjects among the individuals (it recruits them all), or 'transforms' the individuals into subjects (it transforms them all) by that very precise operation ... called *interpellation* or hailing, and which can be imagined along the lines of the most commonplace everyday police (or other) hailing: 'Hey, you there!'"[30] For Althusser, then, a variety of forces, from schools, families, churches, legal institutions, art, and media, all "hail" an individual and "interpellate" that person into a particular ideology. This is the bedrock theory on which this book's ideological foundation rests, but, like the Frankfurt School's view of the culture industry, Althusser's view of ideology gives too much credit to the dominant ideology.

As many have pointed out since Althusser's formulation of ideology in the 1970s, he assumes a passive reception of the dominant ideology's hail. Eagleton pithily points out, "What if we return the reply: 'Sorry, you've got the wrong person?'"[31] Eagleton acknowledges that we must be interpellated as *some* type of subject in society, but not necessarily the subject we are hailed as. Raymond Williams, writing a few years after Althusser, accepts the basic concept of ideology as an "unconscious ... imposed structure."[32] But Williams finds the concept of interpellation too monostic and instead posits a constellation of ideological positions within a single society that represents three differing reactions to hails of ideological state apparatuses.

It is important to understand Williams' three aspects of ideology and his "structure of feeling" concept because *Making the Radical Palatable* relies on them as a model for how change occurs. When this book argues that mainstream theatre holds a place in helping an emergent ideology become assimilated into the dominant ideology, these are terms taken directly from Williams. Thus, while ideology as a whole in this book is an unconscious lens through which we view the world, it can nevertheless be broken down into three important reactions we have to hailing by art, culture, and other ideological state apparatuses. These three ways of interpreting the world, Williams designates the dominant ideology, residual ideologies, and emergent ideologies. Briefly, the dominant ideology is the hegemonic, though not totalizing, world-view that most of the culture agrees upon.[33] A residual ideology was "formed in the past ... but is still active in the cultural process."[34] And, probably most important to understand mainstream theatre's political potency, an emergent ideology is not merely "novel," but genuinely "some new phase in the dominant culture ... and those which are substantially alternative or oppositional to it."[35] For Williams, an emergent ideology comes from a "structure of feeling," a first way of experiencing and articulating "living processes [that] are much more widely experienced."[36] Art is often "among the first indications that such a new structure is forming,"[37] and a difference between a structure of feeling and an emergent ideology is that a structure of feeling is in the present tense, forming, inchoate, whereas an emergent ideology is already to some extent formed and in the past tense. Thus, if mainstream theatre is firmly situated in the culture industry—that is, the dominant ideology's economic and ideological center—and one can trace an emergent ideology becoming more and more a part of the mainstream theatrical productions, that ideological change over time is evidence of mainstream theatre's place in political change. That is the situation in *Making the Radical Palatable*'s case studies, which demonstrate that from 1985 to 2000 the emergent ideology of gay civil rights was in part through mainstream theatre incorporated into the dominant ideology of the U.S. nation.

Mainstream Theatre and the Nation

If a lack of protection from the state, that is, a lack of inclusion in the national imaginary, was deadly for Benjamin and millions of other European Jews, how did gay men's place in the U.S. national imaginary affect their survival during the HIV/AIDS crisis in the 1980s and 1990s? Returning to Hall's theories about decoding in relation to a concrete example of how a gay man might have been hailed in the 1980s during the AIDS crisis is useful to illustrate this question. In 1985 reviews of *The Normal Heart*, a journalist describes HIV/AIDS as a problem caused by the "homosexual lifestyle."[38] If a gay man encountered this article, he would be hailed by it as an agent in the U.S. nation that was producing the catastrophic illness that was devastating his community. He could respond, according to Hall's line of reasoning, in three ways. If the reader accepted the dominant ideology as expressed by the newspaper review, he could internalize the view of the world in which his sexuality was problematic and, even, fatal. If he read the review through a negotiated framework, he might believe that gay men were to some extent responsible for the spread of HIV/AIDS—perhaps he might blame a perceived promiscuity of some gay men, for instance, while believing that not *all* gay men were to blame. Or he might reject the review's ideology altogether. In this oppositional reading, he might blame the statement on a reviewer's homophobia and blame the spread of HIV/AIDS on the inaction of government public health programs. But it is important to note that even when totally in opposition, the reader must nevertheless in some way incorporate the view. That is, the reader must acknowledge that such views exist, even if he is in complete disagreement. Thus, when examining the case studies, if a major paper like the *New York Times* writes a review suggesting that LGBT people are citizens, even a person completely opposed to such a view must accept that the nation's paper of record expressed such a belief. That is part of why newspapers are so important to theories of the nation.

But before understanding the place of media in the national imaginary—which is crucial archival evidence for ideological change in *Making the Radical Palatable*—one must first understand how "nation" has been conceptualized as a performed, imaginary, and changeable entity. Primarily based on Benedict Anderson's foundational text *Imagined Communities*, *Making the Radical Palatable*'s expressed understanding of nation also uses James Carey's media theory, sociologist Jürgen Habermas' social theory, and Bruno Latour's agent-network theory, putting particular emphasis on the power of media in general and newspapers in specific to maintain and change national conceptions at the end of the twentieth century.

In *Imagined Communities*, Anderson defines a nation as "an imagined political community—and imagined as both inherently limited and sovereign ... a community because, regardless of the actual inequality and exploitation that may prevail in each, the nation is always conceived as a deep, horizontal comradeship."[39] That is, a nation is made up of a web of significations that, despite economic realities like those the Frankfurt School identified, is perceived of as essentially unified. But there can be people in that supposedly unified nation who may not be included based on any number of factors: skin color, gender, religion, and sexuality are obvious examples from the United States. An imagined community, as Nadine Holdsworth sums up in her introduction to *Theatre and National Identity: Re-Imagining Conceptions of Nation*, is "activated through cultural practices such as the media, language and the education system."[40] Thus, a nation is not simply all people within a given geographic region. People must be socially integrated to participate in citizenship. In the 1980s and 1990s, gay men in the U.S. fought to integrate themselves into the nation to gain full protection from a public health crisis. But how does the integration process work?

There are two aspects of mass media that make possible Anderson's concept of the nation, both of which are on display in news broadcasting: the transmission and ritual views of communication. The founder of U.S. cultural studies, James Carey, delineates the difference between the two types of communication in his groundbreaking study *Communication as Culture*. The transmission view holds primacy in the U.S. and is viewed as "a process and a technology that would, sometimes for religious purposes, spread, transmit, and disseminate knowledge, ideas, and information farther and faster with the goal of controlling space and people."[41] This view of communication acts as if information is a commodity to be transported and assumes that ideas will be exchanged like goods, filling the receiver's mind with a particular encoded message. This is how the Frankfurt School saw communication. But, crucially for Anderson's concept of nation, there is also the ritual view of communication. Carey writes, "A ritual view of communication is directed not toward the extension of messages in space but toward the maintenance of society in time; not the act of imparting information but the representation of shared beliefs."[42] In this view, communication is a ceremony that creates solidarity. Both the dissemination of information and rituals that create solidarity are necessary for creating Anderson's imagined community.

Though Carey removes ritual communication from an explicitly religious context, the remnants remain, and they help underscore how the ritual view of communication allows new citizens into the national community. Carey quotes sociologist Emil Durkheim's *Elementary Forms of Religious Life*: "Society substitutes for the world revealed to our senses a different world that is a projection of the ideals created by the community."[43] For Carey, that projection and the projected ideals are always works in progress. Similarly, proceeding from the sociological theories of George Herbert Mead and Durkheim, Habermas suggests that while there is internal coherence to a society, "no state, no event, no person is too alien to be drawn into the universal nexus of interactions and transformed into something familiar. ... There can be no social groups so alien that they could not connect up with a given kinship system."[44] In other words, any individual or group can be assimilated into the nation's dominant ideology, as mainstream AIDS theatre helped the LGBT community be assimilated into the U.S. dominant ideology between 1985 and 2000. Holdsworth suggests "that, for many, a 'national' play or performance is embedded in the national fabric and part and parcel of a nation's cultural memory ... But importantly this is not a static process; a national culture—and this includes individual national texts—are organic, and their meanings shift and morph to account for changing times, preoccupations, and levels of national confidence."[45] As the U.S. nation became more "preoccupied" with HIV/AIDS, mainstream theatre became a site that helped to account for this concern and brought the LGBT community, particularly gay men, into the U.S. imagined community. This was done not only onstage, but also through the plays' media receptions.

The study of journalism was Carey's primary field, and he analyzes newspapers to show how a nation is created, maintained, and changed. Given that newspaper reviews are primary documents used by *Making the Radical Palatable* to demonstrate ideological change over time, it is important to understand how newspapers were part of nation formation and transformation in the U.S. at the end of the twentieth century. First, one must acknowledge that reading a newspaper—still done from 1985 to 2000—is an act of both transmission and ritual communication. Transmitting the information of a news story will be affected by the ideologies of the papers' writers, and, hence, will maintain or challenge a reader's ideology. The ritual view of communication understands "reading a newspaper less as sending or gaining information and more as attending a mass, a situation in which nothing new is learned but in which a particular view of the world is portrayed and confirmed. News reading, and writing, is a ritual act and moreover a dramatic one."[46] In other words, while a news story may well transmit new facts about a war, a famine, or a local interest story, "nothing new is learned" in the sense that a reader's ideology, generally, is not challenged. Instead, the ideology is maintained. It is in this sense that Anderson invokes newspaper reading as a constitutive ritual of nation preservation.

Anderson and others point to this performative aspect of newspaper reading as key to how people understand their nation, which is important for grasping how a nation may change its views about who it includes as citizens. Anderson describes reading the newspaper as a "mass ceremony" in which "each communicant is well aware that the ceremony he [or she] performs is being replicated simultaneously by thousands (or millions) of others of whose existence he [or she] is confident, yet of whose identity he [or she] has not the slightest notion."[47] Once again, while not explicitly religious, the word "mass" slips into this description of how the ritual view of communication can transform reading the newspaper into a performative act that binds a nation together. Writing over 20 years later, Latour begins his turning-point work *Reassembling the Social* with the image of newspaper reading,[48] which he too describes as the type of performative

26 *Repairing Reality*

communication necessary to maintain a group. He argues that "if you don't have the festival now or print the newspaper today, you simply lose the grouping, which is not a building in need of restoration but a movement in need of continuation"[49]—meaning, a nation is continually performed, and, if it should stop its performance, it ceases to exist regardless of what archeological remains it leaves. Benjamin wrote of newspapers, "with the indiscriminate assimilation of facts goes the equally indiscriminate assimilation of readers."[50] This returns one to the notions of Habermas and the ability of a society to assimilate anybody, and suggests newspapers' role in it. Therefore, examining the differences in how newspapers reported LGBT characters in mainstream AIDS plays from 1985 to 2000, and analyzing the range of decoding options readers had, shows how gay men were, over time, admitted into the U.S. imagined community.

Epilogue

If one is trying to understand the politics of performance, why study mainstream theatre that is squarely within the culture industry? Why not examine radical performance out of which structures of feeling are more likely to emerge? The reconstruction and recuperation of radical performance is worthwhile and necessary to understand the origins of the radical notions that informed the gay civil rights movement and its response to the HIV/AIDS crisis. But such study does not address changes in the U.S. dominant ideology. As Carey writes, "reality must be repaired for it consistently breaks down: people get lost physically and spiritually, experiments fail, evidence counter to representation is produced, mental derangement sets in—all threats to our models of and for reality that lead to intense repair work."[51] The HIV/AIDS crisis of the 1980s and 1990s led to such a breakdown, and the mainstream theatre of the era took part in repairing reality.

If one wants to understand how the gay civil rights movement made itself palatable to the majority of the U.S. nation, one must uncover moments of change in the dominant ideology. Understanding the culture industry as changeable rather than monolithic; recognizing spectators' power to decode against the dominant ideology's grain; sensing that one need not answer the hegemonic hail in complete agreement; and seeing the nation as a performative, mutable conception that is always in flux allows one to see mainstream theatre not as an inherently conservative, reactionary force for the dominant ideology, but instead as a site of ideological contestation. Ultimately, mainstream theatre in the U.S. at the end of the twentieth century was able to use capitalism to incorporate, package, and sell ideas that began as radical but became palatable to a large, hegemonic audience. In so doing, mainstream theatre supported the emergent ideology of gay civil rights, helped incorporate it into the dominant ideology, and gave LGBT citizens, particularly gay men, a new place in the U.S. nation.

Notes

1. Colin Walmsley, "The Queers Left Behind: How LGBT Assimilation Is Hurting Our Community's Most Vulnerable," *Huffington Post*, 21 July 2015.
2. Ibid.
3. Ibid.
4. Ronald Beiner, *Theorizing Citizenship*, SUNY Series in Political Theory Contemporary Issues (Albany: State University of New York Press, 1995); *Liberalism, Nationalism, Citizenship: Essays on the Problem of Political Community* (Vancouver: UBC Press, 2003); Richard Bellamy, *Citizenship: A Very Short Introduction*, Very Short Introductions (Oxford; New York: Oxford University Press, 2008); Ronald Dworkin, *Freedom's Law: The Moral Reading of the American Constitution* (Cambridge: Harvard UP, 1997); Engin F. Isin and Greg Marc Nielsen, *Acts of Citizenship* (London; New York New York: Zed Books Ltd. Distributed in the USA by Palgrave Macmillan, 2008); Engin F. Isin and Peter Nyers, *Routledge Handbook of Global Citizenship Studies*, Routledge International Handbooks (Abingdon, Oxon: Routledge, 2014); Engin F. Isin and Bryan S. Turner, "Handbook of Citizenship Studies," London; Thousand Oaks: SAGE, 2002; Engin F. Isin and Patricia K. Wood, *Citizenship and Identity*, Politics and Culture: A Theory, Culture & Society Series (London; Thousand Oaks, CA: Sage, 1999); Ruth Lister, *Citizenship: Feminist Perspectives*, 2nd ed. (Washington Square, NY: New York University Press, 2003).
5. Clifford Geertz, "Deep Play: Notes on the Balinese Cockfight," in *The Interpretation of Cultures* (New York: Basic Books, 1973), 448.
6. James W. Carey, *Communication as Culture: Essays on Media and Society* (Boston: Unwin Hyman, 1989), xii.
7. Baz Kershaw, *The Radical in Performance: Between Brecht and Baudrillard* (London: Routledge, 1999), 54.
8. David Román, *Acts of Intervention: Performance, Gay Culture, and AIDS* (Bloomington: Indiana UP, 1998), xx.
9. Elin Diamond, *Performance and Cultural Politics* (London; New York: Routledge, 1996), 3.
10. Matthew Causey and Fintan Walsh, *Performance, Identity, and the Neo-Political Subject*, Routledge Advances in Theatre and Performance Studies (New York: Routledge, 2013), 2.
11. Walter Benjamin et al., *Aesthetics and Politics* (London; New York: Verso, 2007), 139.
12. Terry Eagleton, *Ideology: An Introduction* (New York: Longman, 1994), 46.
13. Max Horkheimer and Theodor W. Adorno, *Dialectic of Enlightenment* (New York: Continuum, 1997), 9.
14. Christopher R. Browning, *Ordinary Men: Reserve Police Battalion 101 and the Final Solution in Poland*, 1st HarperPerennial ed. (New York: HarperPerennial, 1993), 45.
15. In 1971, Zimbardo conducted his notorious Stanford Prison Experiment. In it, he assigned nine students the role of prisoner and nine the role of guard. In just a couple of days, the experiment became distressingly real with a prisoner rebellion, guards using physical punishment, and one prisoner becoming so psychologically distressed that he had to be replaced with an alternate. Zimbardo's findings were that situations are highly influential on human behavior, and his book *The Lucifer Effect: Understanding How Good People Turn Evil* is in

response to the experiment. Philip G. Zimbardo, *The Lucifer Effect: Understanding How Good People Turn Evil*, Random House trade pbk ed. (New York: Random House Trade Paperbacks, 2008).
16. In 1961, at the same time as the trial of Adolf Eichmann, Stanley Milgram began his influential experiments aimed at understanding obedience to authority. In them, an actor pretended to be a scientist conducting an experiment on learning, another actor pretended to be a subject who was given electric shocks when he got answers wrong, and the actual subject of the experiment was a person who had to administer these supposed punishments. No shocks were administered, but the actors pretended to be in pain, and the actor pretending to be a scientist ordered the subject to continue giving the "shocks." The goal of the experiment was to see how many people would follow orders. The results were disturbing. Though subjects showed physical signs of distress following orders, 65% of them did as they were told. The full, fascinating, and distressing results are in *Obedience to Authority: An Experimental View*. Stanley Milgram, *Obedience to Authority: An Experimental View*, 1st ed. (New York; London: Harper & Row, 1974).
17. Browning, *Ordinary Men*, 166–76.
18. István Deák, "A Fatal Compromise? The Debate over Collaboration and Resistance in Hungary," in *The Politics of Retribution in Europe: World War II and Its Aftermath*, ed. István Deák, Jan Tomasz Gross, and Tony Judt (Princeton, NJ: Princeton University Press, 2000), 72; Radu Ioanid, *The Holocaust in Romania: The Destruction of Jews and Gypsies under the Antonescu Regime, 1940–1944* (Chicago, IL: Ivan R. Dee, 2000), 261; Timothy Snyder, "Public Lecture: Bloodlands: Europe between Hitler and Stalin," (Evanston, IL: Northwestern University, 2011); Susan S. Zuccotti, "Surviving the Holocaust: The Situation in France," in *The Holocaust and History: The Known, the Unknown, the Disputed, and the Reexamined*, ed. Michael Berenbaum, Abraham J. Peck, and United States Holocaust Memorial Museum. (Bloomington: Indiana University Press, 1998), 501.
19. Stuart Hall, "Encoding, Decoding," in *The Cultural Studies Reader*, ed. Simon During (London; New York: Routledge, 1993), 102.
20. Hall, "Encoding, Decoding," 103.
21. Hall, "Encoding, Decoding," 104.
22. Horkheimer and Adorno, *Dialectic of Enlightenment*, 129.
23. Horkheimer and Adorno, *Dialectic of Enlightenment*, 128–29.
24. http://www.cdc.gov/mmwr/preview/mmwrhtml/mm5021a2.htm.
25. http://www.archives.gov/research/military/vietnam-war/casualty-statistics.html.
26. Randy Shilts, *And the Band Played On: Politics, People, and the AIDS Epidemic*, 596. New York: St. Martin's Press, 1987.
27. http://www.gmhc.org/about-us/gmhc-hivaids-timeline.
28. Eagleton, *Ideology: An Introduction*, 1.
29. Louis Althusser, "Ideology and the Ideological State Apparatuses," in *Essays on Ideology* (London: Verso, 1984), 36.
30. "Ideology and the Ideological State Apparatuses," in *Essays on Ideology* (London: Verso, 1984), 48.
31. Eagleton, *Ideology: An Introduction*, 145.
32. Raymond Williams, *Marxism and Literature*, Marxist Introductions (Oxford: Oxford UP, 1977), 109.
33. Williams, *Marxism and Literature*, 112.
34. Williams, *Marxism and Literature*, 122.

35. Williams, *Marxism and Literature*, 123.
36. Williams, *Marxism and Literature*, 133.
37. Ibid.
38. Sy Syna, "'The Normal Hear' Offensive and Boring," *New York City Tribune*, April 22 1985.
39. Benedict R. Anderson, *Imagined Communities: Reflections on the Origin and Spread of Nationalism* (New York: Verso, 1991), 6–7.
40. Nadine Holdsworth, "Introduction," in *Theatre and National Identity: Re-Imagining Conceptions of Nation*, ed. Nadine Holdsworth, *Routledge Advances in Theatre and Performance Studies* (New York: Routledge, 2014), 6.
41. Carey, *Communication as Culture*, 14.
42. Carey, *Communication as Culture*, 15.
43. Ibid.
44. Jurgen Habermas, *The Theory of Communicative Action: Lifeworld and System: A Critique of Functionalist Reason*, trans. Thomas McCarthy, Two vols., vol. Two (1987), 158. Boston: Beacon Press, 1987.
45. Holdsworth, "Introduction," 6.
46. Carey, *Communication as Culture*, 16.
47. Anderson, *Imagined Communities: Reflections on the Origin and Spread of Nationalism*, 35.
48. Bruno Latour, *Reassembling the Social: An Introduction to Actor-Network-Theory* (Oxford; New York: Oxford University Press, 2005), 27.
49. Latour, *Reassembling the Social*, 37.
50. Walter Benjamin, "The Newspaper," in *The Work of Art in the Age of Its Technological Reproducibility, and Other Writings on Media*, ed. Michael William Jennings, Brigid Doherty, and Thomas Y. Levin (Cambridge, MA: Belknap Press of Harvard University Press, 2008), 359.
51. Carey, *Communication as Culture*, 24.

Bibliography

Althusser, Louis. "Ideology and the Ideological State Apparatuses." In *Essays on Ideology*, 179 pages. London: Verso, 1984.

Anderson, Benedict R. *Imagined Communities: Reflections on the Origin and Spread of Nationalism*. New York: Verso, 1991.

Beiner, Ronald. *Liberalism, Nationalism, Citizenship: Essays on the Problem of Political Community*. Vancouver: UBC Press, 2003.

———. *Theorizing Citizenship*. SUNY Series in Political Theory Contemporary Issues. Albany: State University of New York Press, 1995.

Bellamy, Richard. *Citizenship: A Very Short Introduction*. Very Short Introductions. Oxford; New York: Oxford University Press, 2008.

Benjamin, Walter. "The Newspaper." Translated by E. F. N. Jephcott. In *The Work of Art in the Age of Its Technological Reproducibility, and Other Writings on Media*, edited by Michael William Jennings, Brigid Doherty, and Thomas Y. Levin, 359–60. Cambridge, MA: Belknap Press of Harvard University Press, 2008.

Benjamin, Walter, Theodor W. Adorno, Ernst Bloch, Bertolt Brecht, and Georg Lukács. *Aesthetics and Politics*. London; New York: Verso, 2007.

Browning, Christopher R. *Ordinary Men: Reserve Police Battalion 101 and the Final Solution in Poland*. 1st HarperPerennial ed. New York: HarperPerennial, 1993.

Carey, James W. *Communication as Culture: Essays on Media and Society*. Boston: Unwin Hyman, 1989.

Causey, Matthew, and Fintan Walsh. *Performance, Identity, and the Neo-Political Subject*. Routledge Advances in Theatre and Performance Studies. New York: Routledge, 2013.

Deák, István. "A Fatal Compromise? The Debate over Collaboration and Resistance in Hungary." In *The Politics of Retribution in Europe: World War II and Its Aftermath*, edited by István Deák, Jan Tomasz Gross, and Tony Judt. Princeton, NJ: Princeton University Press, 2000.

Diamond, Elin. *Performance and Cultural Politics*. London; New York: Routledge, 1996.

Dworkin, Ronald. *Freedom's Law: The Moral Reading of the American Constitution*. Harvard UP, 1997.

Eagleton, Terry. *Ideology: An Introduction*. New York: Longman, 1994.

Geertz, Clifford. "Deep Play: Notes on the Balinese Cockfight." In *The Interpretation of Cultures*. New York: Basic Books, 1973.

Habermas, Jurgen. *The Theory of Communicative Action: Lifeworld and System: A Critique of Functionalist Reason*. Translated by Thomas McCarthy. Two vols. Vol. Two, 1987. Boston: Beacon Press, 1987.

Hall, Stuart. "Encoding, Decoding." In *The Cultural Studies Reader*, edited by Simon During, 90–104. London; New York: Routledge, 1993.

Holdsworth, Nadine. "Introduction." In *Theatre and National Identity: Re-Imagining Conceptions of Nation*, edited by Nadine Holdsworth. Routledge Advances in Theatre and Performance Studies, 1–18: New York: Routledge, 2014.

Horkheimer, Max, and Theodor W. Adorno. *Dialectic of Enlightenment*. New York: Continuum, 1997.

Ioanid, Radu. *The Holocaust in Romania: The Destruction of Jews and Gypsies under the Antonescu Regime, 1940–1944*. Chicago, Ill.: Ivan R. Dee, 2000.

Isin, Engin F., and Greg Marc Nielsen. *Acts of Citizenship*. London; New York: Zed Books Ltd; Distributed in the USA by Palgrave Macmillan, 2008.

Isin, Engin F., and Peter Nyers. *Routledge Handbook of Global Citizenship Studies*. Routledge International Handbooks. Abingdon, Oxon: Routledge, 2014.

Isin, Engin F., and Bryan S. Turner. "Handbook of Citizenship Studies." London; Thousand Oaks: SAGE, 2002.

Isin, Engin F., and Patricia K. Wood. *Citizenship and Identity*. Politics and Culture: A Theory, Culture & Society Series. London; Thousand Oaks, CA: Sage, 1999.

Kershaw, Baz. *The Radical in Performance: Between Brecht and Baudrillard*. London: Routledge, 1999.

Latour, Bruno. *Reassembling the Social: An Introduction to Actor-Network-Theory*. Oxford; New York: Oxford University Press, 2005.

Lister, Ruth. *Citizenship: Feminist Perspectives*. 2nd ed. Washington Square, NY: New York University Press, 2003.

Milgram, Stanley. *Obedience to Authority: An Experimental View*. 1st ed. New York; London: Harper & Row, 1974.

Román, David. *Acts of Intervention: Performance, Gay Culture, and AIDS*. Bloomington: Indiana UP, 1998.

Shilts, Randy. *And the Band Played On: Politics, People, and the AIDS Epidemic*, 596. New York: St. Martin's Press, 1987.

Snyder, Timothy. "Public Lecture: Bloodlands: Europe between Hitler and Stalin." Evanston, IL: Northwestern University, 2011.

Syna, Sy. "'The Normal Hear' Offensive and Boring." *New York City Tribune*, April 22 1985, 6B.
Walmsley, Colin. "The Queers Left behind: How LGBT Assimilation Is Hurting Our Community's Most Vulnerable." *Huffington Post*, 21 July 2015.
Williams, Raymond. *Marxism and Literature*. Marxist Introductions. Oxford: Oxford UP, 1977.
Zimbardo, Philip G. *The Lucifer Effect: Understanding How Good People Turn Evil*. Random House trade pbk ed. New York: Random House Trade Paperbacks, 2008.
Zuccotti, Susan S. "Surviving the Holocaust: The Situation in France." In *The Holocaust and Hstory: The Known, the Unknown, the Disputed, and the Reexamined*, edited by Michael Berenbaum, Abraham J. Peck, and United States Holocaust Memorial Museum., xv, 836 pages. Bloomington: Indiana University Press, 1998.

2 Resistance
The Normal Heart

Prologue

While discussing the "nearly 5,000" total dead from AIDS,[1] reviewers of the 1985 premiere of Larry Kramer's *The Normal Heart* could not fathom that by 2011 nearly 6,000 people would die from the disease daily.[2] Reviews tended to describe the play as "hysterical" and disbelieved its warnings that the disease would continue to spread if not checked by public institutions and activists.[3] After months of resistance from the media, this big-budget and much-marketed production used its position of high visibility to support individuals and organizations fighting the HIV/AIDS epidemic in ways radical performances in marginal venues could not. In the end it was not the news media, the President, the Congress, the National Institute for Health (NIH), or the Center for Disease Control (CDC) that brought public attention to AIDS and all the failures in its management. It was one of the first mainstream plays in the U.S. to take the AIDS epidemic as its topic: *The Normal Heart*. The premiere of Larry Kramer's play generated public recognition of the epidemic and promoted the idea that fighting HIV/AIDS was a national issue, one that anyone "with a normal heart" would care about.[4] Examining its premiere at the Public Theater demonstrates the political vitality of U.S. mainstream theatre and gestures towards a larger theory about the political potential mainstream theatre wields when it hails the public and, particularly, the mass media, demanding some type of recognition of its ideological address. Despite skepticism from many critics about the liberal potential of "the culture industry,"[5] analyzing the mass media reception of *The Normal Heart* shows that the Frankfurt School's pessimism about commercial culture was misplaced. While mainstream theatre may work towards a reformist rather than revolutionary change in the dominant ideology of a culture, mainstream theatre can nevertheless bring about liberal political change. The radical message may be diluted in the culture industry market, but at least the message is relayed to a wide audience. In other words, mainstream theatre can act as a negotiating force between emergent and dominant ideologies, making the radical palatable.

Shameful National Silence

The Normal Heart was born into a moment of shameful national silence about AIDS. In 1981, the CDC declared AIDS an epidemic, but by the fall of 1983, the U.S. federal government had done little to halt the spread of the disease, and even less had been done in New York City, one of the prime sites of transmission. President Ronald Reagan acknowledged the epidemic publically in 1987 only after U.S. HIV/AIDS diagnoses reached 36,058 and the death toll hit 20,849 U.S. citizens. Far from inevitable, these tens of thousands of deaths from HIV/AIDS were, as many posit, avoidable.[6] In 2015, no one questions that U.S. government institutions, the media, and even LGBT activists failed to safeguard the public from the AIDS epidemic in the 1980s. As one of the characters says in *The Normal Heart*, "There's not a good word to be said for anybody's behavior."[7] Taken as a given now, in 1985 the line in Kramer's play still stung. Government agencies, the media, and especially the Reagan Administration were all unwilling to admit there was an epidemic, let alone accept responsibility for the resultant deaths. The *San Francisco Chronicle* was the only newspaper to give the disease major and consistent coverage, led by staff reporter Randy Shilts who would later become the foremost chronicler of AIDS in the 1980s with his magisterial work *And the Band Played On*. San Francisco had a "torpid" program for AIDS, but even that was more than the paltry $24,500 that New York City allotted to fighting the spread of the illness.[8] By the end of 1983, when New York City allocated this small amount of public health spending, more than 1,000 people had died of AIDS in the city. Yet these thousand New York deaths in 1983 did nothing to convince city or country leadership to fight AIDS. Instead, two years later, Larry Kramer's play took the country to task and created a vital awareness of the epidemic.

Though *The Normal Heart* was not the first play to take on the topic of AIDS—there were "such artists, playwrights, and theatre collectives as Robert Chesley, Jeff Hagedorn, Rebecca Ranson, and San Francisco's A.I.D.S. Show Collaborators, among others, whose AIDS performances were produced as early as 1983"[9]—*The Normal Heart* was one of the first to receive major press coverage and, thereby, challenge the dominant ideology's blindness to the AIDS epidemic. One reason performances before *The Normal Heart* remained relatively obscure is that they "were simply that, performances without opening nights, world premieres, or the critical review process."[10] For the most part mainstream newspaper and magazine critics were unaware of the various performances about AIDS already in circulation throughout the early 1980s and discussed *The Normal Heart* as if it were the first. The critical attention directed towards *The Normal Heart* was unprecedented for any cultural text about AIDS at the time.[11] But as *The Normal Heart* was produced at a mainstream venue and employed well-known artists as director, actors, and technical designers, a lack of media coverage would actually have been more unusual than the attention it received.

Further complicating *The Normal Heart*'s status as the "first" play dealing with the AIDS epidemic is the premiere of William Hoffman's *As Is* one month before the opening of Kramer's play. *As Is* depicts two gay lovers who have broken up: one now has AIDS, the other is healthy and returns to take care of his ex-lover "as is."[12] Its focus is much more on the personal aspects of a gay relationship than on the politics of AIDS, particularly suggesting that the gay community must take care of its own, unlike Kramer's demand that gay men be part of the U.S. imagined community. *As Is* did not have the critical, angry stance of *The Normal Heart*. Because *As Is* made no attempt at activism, it garnered few reviews about AIDS and more that reacted to the play's supposed promotion of a "gay lifestyle." As such, *As Is* made less of a dent than *The Normal Heart* in the dominant ideology's refusal to acknowledge AIDS. *The Normal Heart*, then, was not the first or only play to include AIDS in its plot. It was the first mainstream play to take the mismanagement of the AIDS crisis as its central concern, and it generated a flood of press about the disease in both gay and mainstream publications, including major reviews in all the New York national papers.

None of this would have occurred, however, without a theatre searching for a play that explicitly addressed the contemporaneous AIDS crisis. After Kramer finished a draft of the script in 1984, he had trouble finding a theatre willing to take a risk on his play. Through the Gay Men's Health Crisis (GMHC)—an AIDS advocacy groups co-founded by Kramer before he was kicked out of it for his militant tactics—Kramer knew Emmett Foster, "an Administrative Assistant to Joseph Papp, the celebrated founder-producer of the New York Shakespeare Festival/Public Theater."[13] Foster forwarded the script to Gail Merrifield Papp, head of the Public Theatre's Play Department at the time. She read it and initiated frequent discussions with Kramer. He revised the script based on her questions, and, despite Kramer's impatience, she would not show it to Joseph Papp until she was satisfied with the script's quality.

In the meantime, Joseph Papp was coming to realize that the media's response to AIDS was inadequate, particularly in New York City, and he ached to find a script that explicitly addressed the contemporaneous AIDS crisis. Papp had a history of fighting for political causes—he was red-baited during the McCarthy era, which led to his firing at CBS, for instance. After a prominent fight with New York Parks Commissioner Robert Moses over Papp's free productions of Shakespeare in Central Park, Papp was viewed as a man whose art and politics collided.[14] He became painfully aware of the media's silence regarding AIDS when on April 30, 1983, the GMHC held a sold-out benefit at Madison Square Garden that received only a modicum of press coverage. All 17,000 seats sold out in advance, and the program included such public figures as Leonard Bernstein and Mayor Koch. "The night was shaping up as the biggest gay event of all time ... put[ting] $250,000 into the treasury of Gay Men's Health Crisis."[15] As extravagant as all this was, Emmett Foster told Papp:

> 'Something horrible has happened. Last night GMHC had its fundraiser and no one followed up.' [Foster] told him the whole story. Joe said 'This is not right. Something has to be done. When I get back to the office, I'll call the papers and ask them why it wasn't covered.' [Foster] started crying in the car because [he] was so moved that [Papp] had so much power and could use it. Everybody else was like 'What happened?' They didn't know what to do, whereas Joe picked up the phone.[16]

Further, in December of 1984, Joseph Papp received a letter from Victoria Hamburg and Terry Beirn. They represented the media committee of the AIDS Medical Foundation, and they asked Papp to "enlist some of the great talent and courage of the theatrical community to help battle this disease [AIDS]."[17] Thus, Papp was well-primed to receive the draft of *The Normal Heart* from Gail Merrifield Papp in January 1985.

Despite the play's continued dramaturgical shortcomings, Papp soon realized it was the vehicle he sought to promote public knowledge about the AIDS epidemic. He described his first reading of the script this way:

> So I pick it up and I read the first twenty pages and I put it down and say 'Gail, I can't get through this play. It's overwritten, it's overblown.' She didn't say a word, so I pick it up again a day or so later and plow my way through the play, and at each point I put it down, I say, 'I can't get any further with this. There's a moment here and there, but some of the stuff is so poor, and so outrageous.' Finally I get through the whole thing and say, 'This is one of the worst things I've ever read'—and I'm crying. I was crying! Could you believe that? I was so moved, because there was so much feeling in the play. The heart of *The Normal Heart* was beating there.[18]

After that, Joseph Papp and Larry Kramer met and opening night was set for April 21, 1985, nearly four years after the CDC declared AIDS an epidemic. After Kramer left, Joseph Papp "called Literary Manager Bill Hart into his office. 'Someone has to get control of the structure,' he said confidentially. 'Meet with him. See what you can do.'"[19] Based on those meetings, the script changed substantially. In fact, over two hours of text were cut,[20] but the importance of the script always rested in its ability to forward information about AIDS, rather than in its literary value.

As the production neared opening night, Papp and the Public Theater staff braced themselves for the controversy that would come with attacking the dominant ideology in a mainstream setting. New York City owned both spaces in which the Public Theater performed: the building in lower Manhattan and the space in Central Park. Therefore, Mayor Koch, who the play attacked by name, was Papp's landlord. The play also chastised many other New York institutions and national organizations. Papp instructed the

Public's lawyers to prepare notes regarding potential libel issues. The notes were broken into five categories:

1 New York Times: 13 incidents
2 Mayor: 14 times
3 Mayor's asst/Hiram Keebler: 5 incidents
4 Commissioner of health: 3 incidents
5 Affiliations mentioned in dialogue: The Native, Health Dept, Citibank, New York Times, Washington Post, Time, Newsweek, New England Journal of Medicine, Village Voice, Donahue, CBS/Dan Rather, Today Show, NIH, CDC [sic.][21]

According to the lawyer's report, despite the references in the play to actual people and organizations, the Public was not in danger of being sued. Nevertheless, Joseph Papp called Mayor Koch and the *New York Times*. Papp relates his call to the Mayor this way:

> I said 'Mister Mayor, I have a play here about AIDS. I'm going to put it on. The playwright criticizes you and the administration. Whether it's true or not, he wrote it. He says it's true. I'm not going to be a censor, and I just wanted to let you know.' He says 'Fine, Joe, thank you for telling me.' Very pleased.[22]

This crucial call helped lead to a surprise announcement from the Mayor on the eve of the play's production, designed to take the sting out of the play's accusations. The warning allowed Mayor Koch to plan an appropriately timed release of new funds to combat AIDS as well as a press conference touting these measures. Papp's call and the play seem to have led directly to the Mayor's newfound interest in the epidemic.

Papp's call to the *New York Times* editor did not go nearly as smoothly, though Papp's determination to challenge the dominant ideology's silence about AIDS over-ruled any desire not to offend the powerful "paper of record." Kramer voices one of his major grievances against the *Times* in a piece of dialogue comparing its coverage of the AIDS epidemic to that of a poisoned Tylenol scare. A character says, "Have you been following the Tylenol scare? In three months there have been seven deaths, and the *Times* has written fifty-four articles. The month of October alone they ran one article every single day. Four of them were on the front page. For us—in seventeen months they've written seven puny articles. And we have a thousand cases!"[23] After the Public's lawyers checked the accuracy of Kramer's accusations, Papp called his friend Arthur Gelb at the *New York Times*:

> I said, 'Artie, listen, I'm doing a play here, and it's critical of the *Times*.'
> He says, 'What do you mean! We were the first ones to put that thing in the paper! Didn't we have it on June 27th? We had the story on this thing. How can you say that?'

'No,' I said, 'it was not June 27th. It was August. Mind you, Artie, I didn't write the play. I'm putting on the play because it's an important theme and subject. If you think he's wrong, sue him.'[24]

Two important aspects of Papp's decision to produce this play can be seen in this exchange. First, one can see his bravery and forthrightness. He said, "It's important," and to him its political import made it worth the various risks of production. Second, one can see Papp's good business sense in calling the *Times* and suggesting that, ultimately, the claims made by the play were Kramer's and not the Public's. This limited the Public's liability and allowed continued good relations between his institution and a newspaper that can make or break theatres. Hence, this anecdote shows the bravery and pragmatism—an oscillation between radical and palatable—that Papp practiced hand in hand while producing a play that overtly challenged the dominant ideology. Into this hostile environment, *The Normal Heart* opened on April 21, 1985.

The Writing on the Wall

The plot of *The Normal Heart* follows the story of Ned Weeks, a writer who begins a volunteer organization to combat the spread of a mysterious disease that preys mainly on gay men. AIDS and the Gay Men's Health Crisis are never mentioned, but the accounts are very similar to the actual disease and organization. Because of Ned's confrontational style of activism, he is forced out of the advocacy group he helped start. Along the way, Ned meets Felix, a gay reporter at the *New York Times*, and they fall in love. When Felix is diagnosed with the disease, Ned cares for him until Felix dies. This love and dedication on Ned's part helps reconcile Ned and his straight brother, Ben, who up until then cannot understand Ned's "gay lifestyle." Nearly every scene in this simple story contains a monologue, generally from Ned, about the seriousness of the disease and the failure of those around him to prevent it, giving the play an agitprop tone. Regardless of its didacticism—or perhaps because of it given the media silence on the topic of AIDS and the public's curiosity—it became the Public Theatre's longest-running production, a title it still holds in 2015.

Scholarship on *The Normal Heart* often posits the production's success on the premiere coinciding with historical events that made AIDS a broadly covered news story, but a more sound explanation is *The Normal Heart*'s acceptance by mainstream audiences and the news media not as great art but as necessary documentary theatre. In his history of AIDS theatre, *Acts of Intervention*, David Román credits the achievements of *The Normal Heart* to, "remarkable shifts in both the quantity and nature of depictions of AIDS [that] took place," from, "*Life* magazine's notorious July cover story, 'Now No One Is Safe from AIDS,' to Rock Hudson's public announcement and subsequent AIDS death."[25] However, the events Román lists happened months after the April 1985 opening of *The Normal Heart*. Examining the text and conditions of reception during the spring of 1985 shows that *The Normal Heart*'s advertising, content, and review process buried any claims of high art underneath an argument for the play's political relevance, and this was the foundation for the play's accomplishments.

The marketing strategy taken by the Public Theatre for *The Normal Heart* highlighted the significance of the play's information. A week before opening, the Public Theatre took out a quarter-page advertisement in the *New York Times* theatre section. In it, white writing blazed against a black background: "At least 300,000 Americans have already been infected by the AIDS virus, according to Dr. James Curran who heads the AIDS program at the Centers for Disease Control." Below the large quote was a small logo of *The Normal Heart* and the play's tag-line: "A play about the most serious public health crisis of the 20th century."[26] This advertisement frames the production as a serious discussion about the AIDS epidemic more than as a piece of art. For instance, the ad makes no claim that the play is well-written, riveting, or a great piece of theatre. This strategy proved sound, for it continued after opening night when the Public put a new half-page advertisement in the *New York Times*. This second advertisement was made primarily from reviewers' quotes with a block of text in a bigger, more dramatic font written across and obscuring all the review citations. The text obscuring the review pull-quotes read, "Once in every ten years or so a play comes along that fulfills my original idea of what role my theater must play in society. 'The Normal Heart' is that play—Joseph Papp."[27] In this advertisement, the political role of the play literally overshadowed the reviewers' opinions about its artistic merit.

Framing the play as educational rather than artistic continued even in the physical space of the production. Audience members would have carried various amounts of knowledge about the disease, from GMHC volunteers who knew tremendous amounts to people who had never heard of the syndrome,[28] but they all first encountered the Public's imposing red- and brown-bricked Renaissance Revival facade before entering the large lobby with its vaulted ceiling. The Public's architecture would have continued the advertising's argument of the play's grandiosity. *The Normal Heart* was no piece of outsider art in a small loft space. Once inside, various pamphlets about AIDS greeted spectators: information from the AIDS Medical Foundation, GMHC, AIDS Resource Center, Health and Human Services, Children and AIDS, and the American Red Cross Home Attendant Program. There were also a study guide prepared by the AIDS Medical Foundation, a printed directory of organizations and addresses where audience members could send donations, and a reproduced list of suggestions about how audience members could get involved in volunteering to help find a cure for AIDS and to care for its victims. All of this was located in a literature rack in the center of the hallway between the two sets of stairs that led from the lobby to the Anspacher Theatre.[29] A sign-in book invited audience members to leave their names and addresses. This information provided various AIDS support groups data for their direct-mail campaigns. Most notably, inside the programs was an insert that read:

> 'What you can do!'
> 1. Go downstairs to our lobby and buy a 'Normal Heart' Tee Shirt, button or the actual published script. The proceeds will go to AIDS research and the care of its victims.
> 2. Get the facts about AIDS by picking up the pamphlets on display. Education and Funding are two of the strongest tools we can use to fight this dreaded disease.
> 3. Donate money to one or all of the various organizations that are involved in combating AIDS. Pick up a list that we have prepared of organizations that need your financial help.
> 4. Volunteer your time to one of the organizations now involved in the research of AIDS, the care of its victims, or educating the public through the various AIDS HOTLINES.
> 5. Tell your friends, family, colleagues, and students to come see 'The Normal Heart.' There is a 50% DISCOUNT for groups of ten or more. Please contact Clifford Scott in our Group Sales office, (212) 598-7107.[30]

This supplement to the program gave spectators concrete ways to get involved with the real-life problems the fiction of the play presented to them. Also, and perhaps more important, all of this information hailed spectators as people who would *want* to get involved. It assumed a spectator who would be moved into action by witnessing the needless deaths of young, gay men. The Public Theater, with its imposing architecture lending it an official air, was a site with the ability "to take in, to assimilate, and to render more safe, more marketable, the products of [this] oppositional programme."[31] In the process, The Public Theater's production of *The Normal Heart* may have made the emergent ideology of LGBT civil rights and the need to treat AIDS as an epidemic less "radical," but its mainstream location also made the ideology more visible. And, even without "radical" politics, the production still, in Althusser's word, *interpellated*, or *hailed*, the spectators as activists.[32]

Beyond the pamphlets, the location of the theatre, and the theatre's architecture, the production's merchandise plan also contributed to fashioning spectators into activists. By using the proceeds of merchandise to fund organizations directly related to the political cause of the performance, the production utilized consumerism to further AIDS activism. This strategy contrasts with Baz Kershaw's negative assessment of consumerism in mainstream theatre. Kershaw criticizes the inevitable merchandise surrounding these productions, arguing that "the power of performance is sucked dry by the peripherals of theatre as it is transformed into a service industry with subsidiary retail outlets."[33] *The Normal Heart*, however, used the money of its "retail outlet" to further the production's activism and provided spectators with literature that instructed the "shopper" on other ways to get involved—from philanthropy to volunteering. In this way, the space around *The Normal Heart* did not solely reshape spectators into consumers. Instead, spectators played activists for the few hours they spent inside the Public Theatre, regardless of their post-show follow-through. The Greenwich Village location also contributed to spectators' activist role-playing. As the Village is generally seen as New York's location for intellectuals and rebellious artists, the geographic placement of the theatre framed the spectator as activist rather than shopper—even if the Village was rapidly becoming a shopping district by the 1980s. This setting and the activist paraphernalia within the Public Theatre, though unmentioned by reviewers, no doubt affected their experience of the play as well, as it would anyone viewing the production. Thus, while the consumerism surrounding the play did not radically challenge the dominant capitalist culture and played into the neighborhood's rapid gentrification at the end of the twentieth century, allowing spectators to donate money through purchase and to play at activism for an evening nevertheless challenged the dominant ideology's complacency about the AIDS epidemic.

After walking past the educational pamphlets about AIDS and the mailing lists for various non-profit organizations, spectators entered LuEsther Hall, a long performance space with a high ceiling, on the walls of which was more educational information. The set design by Eugene Lee and Keith Raywood surrounded the audience "with walls covered with numbers and names, state by state, city by city, of AIDS victims."[34] According to Howard Kissel, "these numbers are the real setting against which the action takes place."[35] Like a "Brechtian kaleidoscope," these numbers were constantly updated throughout the run of the production.[36] As literary critic Gregory Gross describes it, "these Brechtian announcements flash numbers all over the stage and audience—numbers about AIDS cases, numbers about AIDS deaths, numbers of news articles printed in major papers, numbers of dollars spent, numbers of various dates and some corresponding and contrasting numbers related to the 1982 Tylenol scare. Along with the numbers, people's names appear in the fashion of the Vietnam Veterans Memorial in Washington, D.C."[37] Combined with the script and the concrete steps offered in the program and lobby, these Brechtian elements in the design made spectators aware of the world outside of the fiction and prodded them towards taking action after leaving the theatre. However, the production combined the potential for radical performance in Brechtian design with a more palatable realism-influenced style for its script and direction.

As directed by Michael Lindsey-Hogg at the Public Theater in 1985, the acting and production were based in the traditions of realism, except for the writing on the walls of the theatre surrounding the audience. Spectators sat on two sides of the theatre "basketball-court style."[38] In the intimate space, spectators were close to the action on stage, and they could watch audience members across the stage "squirm as some particularly painful moment" was played out.[39] One reviewer described the sensation of "looking down as in an operating room."[40] If there was no "fourth wall" because of the alley configuration, and if simple set pieces were meant to convey an entire setting—a hospital bed to represent a hospital room, for instance—the production's concept was not to be symbolic but to suggest a realist set simply. This direction seemed an appropriate choice because the script itself is not often symbolic, preferring instead to chastise actual public figures and institutions such as Mayor Koch, the *New York Times*, and the CDC. In fact, literary critic Joel Shatzky attributes the production's "electrifying effect" on audiences to the playwright not treating "the AIDS epidemic in symbolic terms."[41] He explains that because the play was produced at a time when the epidemic was so real, symbolism was unnecessary and would have taken away from the strength of the work.

Only one moment in the text is expressly symbolic, and it stands out mightily from the rest of the play's didactic tone. Late in the play, after Felix takes ill and refuses food, Ned throws recently bought groceries to the floor, one by one, until a carton of milk explodes onstage.[42] This scene stands out because it is one of the few without a monologue of statistics and numbers. Instead, there is a visual representation of waste and death. It must have been striking, for many of the reviews of *The Normal Heart* address it. John Simon, writing for *New York*, writes that "we can choke back our sobs over a gallant death, but cry rightly over a carton of spilt milk."[43] Likewise, Michael Sommers, in the gay biweekly newspaper, the *New York Native*, explains that, "the impact of a quart of milk splattered all over the place is indescribably shocking."[44] It is, perhaps, the key moment of emotional resonance within the play.

The power of an exploding carton of milk comes from the scene's deeply emotional content within the context of so many numbers and statistics. Gregory Gross points out that the play moves "from the big to the small, from the abstract to the concrete and from the general to the highly personal,"[45] and this is exactly what occurs when the milk carton shatters and sprays its contents across the stage. After nearly two hours of long monologues full of statistics of the dead and dying, tirades about the numbers of newspaper articles or amounts of funding, Ned finally says:

> Felix, I am so sick of statistics, and numbers, and body counts, and how-manys, and Emma [Felix's doctor]; and every day, Felix, there are only more numbers, and fights—I am so sick of fighting, and bragging about fighting, and everybody's stupidity, and blindness, and intransigence, and guilt trips. You can't eat the food? Don't eat the food. Take your poison. I don't care. You can't get up off the floor—fine, stay there. I don't care. Fish—fish is good for you; we don't want any of that, do we? (*Item by item, he throws the food on the floor*) No green salad. No broccoli; we don't want any of that, no sir. No bread with

seven grains. Who would ever want any milk? You might get some calcium in your bones (*The carton of milk explodes when it hits the floor.*) You want to die, Felix? Die! ... Felix, please don't leave me.[46]

This scene progresses from the utter frustration that his partner will not fight, represented in the line, "Die!," to the equal fear of his partner's impending death, shown in Ned's line, "Felix, please don't leave me." After throwing the milk, seeing it explode all over the stage, and shouting, "Die!" at the cowering Felix, Ned falls to the floor and Felix crawls through the milk and debris to hold him. Covered in detritus, the couple sits in spilt milk in a hopelessly lethal situation.

This scene is only a few minutes from the end of the play, and by this point the audience shares Ned's frustration with the "statistics, and numbers, and body counts" that make up the bulk of the script. It is at this moment of aggravation that the play finally produces a visual representation of the loss of a generation of gay men. What could be a better symbol of waste than spilt milk, the loss of nutrients, and the ability to help one grow? Milk is representative of a maternal, caretaking force that these men's lives lack as they attempt to take care of their own ill. It is a food staple of the young. Its waste mirrors the waste of a young man dying. Seeing Felix crawl through it is akin to watching him crawl through a representation of all the young men's lives cut short. The fact that the milk and debris from the rest of the thrown groceries remains onstage throughout the final scenes of the play is a constant visual reminder of that waste.

Even if that was the only overtly symbolic moment in the play, realism is itself a symbolic representation of life, and Kramer's particular use of realism made *The Normal Heart* especially appealing to a wide range of spectators. David Bergman detects "at least three major strains" in *The Normal Heart*: "the grating soprano of the enraged child, the wounded contralto of the guilt-inducing mother, and the rasping bass of the humiliating father."[47] Bergman continues, "Because I hear these voices coming not only from Kramer's page but also from my own head, I respond to them with an unusual intensity. Kramer's ability to address the subconscious of gay readers accounts in large part for the power he exerts on and the anger he arouses from [them]."[48] While Kramer's ability to cipher the interior voices of a gay man may account for the play's popularity with gay spectators, John Clum argues that "to the straight audience [Kramer] is the representative gay man, the good fairy who will speak for what being gay should mean."[49] Kramer's text simultaneously taps deep into the subconscious of a gay spectator while showing a straight spectator a "role model" of a gay man in keeping with the dominant ideology's values. Key to this "good fairy" mode is the text's emphasis on the affinities between gay and straight men.[50] The decisive example of the text delineating commonality is Ned ultimately finding acceptance from his straight brother after the non-state-sanctioned deathbed marriage ceremony Ned and Felix undergo.[51] Likewise, by "placing the gay community within the bosom of the heterosexual family,"[52] *The Normal Heart* could be accepted that much more readily by mainstream media outlets such as the *New York Times*, which had no "out" LGBT reporter at that time. The title of the play itself is a plea for a type of acceptance more easily given when similarities rather than differences between gay and straight communities are stressed.

While reconciliation between gay and straight cultures might have appealed to some spectators, it did not appeal to many others. Obviously, there were straight spectators who, because of homophobia, religious beliefs, or other reasons, had no desire to see the gay community reconciled with straight culture. The *New York City Tribune*'s review suggested that gay men's "'alternative lifestyle' has developed lethal complications" and that the play is "offensive to anyone except a homosexual who feels that society has an obligation to pick up the tab for the unsavory implications of their 'lifestyle.'"[53] From the other side of the political spectrum, however, there are completely different reasons for being uncomfortable with the reconciliation desired in *The Normal Heart*. Clum suggests that, via his relationship with Felix, Ned "place[s] his homosexuality within a paradigm that straight Ben understands."[54] Instead of supporting his brother's civil rights, Ben supports Ned's entrance into the institution of marriage, and, for Clum, "herein lies the subtext of *The Normal Heart*: the paradigm of marriage validates homosexuality."[55] This is a way in which the script is not radical, but, in fact, palatable to the dominant ideology. It also, 30 years later, appears a prescient, winning strategy, for white, privileged gay men such as Ned and his creator. By stressing affinities between gay and straight communities, Kramer overlooks legitimate differences and, while this is pleasing to some, it offends others. However, by stressing the resemblances over differentiations, the play received the mainstream support necessary to relay its overarching message, which was not about LGBT civil rights, but about the AIDS epidemic.

Given the production's efforts at AIDS education, a more biting critique can be made of the play's condemnations of promiscuity—such as its statement that "having so much sex makes finding love impossible."[56] While promiscuity certainly does not help abate the spread of any sexually transmitted disease, *The Normal Heart* does not acknowledge that gay sex did not cause AIDS. More accurately, "the dissemination of the HIV virus was assisted by the failure to take seriously the first prognoses of the epidemic's gravity, and by delayed programmes of political education and medical information."[57] And while the play's portrayal of two gay men entering the paradigm of marriage may have accessed the sympathy of the dominant ideology, marriage—whether gay or straight—does not stop affairs, promiscuity, or the spread of sexually transmitted diseases. While educating the public that promiscuity could potentially lead to AIDS was absolutely essential in the 1980s, blaming AIDS on promiscuity is dangerously similar to the *New York City Tribune*'s review that blamed AIDS on a "gay lifestyle."[58] Furthermore, the play claims that, "there's absolutely no such thing as safe sex."[59] Perhaps earlier in the HIV/AIDS crisis this line could be excused, but in 1985 enough was known about the disease to educate spectators about the effectiveness of condom use. As early as 1982 there was advice about the use of condoms to promote a safer way of having sex. For example, Michael Callen's 40-page pamphlet *How To Have Sex in an Epidemic: One Approach* was published in 1982 and reviewed in the *New York Review of Books*.[60] In *The Normal Heart,* there is no discussion how one could have relatively safe sex. Instead, the play created a marriage/promiscuity binary at the heart of AIDS. However, this binary made the play's message easier for the dominant ideology to assimilate, as did the play's representation of AIDS as an omnipotent force against which no effective tactics existed.

The lack of discussion about steps sexually active people could take to halt the spread of AIDS contributes to what Román sees as one of *The Normal Heart*'s "conventional concepts of dramatic tragedy." They present "AIDS as a totalizing and inescapable condition, a condition with little or no agency to fight the powers contributing to the epidemic and with little or no hope for those affected."[61] While this is a valid critique of the script, it ignores some of the material aspects of the Public Theater production, such as the long lists of ways to get involved that greeted spectators both coming and going from the theatre. The script may present AIDS as a totalizing force, but the dialogue's failure to address ways to be sexually active in a less hazardous way does not mean the production gave actors and spectators no agency in this epidemic. The literature in the lobby and program gave extremely specific actions spectators could take to fight AIDS. The very act of presenting the play, seeing the play, and informing spectators of organizations to which one could donate money or time offered the actors and spectators actions to take beyond what the script offered.

This is exactly the type of action Brecht hoped his theatre would inspire in audience members, and much is made of the Brechtian elements of the staging in contemporaneous reviews of and later critical writing on *The Normal Heart*. Almost all these references to Brecht deal with the statistics, names, and facts written on the walls of the set. Clum attributes this mixture of a realistic script with a Brechtian set to "Kramer's political confusion" and sees it as a failure in consistency of form.[62] There is no need to see this inconsistency as a failure, however. Both the realism and the alienation are necessary to give the spectators a dual awareness of the reality of the fiction and the reality outside the theatre. Unlike Clum, D.S. Lawson suggests Kramer abandons stage realism altogether for a completely alienating production and in so doing isolates "his characters and their actions from a recognizable landscape ... and projects an image of homosexual men as pariahs, outcasts from a world whose ideology is so well perpetuated in literary and dramatic realism."[63] But Kramer does not discard realism. The script is quite realistic, and in the Public's production, the acting and direction were all in the realistic tradition. The only non-realistic aspect of the production is the writing on the walls, and this single element is not enough to separate the characters "from a recognizable landscape." While the numbers may produce an alienating effect, spectators were also absorbed by the realist acting of a realist text on the minimalist but ultimately realism-based set. Watching this production, a spectator would move back and forth between alienation and absorption.

It is important to remember that Brechtian "alienation"—understood through the writings of Min Tian, Viktor Shklovsky, Craig Kinzer and Mary Poole[64]—need not mean that a spectator or actor is somehow emotionally disengaged from the production, as Brecht (mis)interprets Chinese acting.[65] Instead, following Shklovsky's statement that "art exists to help us recover the sensation of life,"[66] alienation awakens senses dulled from habit. In fact, "alienation" can actually *increase* emotional engagement between spectators and actors. As Kinzer and Poole write, "the experience of actors and spectators implies that the key to Brecht's notion of alienation can be viewed less a question of *increasing* the distance between actor and character as *decreasing* the distance between actor and audience."[67] The decrease in distance between actor and audience is accomplished through reminding the audience of the reality of life outside the reality of the play. There were real-life echoes in *The Normal Heart* that made the spectators aware of the contemporaneous crisis outside the theatre.

The Normal Heart is set in 1983, two years before its first performance date, and that slight difference in time collided fictional time and non-fictional time to create this type of alienation. Anne Giudici Fettner, a medical journalist who covered HIV/AIDS early in the 1980s, reported in a review for *The New York Native*, "When Joel Grey [the actor playing Ned Weeks] shouted something about there already being 40 deaths in New York City alone, all eyes cut to the number '4280' hanging over center stage. And shuddered." The spectators not only had the number "4280" to turn their eyes to, they also had each other. Because they were seated in an alley configuration, spectators observed others' reactions. Fettner's review depicts spectators psychologically absorbed by events onstage, then alienated by the writing on the wall, and the shuddering emotional response thereby created. In *The Normal Heart* "what is testimonial and what is fictive ... collide," and the explosion caused by that collision—such as the writing on the wall versus the words spoken by the actors—generated much of the production's political power. Gross writes that the early plays about AIDS "are history plays performed in the midst of their own history. The players, the spectators, and those walking around outside the theatre stand engaged in the same situation."[68] This self-consciousness of living history allowed audience members to forge a community that mourned the actual dead and ill. Spectators performed that mourning alongside the artists who enacted a ritual of mourning in their fictional setting for the fictional deceased and dying.

In the moments when fictional time and non-fictional time collided, a community formed, not only among spectators, but also with the actors, and the production became a ritual that was about remembering the dead and refusing to be silent about how to save the living. J. Robert Cox argues that this type of alienation, which becomes a co-performance both by actors and spectators, can produce "remembrance and a refusal of silence" and in the process "re-position 'audience' as this larger community of memory/speech."[69] This was, as Joseph Roach puts it, one of those times when a production made "publicly visible through symbolic action both the tangible existence of social boundaries and, at the same time, the contingency of those boundaries, their constructedness, their anxiety-inducing instability."[70] *The Normal Heart* showed the horrible consequences of "social boundaries" that allowed a disease to run amok because of a widespread early belief that it mainly affected gay men. But the production also showed the "contingency" of those boundaries, and the production and the literature in racks outside the theatre displayed how to help change those boundaries and how to help save lives. As this community of actors and spectators performed mourning, it re-imagined its boundaries outside the theatre to include those who were dead or ill because of AIDS. This re-imagining, caused by alienation, combined with the opportunities to get involved described in the lobby, inspired action among its audience members.

If this seems too hypothetical, examine the eyewitness account of the Public's literary manager, Bill Hart: "There was something about this ritual going on downtown night after night after night in the theater. There was a kind of testifying going on, a kind of witnessing."[71] The audience was testifying against the national silence surrounding the AIDS epidemic and witnessing the consequences of that silence. The production, the information in the lobby, and the script all hailed spectators as people who cared about the AIDS crisis and wanted to do something about it. Though this emergent ideology had been expressed in the alternative, "gay" theatre,[72] when it was presented by *The Normal Heart* in a mainstream theatre setting, it was amplified by the national media. This amplification helped integrate the emergent ideology that AIDS was a crisis in need of attention into the dominant ideology, as can be seen in the production's reviews.

War During Peacetime

Journalists by and large rehearsed the view first espoused by the Public Theatre's advertising that *The Normal Heart* was educational, not artistic. The production's 21 reviews fall into three main categories. Three reviews suggest that it is a bad play with no redeeming qualities.[73] Three more argue that it is a good play with good politics.[74] And the remaining 15, including those in the most mainstream national periodicals such as the *New York Times*, see *The Normal Heart* as a bad play that is redeemed by its necessary social message.[75]

The reviews that came out on April 22, 1985, the day after opening night, were generally negative about the aesthetic value of the play, but their reactions to the play's politics and message were a mix of agreement and denial. Frank Rich, perhaps the most important critic then at the *New York Times*, wrote a review that included more information about the AIDS crisis than the *New York Times* published in the first four years of the epidemic. Rich wrote that *The Normal Heart* is "the most outspoken play around" and that its subject "justifies its author's unflagging, at times even hysterical, sense of urgency."[76] The justification for the "urgency" is the "foot-dragging" of "the Governmental, medical and press establishments ... [New York] Mayor Koch, various prominent medical organizations, the *New York Times* ... [and] most of the leadership of an unnamed organization apparently patterned after the Gay Men's Health Crisis."[77] Rich's synopsis of the play's content and amplification of its emergent ideology provided information to the readership of the *New York Times* and gave legitimacy to a worldview that saw AIDS as a real threat and condemned official faltering. While the subject is "urgent," Rich blasts the play's "pamphleteering tone" that "is accentuated by Mr. Kramer's insistence on repetition ... and on regurgitating facts and figures in lengthy tirades."[78] In the end, Rich does praise this "shrill" play, in part for the text on the walls, "While one wishes that the play's outrage had been channeled into drama as fully compelling as its cause, the writing on the theater's walls alone could drive anyone with a normal heart to abandon what Mr. Kramer calls the 'million excuses for not getting involved.'"[79] Just like the literature in the lobby did for spectators, this review hailed its readers as people who cared about the AIDS crisis. Given the lacuna of information about the epidemic in the media, including the *New York Times*, Rich's review was a shot across the bow of the dominant ideology's suppression of information about the malady.

The play also prompted two concrete political effects the day after its opening. First, as the play attacks the *New York Times* by name, the paper responded next to Rich's review with "a denial of Kramer's accusation that the [*New York*] *Times* had failed to cover AIDS and the defense that the newspaper had sent a member of the science staff to cover the story as soon as it had been informed of the existence of the disease."[80] Regardless of the veracity of this claim, which is highly debatable, *The Normal Heart* forced the *New York Times* into defending its policies; at the very least, the newspaper now admitted in print the importance of AIDS. The second tangible political effect the day after the play's opening was press coverage of a surprise announcement by Mayor Koch—one potentially in the works since the mayor's conversation with Joseph Papp during which the producer warned Koch about the play's attacks:

> Just hours before the first preview performance, as photocopied scripts of *The Normal Heart* circulated among the city's news organizations, Mayor Ed Koch hurriedly called a press conference to announce "a

comprehensive expansion of city services" for local AIDS patients. Koch shifted responsibility for AIDS from Health Commissioner Sencer to Deputy Mayor Victor Botnick and instituted the plans for coordinated care and long-term facilities that had been proposed years before by AIDS clinicians. Included in the new $6 million program were pledges of expanded home and hospice care, day-care programs for children with AIDS, and funds for ten interdisciplinary patient care teams at hospitals with large AIDS caseloads.[81]

The mayor's actions were reported in the media on the same day as the first reviews of *The Normal Heart*. That means on April 25, 1985, the *New York Times* included Rich's review, the paper's defense of its AIDS reporting, and an account of the mayor's newfound interest in AIDS. These political events coterminous with the first performance of *The Normal Heart* sought to lessen the impact of the play's accusations. Such direct political effects from mainstream theatre are admittedly rare, but their scarcity in no way lessens the fact that this mainstream play had the potential to unleash them. Further, less verifiable effects of mainstream theatre are far more abundant. In the case of *The Normal Heart* the statements made by the *New York Times* and Mayor Koch affected the reception of the play, lending the production an air of activist journalism rather than art, augmenting the narrative already created by advertising and reviews.

In a number of reviews from April 25 to May 15, 1985—including a second *New York Times* review, this one by Mel Gussow[82]—the dramaturgical shortcomings of *The Normal Heart* continued to be noted, but less and less so as its political importance became the focal point. In Gussow's *New York Times* article, which to some extent revised Rich's earlier review, he compared Kramer's hero Ned Weeks to Ibsen's hero of *An Enemy of the People*, Thomas Stockmann. In Gussow's opinion:

> The principal problem in 'The Normal Heart' is not Acquired Immune Deficiency Syndrome (a subject that is not mentioned by name in the course of the play), or even the broader question of a bias against homosexuals. As Ned affirms, 'This is not a civil rights issue. This is a contagion issue.' In common with Stockman [sic], he is trying to staunch an epidemic. He is a whistleblower and he is surrounded by people who are worried about their careers, their images and their sex lives. Life itself is at stake.[83]

While Gussow criticized Kramer for not having the "irony" of Ibsen, he praised *The Normal Heart*'s "polemic purpose,"[84] and his review hailed readers as people who would care about the AIDS epidemic over petty concerns.

Michael Feingold, writing for the liberal *Village Voice,* also compared the play to *An Enemy of the People* and wrote that Ibsen saw "the idealist as both necessary and a problem."[85] According to Feingold, Kramer instead used Ned as "strictly an author's mouthpiece" thereby limiting the literary value of the script.[86] Feingold ended his review by writing that "*The Normal Heart* can't solve the problems of the gay community any more than it can discover a cure for AIDS. What it can do is what any usable piece of political theatre does: nag at the viewers, rouse them to the prospect of accomplishing something. Kramer in person, like his hero, may be part of the problem; his play is at least a tiny part of the solution."[87] *The Normal Heart* was again seen as dramaturgically flawed, but it could "rouse" viewers. And, though the review does not mention them, the production presented spectators with clear actions to take in the lobby displays. This production did more than "nag." It hailed spectators as activists.

Even reviewers who experienced the writing of *The Normal Heart* as "more of a tract than a play" admitted its political import.[88] Clive Barnes described the play this way in the *New York Post*, which was then owned by the conservative media baron Rupert Murdoch. Barnes further asked, "How many people of the thousands who will see the play, and be stirred by its sheer intensity and passionate concern, would have read the tract?"[89] Additionally, would Barnes address a tract in the sensationalist *New York Post*? Would a tract receive 21 newspaper reviews and an advertising campaign? John Simon, writing for *New York*, which was also owned by Murdoch, argued that "what could have been a mere staged tract—and, in its lesser moments, is just that—transcends often enough into a fleshed-out, generously dramatized struggle, in which warring ideologies do not fail to breathe, sweat, weep, bleed—be human."[90] In 1985, arguing that gay men were "human" was quite remarkable, especially for a mainstream owned by the conservative Murdoch, and admitting gay men into the human fold would have challenged the ideologies of many mainstream readers. All this from a play that, according to some, read more like a tract. Even negative reviews in press organs unfriendly to the play's politics could spread the play's message. The review in *The Christian Science Monitor* is a prime example.

While *The Christian Science Monitor* often claims independence from its eponymous religion, notable employment confrontations in the early 1980s demonstrate that—legally, at least—*The Christian Science Monitor* then defined itself as a publication of the Christian Scientist sect. At the heart of these legal battles is testimony from high-ranking employees of *The Christian Science Monitor* defining the journal as a religious text rather than a secular news source.[91] The *Monitor*'s executives argue under oath that the journal's mission is "more effectually promoting and extending the religion of Christian Science."[92] That religion, as stated in court, explicitly included the Christian Science teaching that "homosexuality is a deviation from the moral law."[93] Therefore, one would not expect a sympathetic review of *The Normal Heart* from this periodical.

Nevertheless, *The Christian Science Monitor*'s short, disapproving review of *The Normal Heart* did more to inform its readers about AIDS than any prior article in its pages. It found the play to be "one-sided" and argued that "Mr. Kramer attempts unsuccessfully to combine a plea for responsible official awareness and treatment of a tragic health disaster with a propaganda pitch for society's unreserved acceptance of homosexual lifestyles."[94] However, the article also declared AIDS "a tragic health disaster," and, far more important, the article defined AIDS in its first paragraph, suggesting that readers were not familiar with the epidemic.[95] In fact, this is the first use of the term "acquired immune deficiency syndrome" in the *Christian Science Monitor*, making the review of *The Normal Heart* the publication's first AIDS coverage. Thus, the reviewer, as much as he disliked the play, added to readers' knowledge of the world, explaining this new and deadly disease. By calling it a "tragic health disaster," he also implicitly argued for fighting its spread, an action previously not undertaken by the government. Again, while many non-mainstream performances about HIV/AIDS had already occurred, *The Normal Heart* was the first that—due to its mainstream position—incited a review from *The Christian Science Monitor*. To not review the play that was the talk of the town would be bizarre for a major news source, regardless of its editorial point of view. *The Normal Heart* was a part of the culture industry in a way that alternative HIV/AIDS performances were not. And because it was embedded in capitalist structures, *The Normal Heart* was positioned to deploy emergent ideological principles into the mainstream. Though one ordinarily credits alternative, radical theater with being able to do this type of political work, it was precisely because *The Normal Heart* was in the mainstream that it was able to be so effective and to coerce journals like *The Christian Science Monitor* to acknowledge the AIDS epidemic.

In May, as the buzz surrounding the play was turning into sold-out crowds and the first extensions of the run, *The Normal Heart* received some positive reviews regarding its aesthetics from the popular national magazines *Newsweek* and *Time*, but these articles did little to promote the production's AIDS activism. Instead, they promoted an ideology that gay men are human, which, while not Kramer's primary mission, was a critical part of fighting AIDS. Jack Kroll wrote for *Newsweek* that "Kramer produces not a series of debates but a cross fire of life-and-death energies that illuminate the many issues and create a fierce and moving human drama."[96] *Time* seconded that opinion when its review asserted that what made *The Normal Heart* "so deeply affecting is that [it] portrays anguish and doom in individual human terms and enables audiences of every sexual inclination to grasp a common bond of suffering and mortality."[97] Because these positive reviews did not prominently mention the AIDS epidemic they did less to spread the play's main message. However, these reviews posit the "common bond" between people regardless of "sexual inclination" that no doubt challenged many readers' ideologies. And in 1985 hysteria about AIDS led to the violation of some gay men's civil rights, so keeping their humanity at the forefront was critical for fighting AIDS.

An article appearing in late May 1985 in the *New York Native* describes some of the panic felt by the straight public and the ways that even supposed allies could abuse gay men's civil rights. It is worth quoting at length:

> A few weeks ago [my straight roommate] told me she wanted me to move out because she was afraid I was going to give her AIDS. Understand, now, that my health is perfectly fine, as both my doctor and insurance company will attest. But *her* doctors tell her that while sexual intercourse seems to be how the virus is transmitted, there's no way of knowing the long-term effects of her sharing a bathroom and kitchen with a gay roommate. After all, he may be healthy *now*, her doctors say, but what if something's incubating away in his bloodstream? So this well-educated, cultured, and altogether lovely woman, a lawyer, gave me two weeks to clear out of the house. Too shocked and heartsick to even argue, I packed and left.
>
> Ned Weeks, the outspoken journalist in Larry Kramer's new play *The Normal Heart*, fears that the AIDS crisis could easily turn into another Holocaust, with gays railroaded into plague camps and worse. Weeks is dismissed by his associates as being hysterical. I thought so, too, and then three days after I saw the play, I had that little talk with my roommate. My God, if the woman I've lived with for all these years now believes that I'm a human time bomb threatening her existence, what're those yahoos in East Jesus, Missouri, thinking? Or the ones in Washington, D.C.?[98]

If the author seems paranoid, note that in 1986 conservative activist Lyndon LaRoche promoted California's Proposition 64, which asserted, based on no evidence, that AIDS could be transmitted by mosquitoes, casual contact, and respiratory infections. Proposition 64 would have created mandatory AIDS testing for gay men and AIDS quarantine camps. While no AIDS camps ever came into existence, the anecdote this author relates about his roommate captures the fear and anxiety surrounding AIDS at the time *The Normal Heart* was produced. His story highlights the necessity for the mainstream media, even if only in reviews of a play, to categorize AIDS patients as "human," as reviews of *The Normal Heart* did.

On July 25, 1985, over three months after *The Normal Heart* opened at the Public Theater, the famously masculine movie star Rock Hudson announced that he had AIDS. On July 28, 1985, "AIDS was on the front page of virtually every Sunday morning paper in the United States."[99] As Dr. Michael Gottlieb, an immunologist at UCLA who worked on AIDS cases from the beginning, wrote, "There was AIDS before Rock Hudson and AIDS after."[100] Hudson's announcement created drastically increased frequency and improved quality of AIDS coverage in the media. This awareness of the disease created a new frame for *The Normal Heart*: historical document. Instead of doubting the play's "hysteria," articles now wrote about its factual chronicle. One review in October in the *New York Native* optimistically suggested, "Someday [*The Normal Heart*] is going to be a standard script to be read in high schools."[101] The success of the *The Normal Heart* was due to its perceived nature as living journalism, and from within that paradigm it succeeded in its mission to transmit information about the HIV/AIDS epidemic to a largely ignorant public.

Epilogue

By disseminating information through reviews, performances, and pamphlets in the theatre lobby, *The Normal Heart* informed U.S. citizens about the AIDS crisis and hailed spectators and readers as people who cared about the epidemic and wanted to check its spread. Though this emergent ideology had been expressed in the alternative, "gay" theatre,[102] when it was presented by *The Normal Heart* in a mainstream theatre setting, it was amplified by the national media. This extension of the information across space also became integrated into the media's ritual mode of communication that promoted a shared ideology.[103] The result was the integration into the dominant ideology of the emergent ideology that AIDS was an emergency in need of attention. This incorporation of an emergent ideology into the dominant one demonstrates the central role mainstream theatre held in the U.S. political process. But what of the thousands of lives lost to HIV/AIDS during the mainstream media's silence before *The Normal Heart*?

The writing on the AIDS crisis of the 1980s is filled with war metaphors. Shilts begins the epilogue to *And the Band Played On* with an epigraph by Hermann Hesse: "There was no need to think at all of any reader but myself, or at the most, here and there another close war-comrade, and I most certainly never thought then about the survivors, but always about those who fell in the war. While writing it, I was as if delirious or crazy, surrounded by three or four people with mutilated bodies—that was how this book was produced."[104] This epigraph shows how gay men felt like they were at war during the early years of the AIDS epidemic, despite the general public's ignorance. Joseph Papp recalled that:

> Every night, at the end of *The Normal Heart*, ten, twelve or fifteen young men would sit there and be unable to move, absolutely stunned. Sit in their chairs, not leave. What would happen is, several other people in the audience, mostly men, would go over and sit with that person. Downstairs, another play called *Tracers* was running—a moving portrayal of young men dying in Vietnam. Exactly the same thing. All the Vietnam veterans would come over to a veteran, sit there and put an arm around him. You could have duplicated those two scenes. They both dealt with the same thing—buddies under fire, under threat of death.[105]

Those who fought AIDS during the early 1980s suffered a war of which most of the country was unaware, a war during peacetime, and *The Normal Heart* was one of the first major actions that helped combat apathy, homophobia, and ignorance.

Notes

1. Jack Kroll, "Going to the Heart of AIDS," *Newsweek*, May 13 1985.
2. Gay Men's Health Crisis, "Homepage," Gay Men's Health Crisis, www.gmhc.org.
3. Frank Rich, "Theatre: 'The Normal Heart,' by Larry Kramer," *New York Times*, April 22 1985.
4. Mel Gussow, "Confronting a Crisis with Incendiery Passion," ibid., April 28.
5. Max Horkheimer and Theodor W. Adorno, *Dialectic of Enlightenment* (New York: Continuum, 1997), 94–136.
6. Randy Shilts reminds us, "The AIDS epidemic, of course, did not arise full grown from the biological landscape; the problem had been festering throughout the decade. The death tolls of the late 1980s are not startling new developments but an unfolding of events predicted for many years. There had been a time when much of this suffering could have been prevented, but by 1985 that time had passed ... The bitter truth was that AIDS did not just happen to America—it was allowed to happen by an array of institutions, all of which failed to perform their appropriate tasks to safeguard the public health. The failure of the system leaves a legacy of unnecessary suffering that will haunt the Western world for decades to come" Randy Shilts, *And the Band Played On: Politics, People, and the AIDS Epidemic* (New York: St. Martin's P, 1987), xxi–xxii.
7. Larry Kramer, *The Normal Heart and the Destiny of Me* (New York: Grove Press, 2000), 116.
8. Shilts, *And the Band Played On*, 380.
9. David Román, *Acts of Intervention: Performance, Gay Culture, and AIDS* (Bloomington: Indiana UP, 1998), xx.
10. Román, *Acts of Intervention*, xxii.
11. Román, *Acts of Intervention*, 58.
12. William M. Hoffman, *As Is* (New York: Random House, 1985).
13. Gail Merrifield Papp, "Larry Kramer and the Public Theatre," in *We Must Love One Another or Die: The Life and Legacies of Larry Kramer*, ed. Lawrence Mass (London: Cassell, 1997), 257.
14. Papp, "Larry Kramer and the Public Theatre," 258.
15. Shilts, *And the Band Played On*, 282.
16. Papp, "Larry Kramer and the Public Theatre," 259.
17. Victoria Hamburg and Terry Beirn, December 17 1984.
18. Papp, "Larry Kramer and the Public Theatre," 8.
19. Papp, "Larry Kramer and the Public Theatre," 261.
20. Papp, "Larry Kramer and the Public Theatre," 265.
21. Anonymous, "New York Shakespeare Festival Records. Series II: Play Department Files 1962–1992, Series II: Play Department 1962–1992, Sub-Series 3 Playwrights," in *The Normal Heart Larry Kramer 1984–1988* (New York Public Library Archive: Lincoln Center 1984–1988).
22. Papp, "Larry Kramer and the Public Theatre," 264.
23. Kramer, *The Normal Heart and the Destiny of Me*, 75.
24. Papp, "Larry Kramer and the Public Theatre," 264–65.
25. Román, *Acts of Intervention*, 60.

26. Public Theatre, "Pre-Opening *Normal Heart* Advertisement," *New York Times* 1985.
27. Public Theatre, "Post-Opening *Normal Heart* Advertisement," *New York Times* 1985.
28. If it seems unlikely that in April of 1985 there could be people who had still never heard of AIDS, remember that in February 1985 "the official position of New York City was that the AIDS epidemic was not yet a crisis" even though the city's "cases surpassed 3,000" (Shilts, *And the Band Played On*, 533). And media coverage of New York City's crisis was scarce: "the first series of newspaper articles investigating New York's response to the AIDS epidemic was published, not in New York, but in the *San Francisco Chronicle*," (*And the Band Played On*, 533–34).
29. Anonymous, "New York Shakespeare Festival Records. Series II: Play Department Files.
30. Ibid.
31. John Bull, "The Establishment of Mainstream Theatre," in *Cambridge History of British Theatre* (Cambridge: Cambridge UP, 2004), 329.
32. "Ideology and the Ideological State Apparatuses." In *Essays on Ideology*, 179 pages. London: Verso, 1984.
33. *The Radical in Performance: Between Brecht and Baudrillard* (London: Routledge, 1999), 47.
34. Michael Sommers, "Casualties," *New York Native*, May 20 1985, 45.
35. Kissel Howard, "Untitled," *Women's Wear Daily* 1985, 14.
36. Ann Giudici Fettner, "Heart Minus Snarl," *New York Native*, October 21–27 1985, 40.
37. Gregory Gross, "Coming up for Air: Three AIDS Plays," *Journal of American Culture* 15(1992): 64.
38. Michael Feingold, "Part of the Solution," *Village Voice*, April 30 1985, 105.
39. Ibid.
40. Gussow, "Confronting a Crisis with Incendiery Passion," 2: 24.
41. Joel Shatzky, "AIDS Enters the American Theatre: *As Is* and *the Normal Heart*," in *AIDS: The Literary Response*, ed. Emmanuel S. Nelson (New York: Twayne Publishers, 1992), 134.
42. Kramer, *The Normal Heart and the Destiny of Me*, 113.
43. Simon John, "Untitled," *New York* 1985, 92.
44. Sommers, "Casualties," 45.
45. Gross, "Coming up for Air: Three Aids Plays," 65.
46. Kramer, *The Normal Heart and the Destiny of Me*, 113.
47. Bergman, "Larry Kramer and the Rhetoric of AIDS," 179.
48. Bergman, "Larry Kramer and the Rhetoric of Aids," 180.
49. John Clum, "Kramer vs. Kramer, Ben and Alexander: Larry Kramer's Voices and His Audiences," in *We Must Love One Another or Die: The Life and Legacies of Larry Kramer*, ed. Lawrence Mass (London: Cassell, 1997), 202.
50. Nicholas de Jongh, *Not in Front of the Audience: Homosexuality on Stage* (London and New York: Routledge, 1992), 183.
51. Kramer, *The Normal Heart and the Destiny of Me*, 117.
52. Bergman, "Rhetoric." #179.
53. Syna, "'The Normal Hear' Offensive and Boring," 6B.
54. John M. Clum, "Kramer," 209.
55. Ibid.

56. Kramer, *The Normal Heart and the Destiny of Me*, 51.
57. de Jongh, *Not in Front*, 183.
58. Syna, "'The Normal Hear' Offensive and Boring."
59. Kramer, *The Normal Heart and the Destiny of Me*, 71.
60. Callen, *Surviving AIDS* (New York: Harper Collins, 1990).
61. Román, *Acts of Intervention*, 238.
62. John M. Clum, *Still Acting Gay: Male Homosexuality in Modern Drama* (New York: St. Martin's Griffin, 1992), 64.
63. D.S. Lawson, "Rage and Remembrance: The Aids Plays," in *Aids: The Literary Response*, ed. Emmanuel S. Nelson (New York: Twayne Publishers, 1992), 142.
64. Kinzer, Craig, and Mary Poole. "Brecht and the Actor." *Communications from the International Brecht Society* 20, no. 1,2 (October 1991): 79–84.
65. Min Tian, "Alienation-Effect for Whom? Brecht's (Mis)Interpretation of the Classical Chinese Theatre," *Asian Theatre Journal* 14, no. 2 (1997).
66. qtd in Robert E. Scholes, *Semiotics and Interpretation* (New Haven: Yale UP, 1982), 48.
67. "Brecht and the Actor," *Communications from the International Brecht Society* 20, no. 1,2 (1991).
68. Gross, "Coming up for Air: Three Aids Plays," 63.
69. Robert J. Cox, "Performing Memory/Speech: Aesthetic Boundaries and "the Other" in *Ghetto* and *the Normal Heart*," *Text and Performance Quarterly* 12, no. 4 (1992): 386.
70. Joseph Roach, "Normal Heartlands," ibid.: 378.
71. Papp, "Larry Kramer and the Public Theatre," 266.
72. Michael Paller, "Larry Kramer and Gay Theater," ibid., 238; Román, *Acts of Intervention*, xx, 64.
73. Frank Rich, "Theatre: 'The Normal Heart,' by Larry Kramer; John Beaufort, "Review: The Normal Heart," *The Christian Science Monitor*, April 29 1985; Syna, "'The Normal Hear' Offensive and Boring."
74. Douglas Watt, "The Tragedy of AIDS" *Daily News*, April 22 1985; Sommers, "Casualties; Kissel, "Untitled."
75. Allan Wallach, "Drama of Official Apathy Towards AIDS," *Newsday*, April 22 1985; Robert Massa, "T-Cells and Sympathy: Making Theatre out of AIDS," *The Village Voice*, April 23 1985; Michael Kearns, "Gay Dramatists Pen New Works Responding to 'Age of Aids'," *The Advocate*, January 22 1985; Fettner, "Heart Minus Snarl; Leora Manishchewitz, "'Normal Heart' Takes an Unsparing Look at AIDS," *Villager*, April 25 1985; Gussow, "Confronting a Crisis with Incendiery Passion; Feingold, "Part of the Solution; Liz Smith, "Untitled," *Daily News*, May 1 1985; Clive Barnes, "Plague, Play and Tract," *New York Post*, May 4 1985; "Joel Gray Adds Love to the AIDS Equation," *New York Post*, October 8 1985; Simon, "Untitled; Humm, "Review: The Normal Heart," *Variety*, May 15 1985; Kroll, "Going to the Heart of AIDS; William A Henry III, "A Common Bond of Suffering: Shows About AIDS Make Good Drama as Well as Propoganda," *Time*, May 13 1985; Humm, "Review: The Normal Heart; Holly Hill, "Dreadful Subject Drained of Nastiness and Sickly Content," *London Times*, May 29 1985.
76. Rich, "Theatre: 'The Normal Heart,' by Larry Kramer," C17.
77. Ibid.
78. Ibid.
79. Ibid.

56   *Resistance*

80. Shatzky, "AIDS Enters," 133.
81. Shilts, *And the Band Played On*, 556.
82. It is not normal for the *New York Times* to have two reviews of the same play, but this is what happened in the case of *The Normal Heart*.
83. Gussow, "Confronting a Crisis with Incendiery Passion."
84. Ibid.
85. Feingold, "Part of the Solution," 105.
86. Ibid.
87. Ibid.
88. Barnes, "Plague."
89. Barnes, "Plague," 17.
90. Simon John, "Untitled," 92.
91. First, in 1983, after refusing Mark Feldstein employment because he was not a member of the Christian Science religion, *The Christian Science Monitor* successfully argued in the United States Circuit Court D "that the *Monitor* is a religious activity of a religious organization and is therefore entitled to discriminate in its employment practices in favor of co-religionists" A. David Mazzone, "Feldstein V. Christian Science Monitor," www.leagle.com, http://www.leagle.com/decision/19831529555FSupp974_11373.xml/FELDSTEIN%20v.%20CHRISTIAN%20SCIENCE%20MONITOR. According to the testimony of Michael West, then Treasurer of the Christian Science Church and Trustee of the Christian Science Publishing Society, "the *Monitor* is published by the Christian Science Publishing Society, an organ of the Christian Science Church. Both the Publishing Society and the Monitor were founded by Mary Baker Eddy, the founder of the Christian Science faith. The deed of trust of the Publishing Society declares as its purpose 'more effectually promoting and extending the religion of Christian Science'" ibid. Finally, the judge finds "that the Monitor is a religious activity of a religious organization, [thus] I find that it is permissible for the Monitor to apply a test of religious affiliation to candidates for employment" ibid. One of those tests would be whether its employees were gay, as was the case when *Christian Science Monitor* reporter Christine Madsen was fired because she was a lesbian.

    The *Monitor* fired Madsen in 1982, and the Massachusetts Supreme Court upheld the paper's right to do so in 1985. The *Monitor*'s argument hinged on its religious affiliation. The case's decision reads that "Warren D. Silvernail, personnel manager of the Church averred that '[t]he Church's personnel office [was] in charge of the personnel functions at the Church and its religious activities including The Christian Science Publishing Society which publishes the Christian Science Monitor' ... [and that evidence to this effect included] portions of the Employee Handbook, providing, in relevant part, that 'the policy of The Mother Church [is] to employ only members of the Church in all of its activities, including The Christian Science Publishing Society ...'; and of the plaintiff's employee badge labeled 'The First Church of Christ, Scientist, Boston'" Joseph Nolan, "Christine Madsen vs. Robert Erwin & Others, Trustees, & Others," www.Masscases.com, http://masscases.com/cases/sjc/395/395mass715.html. And, in fact, Madsen herself "did not contradict the fact she was a Church employee in her affidavit." Ibid. What is more, according to the court records, part of the *Christian Science* Monitor's evidence for it being a religious organization included "a memorandum regarding sexual morality [that] 'was distributed on

or about August 8, 1974 to all Church employees, including those working for The Christian Science Monitor'" ibid. This memorandum dictated that "'homosexuality is a deviation from the moral law' as expounded by the Christian Science Church, and that every employee of the Church is expected to uphold the Church's standard of morality" ibid. Thus, while the *Christian Science Monitor*'s website claims that it is an independent news source rather than a religious publication ("About the Christian Science Monitor," The Christian Science Monitor, http://www.csmonitor.com/About/The-Monitor-difference.), in the early 1980s it legally defined itself as a religious publication in order to discriminate against those outside its sect.
92. Mazzone, "Feldstein V. Christian Science Monitor."
93. Nolan, "Christine Madsen vs. Robert Erwin & Others, Trustees, & Others."
94. Beaufort, "Review: The Normal Heart," 2.
95. Ibid.
96. Kroll, "Going to the Heart of AIDS," 87.
97. Henry III, "A Common Bond of Suffering: Shows About Aids Make Good Drama as Well as Propoganda," 85.
98. Sommers, "Casualties," 45.
99. Shilts, *And the Band Played On*, 578.
100. *And the Band Played On*, 585.
101. Fettner, "Heart Minus Snarl," 40.
102. Paller, "Gay Theater," 238; Román, *Acts of Intervention*, xx, 64.
103. For more on ritual communication, ideology, and the media, see: James W. Carey, *Communication as Culture: Essays on Media and Society* (Boston: Unwin Hyman, 1989).
104. Shilts, *And the Band Played On*, 583.
105. Papp, "Larry Kramer and the Public Theatre," 266–67.

Bibliography

"About – the Christian Science Monitor." The Christian Science Monitor, http://www.csmonitor.com/About/The-Monitor-difference.
Anonymous. "New York Shakespeare Festival Records. Series II: Play Department Files 1962–1992, Series II: Play Department 1962–1992, Sub-Series 3 – Playwrights." In *The Normal Heart / Larry Kramer 1984–1988*. New York Public Library Archive: Lincoln Center, 1984–1988.
Althusser, Louis. "Ideology and the Ideological State Apparatuses." In *Essays on Ideology*, 179 pages. London: Verso, 1984.
Barnes, Clive. "Joel Gray Adds Love to the AIDS Equation." *New York Post*, October 8 1985, 61.
———. "Plague, Play and Tract." *New York Post*, May 4 1985.
Beaufort, John. "Review: The Normal Heart." *The Christian Science Monitor*, April 29 1985, 28.
Bergman, David. "Larry Kramer and the Rhetoric of AIDS." In *AIDS: The Literary Response*, edited by Emmanuel S. Nelson, 175–86. New York: Twayne Publishers, 1992.
Bull, John. "The Establishment of Mainstream Theatre." In *Cambridge History of British Theatre*, 326–48. Cambridge: Cambridge UP, 2004.
Callen, Michael. *Surviving AIDS*. New York: Harper Collins, 1990.

Carey, James W. *Communication as Culture: Essays on Media and Society*. Boston: Unwin Hyman, 1989.

Clum, John M. "Kramer vs. Kramer, Ben and Alexander: Larry Kramer's Voices and His Audiences." In *We Must Love One Another or Die: The Life and Legacies of Larry Kramer*, edited by Lawrence Mass, 200–14. London: Cassell, 1997.

———. *Still Acting Gay: Male Homosexuality in Modern Drama*. New York: St. Martin's Griffin, 1992.

Cox, J. Robert. "Performing Memory/Speech: Aesthetic Boundaries and 'the Other' in *Ghetto* and *the Normal Heart*." *Text and Performance Quarterly* 12, no. 4 (1992): 385–90.

de Jongh, Nicholas. *Not in Front of the Audience: Homosexuality on Stage*. London and New York: Routledge, 1992.

Feingold, Michael. "Part of the Solution." *Village Voice*, April 30 1985, 105.

Fettner, Ann Giudici. "Heart Minus Snarl." *New York Native*, October 21–27 1985, 40.

Gay Men's Health Crisis. "Homepage." Gay Men's Health Crisis, http://www.gmhc.org.

Gross, Gregory D. "Coming up for Air: Three AIDS Plays." *Journal of American Culture* 15 (1992): 63–67.

Gussow, Mel. "Confronting a Crisis with Incendiery Passion." *New York Times*, April 28 1985, B3.

Hamburg, Victoria, and Terry Beirn. December 17 1984. Henry III, William A. "A Common Bond of Suffering: Shows About AIDS Make Good Drama as Well as Propoganda." *Time*, May 13 1985, 85.

Hill, Holly. "Dreadful Subject Drained of Nastiness and Sickly Content." *London Times*, May 29 1985.

Hoffman, William M. *As Is*. New York: Random House, 1985.

Horkheimer, Max, and Theodor W. Adorno. *Dialectic of Enlightenment*. New York: Continuum, 1997.

Humm. "Review: The Normal Heart." *Variety*, May 15 1985, 106.

Kearns, Michael. "Gay Dramatists Pen New Works Responding to 'Age of AIDS'." *The Advocate*, January 22 1985.

Kershaw, Baz. *The Radical in Performance: Between Brecht and Baudrillard*. London: Routledge, 1999.

Kinzer, Craig, and Mary Poole. "Brecht and the Actor." *Communications from the International Brecht Society* 20, no. 1,2 (October 1991): 79–84.

Kissel, Howard. "Untitled." *Women's Wear Daily*, 1985, 14.

Kramer, Larry. *The Normal Heart and the Destiny of Me*. New York: Grove Press, 2000.

Kroll, Jack. "Going to the Heart of AIDS." *Newsweek*, May 13 1985, 87.

Lawson, D.S. "Rage and Remembrance: The AIDS Plays." In *AIDS: The Literary Response*, edited by Emmanuel S. Nelson, 140–54. New York: Twayne Publishers, 1992.

Manishchewitz, Leora. "'Normal Heart' Takes an Unsparing Look at AIDS." *Villager*, April 25 1985, 13.

Massa, Robert. "T-Cells and Sympathy: Making Theatre out of AIDS." *The Village Voice*, April 23 1985, 110.

Mazzone, A. David. "Feldstein v. Christian Science Monitor." http://www.leagle.com, http://www.leagle.com/decision/19831529555FSupp974_11373.xml/FELDSTEIN v. CHRISTIAN SCIENCE MONITOR.

Nelson, Emmanuel S. "Introduction." In *AIDS: The Literary Response*, edited by Emmanuel S. Nelson, 1–10. New York: Twayne Publishers, 1992.
Nolan, Joseph. "Christine Madsen vs. Robert Erwin & Others, Trustees, & Others." http://www.Masscases.com, http://masscases.com/cases/sjc/395/395mass715.html.
Paller, Michael. "Larry Kramer and Gay Theater." In *We Must Love One Another or Die: The Life and Legacies of Larry Kramer*, edited by Lawrence Mass, 235–55. London: Cassell, 1997.
Papp, Gail Merrifield. "Larry Kramer and the Public Theatre." In *We Must Love One Another or Die: The Life and Legacies of Larry Kramer*, edited by Lawrence Mass, 256–70. London: Cassell, 1997.
Public Theatre. "Post-Opening *Normal Heart* Advertisement." *New York Times*, 1985.
———. "Pre-Opening *Normal Heart* Advertisement." *New York Times*, 1985.
Rich, Frank. "Theatre: 'The Normal Heart,' by Larry Kramer." *New York Times*, April 22 1985, C17.
Roach, Joseph. "Normal Heartlands." *Text and Performance Quarterly* 12 (October 1992): 377–84.
Román, David. *Acts of Intervention: Performance, Gay Culture, and AIDS*. Bloomington: Indiana UP, 1998.
Scholes, Robert E. *Semiotics and Interpretation*. New Haven: Yale UP, 1982.
Shatzky, Joel. "AIDS Enters the American Theatre: *As Is* and *the Normal Heart*." In *AIDS: The Literary Response*, edited by Emmanuel S. Nelson, 131–39. New York: Twayne Publishers, 1992.
Shilts, Randy. *And the Band Played On: Politics, People, and the Aids Epidemic*. New York: St. Martin's P, 1987.
Simon, John. "Untitled." *New York*, 1985, 91–92.
Smith, Liz. "Untitled." *Daily News*, May 1 1985, 10.
Sommers, Michael. "Casualties." *New York Native*, May 20 1985, 45.
Syna, Sy. "'The Normal Hear' Offensive and Boring." *New York City Tribune*, April 22 1985, 6B.
Tian, Min. "Alienation-Effect for Whom? Brecht's (Mis)Interpretation of the Classical Chinese Theatre." *Asian Theatre Journal* 14, no. 2 (Fall 1997).
Wallach, Allan. "Drama of Official Apathy Towards AIDS." *Newsday*, April 22 1985, 17.
Watt, Douglas. "The Tragedy of AIDS." *Daily News*, April 22 1985, 38.

3 Assimilation
Angels in America

Prologue

"*Save us!*" wrote *New York Observer* critic John Heilpern about the 1993 Broadway premiere of *Angels in America*.[1] Save us from the murderous HIV/AIDS policies of the Ronald Reagan and George H.W. Bush Administrations. Save us from the marginalization of gay characters by the U.S. culture industry. And save us from a nation that forces gay men to die "secret deaths" from HIV/AIDS, as one character from the play puts it.[2] Heilpern's representative review demonstrates a desire for change wholly in keeping with the political moment. It also provides a striking contrast to reviews of earlier plays that took gay men and AIDS as their subjects. Though *Angels in America* follows two gay couples and ends with one gay character declaring, "We will be citizens,"[3] the play was not greeted as gay propaganda, as were earlier AIDS plays such as *The Normal Heart*. Instead, *Angels in America* was hailed as mainstream art with its prediction of gay citizenship. This reception was because of the play's horizon of expectations. Every aspect of the production suggested it was a thoroughly mainstream play, from its Broadway location, to its advertising in the *New York Times*, to its glowing reviews. And because the play was situated so squarely in the mainstream, its prophecy of gay citizenship and its fulsome critical reception suggested that the play could expand the U.S. imagined community to include gay men.

But the salvation craved by critics reviewing *Angels in America* was not based solely on the play's graphic exploration of AIDS and gay men's relationships. Many plays with similar subjects had already been produced and elicited different reactions. Between 1985 and 1994 "over sixty plays had opened in New York that either took people with AIDS as their principal subject or in which some aspect of the AIDS epidemic played an important part."[4] Instead, what provoked critics' hyperbolic hopes was *Angels in America*'s inexorable intertwining with the historical moment, particularly President Bill Clinton's election, and a perceived shift in national politics towards more inclusive policies for LGBT communities.

Examining the historical context of *Angels in America*'s early productions, the play's Broadway premiere, and its Broadway reception demonstrates how the play's text and acceptance by the culture industry created a space for gay men in the dominant ideology's imagined community. Benedict

Anderson suggests that a nation is "an imagined political community, ... imagined as both inherently limited and sovereign,"[5] while Joseph Roach and Robert Cox show how theatre helps circumscribe and, occasionally, redraw these imagined boundaries.[6] *Angels in America* utilized its mainstream platform to reimagine the national boundary to include gay men within it. While including gay men in the U.S. imagined community in 1993 may seem radical, the play contained other, more conservative, aspects—such as its treatment of race, class, and gender—that made its assimilation of gay men palatable. What's more, the play's similarities to the rhetoric of the Bill Clinton presidential campaign created a symbiosis of message that fostered the play's success. By presenting a prophet of a world in which Clinton's assimilationist campaign promises regarding the LGBT community were made good, the Broadway premiere of *Angels in America* acted as a transition between a structure of feeling and an emergent ideology. In other words, *Angels in America* was "a kind of feeling and thinking which is indeed social and material" but not yet fully realized in the political arena.[7] The structure of feeling/emergent ideology *Angels in America* presented was an imagined community in the U.S. that included gay men, one in which gay men were citizens, not ignored by the government, and not left to die "secret deaths" by the tens of thousands. While assimilationist rather than radical, *Angels in America* nevertheless utilized its high position in the culture industry to expand the U.S. imagined community to include gay men.

The Road to Broadway

After the lethal and reprehensible silence about HIV/AIDS in the U.S. from the Ronald Reagan and George H.W. Bush Administrations, LGBT communities and allies in 1992 were understandably excited for what they saw as a sea change on the eve of Bill Clinton's election. Clinton was, after all, the first U.S. presidential candidate to make campaign promises to the LGBT community. This charged atmosphere of optimism was strong in Los Angeles at the Mark Taper Forum's premiere of Tony Kushner's *Angels in America: A Gay Fantasia on National Themes*. The play's full form—that is, both its parts performed together—came into the world literally on the eve of Clinton's election. Instead of crying out from the wilderness, like *The Normal Heart*'s eruption into the Reagan years, the opening of *Angels in America* at the Mark Taper was a messiah of hope for a new era in which LGBT communities would be part of the U.S. imagined community. Clinton insisted his administration would treat LGBT individuals as citizens and would end the military's ban on gays and lesbians serving their country. There was, as yet, no disappointment about Clinton's lack of follow-through on those promises, and *Angels in America* fit the buoyancy of the moment. Theatre scholar David Román, who was in the Mark Taper audience opening night, writes that "to watch *Angels in America* on the eve of the [Clinton] election was to participate in a public ritual of hope."[8] Any opening night audience is generally sympathetic, composed of friends of the artists and producers.[9] Thus, opening night audiences tend to root for a production's success. That is certainly what Román recounts for *Angels in America*'s 1992 Los Angeles premiere: "For many of us at the Mark Taper Forum on the eve of the presidential elections … a shift in the national AIDS ideology seemed possible."[10] This "possible" shift was made material through the ritual of creating and witnessing *Angels in America*, through the evening's articulation of a structure of feeling. Román and his companions at the Mark Taper Forum felt optimistic about Clinton's presidency, and saw their roles as spectators at this play as analogous to their roles as voters in Clinton's election. They thought with Clinton in office, AIDS would be dealt with as a serious problem and, as full citizens, gay men would receive protection by the state from this epidemic, thus entering the U.S. imagined community.

Moreover, given the play's utopian aspirations, spectators likely experienced a utopian performative. As Jill Dolan describes,

> Utopian performatives persuade us that beyond this 'now' of material oppression and unequal power relations lives a future that might be different, one whose potential we can feel as we're seared by the promise of a present that gestures toward a better later. The affective and ideological 'doings' we see and feel demonstrated in utopian performatives also critically rehearse civic engagement that could be effective in the wider public and political realm.[11]

Within the walls of the Mark Taper theatre, spectators witnessed a play that ended emphatically proclaiming that gay men "will be citizens."[12] Outside the theatre, Clinton's election and campaign promises pointed towards a future in which that aspiration could be writ in law. Further, as spectators applauded, they celebrated the "civic engagement" each of them performed to elect Clinton—the labor of campaigning and voting. Thus the hope embodied by *Angels in America* in 1992 Los Angeles transcended the confines of the Mark Taper Forum and expanded to include the "ideological 'doings'" of the Presidential election, hinting at the existence of a utopian performative. Completing the experience, the production received lavishly positive reviews, suggesting *Angels in America* was not solely for a niche LGBT audience. The Los Angeles reception, and an equally positive reception of a London production, convinced producers that *Angels in America* would be a mainstream success in New York City.

By the time *Angels in America* opened on Broadway in May of 1993, its West Coast and London performances had already entered theatre history's annals, and the script had won many accolades, including the Pulitzer Prize. These honors contributed to New York's high expectations for salvation, both artistic and political; they were embodied in *Angels in America*'s place of pride in the Walter Kerr Theatre with the highest ticket prices Broadway had yet seen. The Broadway premiere of *Angels in America* was a mainstream commodity in every sense. Yet, because of the historical context in which it opened on Broadway, because of its position within the culture industry, and particularly because of its reception in the press, its Broadway premiere incorporated gay men into the U.S.'s imagined community. *Angels in America* accomplished this expansion based on its unique production history and its privileged place in the culture industry.

The historical context of *Angels in America* positioned it to be mainstream theatre's voice of gay civil rights. The play connected to actual political events, in part, through its explicit references to the recent past. Though produced on Broadway in 1993, the play's primary 1985–1986 setting[13] alluded directly to President Reagan, Reagan's Attorney General Ed Meese, Reagan's ambassador to the United Nations Jeane Kirkpatrick, and especially to the conservative power broker Roy Cohn.[14] The play's scathing commentary on these figures fit the dominant ideology of the United States represented by the election of Bill Clinton. By positing the Reagan Administration's selfishness, *Angels in America* echoed criticisms lodged by the Clinton campaign against the Republican old guard, criticisms that, for Clinton, led to an easy plurality of the popular vote. Opening on Broadway shortly after Clinton's inauguration, *Angels in America* became central to the new windfall of liberal sentiment. As president, Clinton became a repository of hope for those in and around the gay community who suffered horribly under the AIDS policies of Presidents Reagan and George H.W. Bush. Andrew Sullivan, later writing for the *Advocate*, explained, "[T]he origins of the gay love affair with Clinton are not hard to explain. Back in 1991 and 1992, Clinton was among the first candidates of either party to address the question of gay rights forcefully and eloquently. His promise to end the ban on gay men and women in the military was a stunning promise, unique in American history."[15] While Clinton's infamous "Don't Ask, Don't Tell" policy—which allowed gay men and women to serve in the military as long as they did not reveal their sexual identity—was not satisfying, when *Angels in America* premiered on Broadway, Clinton was still the darling of LGBT civil rights activists. And much like Clinton's election became politically symbolic of the dominant ideology's increased support for LGBT rights, *Angels in America* became culturally symbolic of this movement.

Angels in America's discussion of gay citizenship further linked it to contemporaneous political debates. In a *Time* magazine interview shortly after the Broadway premiere, Kushner asserted: "We're at a historic juncture. In a pluralist democracy, there's a moment when a minority obtains legitimacy and its rights are taken seriously by the other minorities that together make up the majority. That's happening now for gays and lesbians. We're winning, and that gives things a certain electricity."[16] During the early 1990s, whether gay men and women would be allowed to adopt, marry, serve their country, or stand by their loved ones in hospitals, were topics of great currency, and they propelled *Angels in America*'s Broadway premiere to the fore. These discussions bestowed upon *Angels in America* "a certain electricity."

64 *Assimilation*

The fact that *Time* magazine participated in this discourse starkly reveals ideological differences between the Clinton era and that of his predecessors. For example, three years prior to Clinton's election and *Angels in America*'s Broadway premiere, Queer Nation circulated an anonymous manifesto that delineated the activist group's rage. The manifesto stated, "I hate that in twelve years of public education I was never taught about queer people. I hate that I grew up thinking I was the only queer in the world, and I hate even more that most queer kids still grow up the same way."[17] Such isolation post-1993 is hard to imagine given Clinton's campaign promises, the commercial success of *Angels*, and the maelstrom of press coverage both sparked. Yet, while Clinton's assurances ultimately proved empty, *Angels in America* delivered on its promise. It successfully positioned itself as a harbinger of a time in which gay men would be acceptable characters in the culture industry, and this opened space in the U.S. imagined community for gay men. Part of this work was done through the script's many awards.

The pre-Broadway honors helped structure spectators' horizon of expectations, suggesting the play was "art" and therefore worthy of society's attention. These prizes, including a Pulitzer Prize awarded on the eve of the Broadway premiere, framed *Angels in America* as "great literature."[18] Because art is frequently conflated with "universal" appeal, *Angels in America*'s reception more successfully promoted the emergent ideology of gay men's merit of mainstream attention than earlier HIV/AIDS plays that were received as propaganda. *Angels in America*'s reviews, even the negative ones, praised its artistic merit, suggesting, either explicitly or implicitly, that its gay characters belonged in the culture industry, and, hence, in the nation's imagined community.[19] These awards thus contributed to ideological support for gay people belonging center stage, which, in *Angels in America*'s case, was directly in the middle of a for-profit enterprise.

In addition to its touted artistic merit, *Angels in America* also enjoyed "great economic expectations," as described by critic Robert Brustein and revealed by its high-price ticket.[20] Since the play was presented in two parts, with tickets set at $60 per installment, *Angels in America* boasted the most expensive Broadway ticket to date.[21] Shows typically sold out, indicating that spectators believed or hoped that the show was worth the high price. Likewise, the production's cost demonstrated producers' confidence in the show's ability to make money. By December 6, 1993, $3 million was spent on the production, making it then the most expensive non-musical production.[22] Nearly every review commented on these high artistic and economic expectations and maintained that *Angels in America* lived up to them.[23] Changes to the scheduled New York production further highlight the expectations for profit.

Originally, *Angels in America* was slated for production at the Public Theatre, home of *The Normal Heart*'s premiere in 1985. But the play's success prior to New York City caused changes to its venue that establish that its producers believed it was a product with a strong chance of generating profit in the culture industry. Following the play's success in San Francisco, Los Angeles, and London, it bypassed the off-Broadway Public and was produced by Jujamcyn Theatres at the Walter Kerr Theatre on Broadway. Its first part, *Millennium Approaches*, opened on May 4, 1993, and its second part, *Perestroika*, joined it in repertory on November 23, 1993. Likewise, Oskar Eustis, the director of California's Mark Taper and Eureka Theatre productions, was replaced with the New York-based director George C. Wolfe, who broke a previous commitment to take on *Angels in America*. While much of the cast and blocking came from West Coast productions, the New York program did not acknowledge Eustis. This omission prompted one critic to comment, "[Wolfe] also left enough of the L.A. production alone that the omission of any mention of Eustis in the credits seems impolite, if not unjust."[24] This was not the only questionable event surrounding the New York production. JoAnne Akalaitis, the Artistic Director at the Public who lost the production of *Angels in America*, vacated her position soon after this disappointment. Brustein suggests that Akalaitis' inability to secure the play for the Public led to her "departure."[25] Interestingly, in August 1993, Wolfe assumed Akalaitis' previous position at the Public.[26] While the chronology of these events does not prove causality, it is indisputable that Wolfe replaced Akalaitis soon after Wolfe's Broadway production of *Angels in America*. This chain of events, at the very least, suggests that the play was considered an important commodity.

This, then, was the context in which *Angels in America* emerged from its beginnings in California to its Broadway premiere. Knitted with Clinton's election and a promised new era of gay civil rights, the play gave concrete form to a structure of feeling and a utopian performative "gesture[ing] toward a better later."[27] It did so, in part, by criticizing the Reagan Administration, but more so through its reception as art rather than propaganda. With its Pulitzer Prize, its space in the heart of Broadway, and its ambitious economic expectations, the play enlarged the imagined community, at least in the culture industry, of the U.S., to include gay characters struggling for citizenship. In this milieu, the Broadway production of *Angels in America* became a beacon for movement towards gay equality.

A Halo of Gay Civil Rights

When *Angels in America* spread its wings over Broadway, its historical context and prior awards created a space in which every aspect of the production text—from its script to its neighborhood—assumed the halo of promoting gay civil rights. Its plot and cultural position expanded the U.S. imagined community to include gay men, but in a palatable rather than radical manner. By examining the intricacies of its cultural milieu—its physical space, its advertising, its program note, its *mise-en-scène*, its merchandising, and its relation to the Clinton campaign—alongside its massive text, one can see how *Angels in America* interacted with its environment to create a performance of gay civil rights that was acceptable to the contemporaneous dominant ideology.

To understand the ideology promoted by *Angels in America*, one must understand the play's textual content. Consequently, an appropriate first step is a brief recapitulation of the plot. Set in 1985 and 1986 with an epilogue in 1990, the play follows two couples in New York City and the dissolution of their romantic relationships. The relationship of Prior and Louis, a gay male couple, falters under the strain of Prior's illness with AIDS. Meanwhile, Joe and Harper, an opposite-sex Mormon couple recently transplanted from Utah, endure an unhappy marriage. Their relationship disintegrates because of Joe's closeted "homosexuality."[28] Joe's mother, Hannah, moves to New York City from Utah after Joe comes out to her over the phone. Instead of caring for Joe, however, Hannah ends up comforting Harper and Prior. In the interim, Joe and Louis meet, and, over time, begin a romantic relationship. This ends when Louis discovers Joe's mentor is ultra-conservative Roy Cohn whose own struggle with HIV figures prominently. Prior, meanwhile, is nursed by Belize, an African American ex-drag queen. Under his drug regimen, Prior begins either to hallucinate or to see angels. This experience eventually leads Prior to heaven where angels tell him that God has left and that humanity's "movement" is destroying heaven. In some of Prior's hallucinations, he meets Harper high on valium. In their altered states, they reveal each other's secrets, causing Harper to confront Joe about his sexuality. Because of this confrontation, Harper leaves Joe, and heads west, waxing poetic about angels and ozone. Prior refuses to be the angels' prophet of stasis and instead asks for more life, which he is granted. He survives with the AIDS virus into 1990 when a ragtag group of friends is seen arguing politics: Belize, Hannah, Prior, and Louis, who are now platonic friends. In the final moments, Prior speaks directly to the audience, declaring, "We will be citizens."[29] Thus, *Angels in America* explicitly prophesies gay civil rights. But *Angels in America* was not radical performance art. It was made palatable enough for mass consumption and consumerism, in part by governing the production's horizon of expectations. The play's location, advertising, and program note all suggested to potential spectators a wholeheartedly mainstream, and, thus, palatable production.

The mainstream status of *Angels in America* began before audience members even bought their tickets. Before superlative reviews began to circulate, and before publicity for the show drew attention to its accolades, the play's physical location on Broadway, in the Walter Kerr Theatre, cemented its mainstream status and helped spectators in their selection process.[30] In the center of Broadway's theatre district near Times Square, the Walter Kerr was restored in 1990 to resemble a "classic" Broadway theatre with an ornate façade, neo-classical lobby, and velvet-trimmed seats. In the plush, newly renovated theatre, *Angels in America* was geographically and spatially attached to prior canonical productions in the same space, such as *Murder in the Cathedral* by T.S. Eliot, and to Walter Kerr's own Pulitzer-winning criticism and playwriting. To contrast, if the New York premiere of *Angels in America* had been off-Broadway at the Public Theater, the countercultural East Village location would, likewise, have informed its reception. Instead of being hailed as "universal" art on "national themes," *Angels in America* might well have been framed as "gay activism" akin to *The Normal Heart*. The Broadway location, however, left little room to interpret *Angels in America* as anything other than mainstream.

As with the location, the advertising contributed to the play's nearly instantaneous branding as a "classic." On May 16, 1993, shortly after *Millennium Approaches* opened on Broadway, Jujamcyn Theatre published a full-page advertisement in the *New York Times* Sunday arts section.[31] Across the top of the ad, *"Angels in America"* is emblazoned with wings making the first and last A's. Above the title, "A Gay Fantasia on National Themes," is written. But the bulk of the ad is a graceful drawing of a female angel beckoning in flowing white robes, arms outstretched, hands held out, palms up, in benediction. Her wings rise up behind her, echoing the wings that make the A's in the title. Under the image, "More Tony nominations than any play in Broadway history," with a large numeral "9" and a delineation of the Tony nominations with "Best Play" at the top of the list and, below this: "Winner of the 1993 Pulitzer Prize." Finally, the ad cites Frank Rich, then the *New York Times*' most important theatre critic: "Don't even think for a second about missing Tony Kushner's landmark American play, *Angels in America*." At the bottom of the page are box office information and, more prominently, the play's location at the Walter Kerr Theatre.

This advertisement tied the production to the culture industry establishment and thus demonstrated *Angels in America*'s mainstream bona fides. While the advertisement mentions "a gay fantasia," the record-breaking Tony Award nominations establish that this play is not offensive to the gatekeepers of U.S. theatre. Frank Rich's admonition to see the play and the Pulitzer Prize announcement underscore this message. And, crucially, the advertisement's only image depicts a female angel, not a gay man. An angel illustrated as a classically beautiful woman dressed modestly in all white is the stuff of a nineteenth century tableau vivant,[32] not a radical gay screed. The semiotics of this advertisement created a horizon of expectations for spectators of a solidly mainstream play that was, thus, neither radical nor offensive. And once advertisements like this one drew in spectators, the program note continued the message.

The program note has two thrusts promoting the mainstream acceptability of *Angels in America* that resemble the *New York Times* advertisement: first, attaching the play to prizes, and second, utilizing the female angel image to cover gay male bodies. The program note mentions early that *Angels in America* captured "most of the season's major prizes (Pulitzer included),"[33] thereby tying the play to mainstream acceptance. Further, the program note explains that the angel image—central both to the play and its advertising—comes from Kushner's dream after the first death of a friend from AIDS. The note states that Kushner "dreamed the friend had been visited on his deathbed by a beautiful angel."[34] The trope—familiar by 1993—of a young gay man dealing with the terrible loss of a friend is overlaid with non-denominational religious iconography that provides a level of comfort in an otherwise dire situation. It transforms death at the hands of a horrible plague—as AIDS is portrayed in *The Normal Heart*—into death as a transition into the waiting arms of a beautiful, supernatural being. Though the program note never mentions the angel's sex in Kushner's dream, every image of an angel in the advertising and on the program's cover is of a female. This conversion of horror into maternal comfort differentiates *Angels in America* from *The Normal Heart* and is one reason *Angels in America* was more commercially viable.

The program note also has three ways of claiming the play's palatability that go beyond the *New York Times* advertisement. It does so by connecting the play directly to U.S. government financial support; by arguing that its "minority" characters are actually central to U.S. history; and by linking the play to Broadway's hundredth anniversary. The note records that the play first came into being when Oskar Eustis applied for an NEA grant for Kushner to write the play: "With Jesse Helms [the conservative Republican who disapproved of both the NEA and what he perceived as LGBT art] in full filibuster at the time, the entry was something of a half-hearted test for the NEA—only it worked!"[35] This sentence creates in spectators the knowledge that the play they are about to watch was funded by the government, even while the conservative Jesse Helms held sway.[36]

Next, a quotation from Kushner argues that the play's minority characters—gay men, straight women, and African Americans—"are actually the central concerns of the society and American history. To hear Ronald Reagan tell it, it's a history of one straight civilization—but the shape and history of this country have been determined entirely by the way it has dealt with minorities."[37] In other words, despite the straight, white male agenda represented for Kushner by Reagan, the oppression by the U.S. of the country's "minorities" sets the shape of the nation. Through this statement, Kushner puts the characters of his play center stage in U.S. history. And on the next page, the play itself is connected to Broadway's history.

In the pages of the program note is an advertisement congratulating Broadway on its centennial. Text in large letters runs across the top of the page stating, "Happy Birthday Broadway! The Great White Way pulls out all the stops."[38] So while Kushner's quote in the program celebrates minorities in the U.S., the "The Great White Way" is also literally honored. If there was concern that the characters onstage somehow did not belong in the mainstream, there is reassurance with the turn of a page that they are squarely part of a hundred-year tradition of hegemony. The program utilizes these rhetorical strategies to create a horizon of expectations that while the play may appear radical, it is actually palatable. This oscillation is also found in the play's design.

The script has Brechtian possibilities that the Broadway premiere resisted, minimizing alienation and maximizing audience absorption. Even so, alienation was recorded by critics. There was a swinging between a production calling attention to its politics, and an absorbing, entertaining evening out. Frank Rich in the *New York Times* writes: "Mr. Kushner has not revised the text since [Clinton's election]—a crony of Cohn still boasts of a Republican lock on the White House until the year 2000—but the shift in Washington has had the subliminal effect of making 'Angels in America' seem more focused on what happens next than on the past."[39] The line of Cohn's crony likely brought spectators out of the fictional realm and into their own lives, for a moment aware of both. In that instant, "more focused on what happens next than on the past," audiences may have experienced a radical reimagining of the future. But these fleeting moments in the course of a six-hour production probably did little to remove the audience from the absorption in consumerism that director George C. Wolfe desired.

Wolfe's direction—particularly his handling of the simultaneous scenes—sought "universal" art rather than "gay activism" by eliminating some Brechtian tactics. Theatre scholar Janelle Reinelt compares stagings of the script's simultaneous scenes at the Broadway premiere and a later San Francisco production directed by Mark Wing-Davey. Reinelt writes that "in the New York production Wolfe staged the 'split screen' scenes in *Millennium* as simultaneous but discretely separate scenes in stable space. [San Francisco director] Wing-Davey reframed these scenes as interconnected and uncontainable (actors 'violated' one another's stage space to produce this effect of overflowing boundaries)."[40] Wolfe's staging was more in line with mainstream entertainment, like television, which uses split screens semi-regularly. This made the Broadway production more palatable and contributed to its success. Reinelt posits as much when examining a review of the Broadway premiere, which reads: "For all the political rage and the scathing unsanitized horror, the hours zip by with the breezy enjoyment of a great page-turner or a popcorn movie."[41] About this sentence, Reinelt writes, "It is not the popular culture comparisons to popcorn movies that chill ... it is the notion that a good night out in the theatre dishes up politics and genuinely horrible insights in order to accommodate them to the culinary tastes of an audience for whom these things must be rendered palatable."[42] The idea of a play discussing politics and "horrible insights" while being "rendered palatable" may "chill" Reinelt, but palatability is a necessary precondition for a play in the culture industry to support an emergent ideology.

The fact that *Angels in America* used mainstream theatre to support the emergent ideology of gay civil rights should not "chill" one who supports gay men's inclusion in the U.S. imagined community. It should make one celebrate. While there are a few reviews of the Broadway premiere that criticize Wolfe's slick direction, there are many more that compliment it.[43] Wolfe's directing, then, may not meet the Brechtian taste of some—and may hinder the radical potential of the text by rendering it "palatable"—but the directing style of Wolfe contributed to the play becoming a commercial success and thus supported its emergent ideology of gay men being center stage in U.S. theatre's imagined community. In fact, spectators were literally willing to wear the play's ideology on their bodies.

The Walter Kerr lobby boasted a variety of amenities including drinks, snacks, and apparel, such as shirts and hats. Unlike *The Normal Heart*, revenue from *Angels in America*'s merchandise did not go to AIDS activist organizations. The profits went to Jujamcyn Theatres, which fought to get the rights to produce this play and expected to make a profit. The spectators, who purchased record-priced tickets and who bought for-profit souvenirs, were consumers in every sense of Baz Kershaw's critique.[44] There is no room to suggest that spectators who purchased an *Angels in America* t-shirt were contributing to activism, as is possible with shopping spectators at the 1985 premiere of *The Normal Heart* whose dollars went to organizations like the Gay Men's Health Crisis. However, the consumerism at the Broadway premiere of *Angels in America* was supporting the play's emergent ideology of gay men's visibility in the U.S. imagined community by taking it to the streets.

When a spectator buys tickets, he or she "is always buying another's ideology."[45] By purchasing tickets, a spectator implicitly and financially supports the ideology that the production is advertising and that its reviews put forth. It follows that the same would hold true for merchandising. Wearing an *Angels in America* shirt or hat in 1993 may not have constituted activism, but it surely had ideological implications. Theatre patrons wearing merchandise from a play that stated gay men "will be citizens" put that ideology on their bodies with the same fervor music fans demonstrate for bands. A music fan's zeal often denotes attempts to incorporate a band's ideological underpinnings into one's persona—wearing an "alternative" band's shirt to perform one's alienation, or a "pop" star's shirt to display membership in the dominant culture, for example. Thus, instead of writing off the consumerism associated with *Angels in America*'s Broadway premiere, one must instead see that wearing the production's merchandise carried the emergent ideology of gay men's inclusion in the U.S. imagined community outside the theatre. Spectators of *Angels in America* were willing to wear the play's ideology, just as supporters of politicians wear shirts and hats from campaigns. And *Angels in America*'s connection to Bill Clinton's presidential campaign rhetoric helped the public categorize the play as solidly mainstream.

Angels in America and the New Democrat

While *Angels in America* may appear at first glance to be a radically inclusive text supporting LGBT civil rights, it actually reifies the palatable "big tent" coalition building at the heart of the then successful "New Democrat" movement embodied by Bill Clinton's election. *Angels in America* creates an ensemble of characters not considered part of the U.S. imaginary in 1993.

But it does so utilizing four main tactics similar to those of the Clinton campaign: an assimilationist model of democracy; a dismissal of racial politics in favor of economic politics; a faith in a teleological progress inherent in U.S. democracy; and an inclusion of gay men in the U.S. imagined community. Assimilation, dismissal of racial problems, and faith in democracy are hardly radical for the U.S., but the inclusion of gay men within these contexts is at least liberal in the sense of expanding who deserves inclusion in the national imaginary. The vacillation between dominant and emergent ideologies embodies Eve Sedgwick's brilliant axiom "'kinda subversive, kinda hegemonic.'"[46] This type of ideological fluctuation in *Angels in America* is exactly the type of work necessary for a production to create a space in the culture industry that makes the radical palatable.

But it is not the work of the text alone that created the opening in boundaries through which gay men could fit into the U.S. imagined community—to think so would be to fall victim to "the intentional fallacy," the belief that artists' intentions matter more than or as much as their works' cultural location.[47] Instead, a play's political efficacy comes from a combination of text and context. In *Angels in America*'s case, its rhetorical connection to the rising star of Clinton and the New Democrat movement made it exceptionally effective. The play and Clinton's campaign found success through juxtaposition with the Reagan-Bush Administrations.

In 1986, President Ronald Reagan expressed a lethal sentiment for tens of thousands of people hoping that the U.S. government would confront the HIV/AIDS epidemic: "The nine most terrifying words in the English language are 'I'm from the government, and I'm here to help.'"[48] This statement, expressed without irony by the head of the executive branch of the U.S. government, encapsulated what Bill Clinton in 1991 saw as "citizens conditioned by the Reagan-Bush years to believe the federal government was the source of our problems, not the solution."[49] Clinton's goal, and that of the "New Democrats" he led, was to create a big-tent, assimilationist, non-punitive, pro-government voting block. Using that block to get elected would allow them to implement policies that focused on economic solutions to social problems.

As Clinton contended in his 1991 keynote address at the Democratic Leadership Council (DLC) conference, "The Republican burden is their record of denial, evasion, and neglect. But our burden is to give the people a new choice, rooted in old values. ..."[50] Encapsulated in this early framing of Clinton's campaign message is a faith in "old values" combined with a new vision. In the same DLC speech, Clinton stated, "We recognize that we are a community. We are all in this together, and we are going up or down together."[51] By envisioning the entire U.S. as one "community" sharing a destiny, Clinton attempted to create a concept broad enough to include all constituencies. As he said in a 1991 speech, Clinton desired to reach beyond the Republicans' "divisive tactics on racial and gay issues."[52] Clinton's model for assimilation was to emphasize economic problems over identity politics. His view on race in the U.S. was demonstrated by a speech he gave both to a mainly white audience at Macomb County [Michigan] Community College and to a predominantly black audience at the Pleasant Grove Baptist Church in inner-city Detroit. He told both of these audiences that "the problems are not racial in nature. This is an issue of economics, of values."[53] For the LGBT community, Clinton's biggest campaign promise was that if elected, he would see that the military would accept people regardless of sexuality. This promise explicitly reimagines LGBT people as part of the nation's imagined community, and is but one part of the Clinton Campaign's teleological view of U.S. democracy's ever-increasing inclusion. Clinton wound up his 1991 DLC keynote speech arguing that "the future can be better than the past, and that each of us has a personal, moral responsibility to make it so. ... We are not here to save the Democratic Party. We are here to save the United States of America."[54] This epic, utopian ambition, solidly grounded on "old values" (the dominant ideology), but reaching out to new constituencies (emergent ideologies), is similar to if not indistinguishable from *Angels in America*'s wavering between the palatable and the radical.

The monumental scope of the Clinton campaign—"to save the United States of America"—is mirrored in Kushner's subtitle, "A Gay Fantasia on National Themes." The zeal to save the country is demonstrated by the utopian-infused titles of the play's two parts, "Millennium Approaches" and "Perestroika." Millennium is oft linked to spiritual fulfillment and end-of-days paradise. Perestroika represented political changes in the USSR that many hoped in the late 1980s might harken an end of the Cold War. Both Clinton and Kushner pointed towards a brighter future in their political rhetoric, but both, importantly, also looked back to "old values."

In its opening monologue, *Angels in America* explicitly pays tribute to past values. A rabbi presiding over the funeral of Louis' grandmother states that her descendants "do not live in America" but in "the clay of some Litvak shtetl ... because she carried the old world on her back across the ocean."[55] That is Kushner's nod to "old values" carried via ancestors to America. But, echoing the Clinton campaign, Prior's ultimate rejection of stasis and prophecy of gay men's place as citizens is the play's version of Clinton's "new choice." The play also reiterates Clinton's desire for an inclusive U.S. community in which race is not a problem.

Just like Clinton's campaign speeches, *Angels in America* overlooks issues of race in favor of economics. A section of the play declares lines nearly identical to Clinton's speeches at Macomb County [Michigan] Community College and Pleasant Grove Baptist Church.[56] Louis states, "Racists just try to use race here as a tool in a political struggle. It's not really about race."[57] Despite the skepticism of Belize, the lone African American character, the text gives Louis nearly four full pages of dialogue opposed to Belize's periodic interjections. Thus, even if one is skeptical of the ideas expressed by Clinton and Louis that America does not have a race problem, the campaign and play convey the idea and enjoy great success.

Finally, while not a main theme of *Angels in America,* the play does echo Clinton's promise to the LGBT community about military service. Louis gives a two-page disquisition about an opinion on the subject written by his Republican lover, Joe, for a Reagan-appointed judge.[58] Louis calls the opinion "an important bit of legal fag-bashing" because it finds that the U.S. Armed Forces may discriminate against gay men.[59] In this way, the script calls out Republican prejudice against gays in the military, which Clinton's campaign promises juxtaposed.

Consequently, *Angels in America* lined up with the Clinton Campaign rhetoric that handily won the 1992 presidential election. Based on that, *Angels in America* fit the U.S. zeitgeist of 1992–1993. Even if the script appeared radical with its inclusion of gay men in the U.S. imagined community, it fit the ideology for which a plurality of U.S. citizens voted. However, just as the Clinton Administration proved unable or unwilling to make good on all of its campaign promises, the script's palatable rhetoric contains certain limitations that a more radical text may not have. One important concession is that Clinton and Kushner's visions of utopia hinge on assimilation.

Angels of Assimilation

The idea of different groups assimilating into a more uniform American imagined community dates at least to the eighteenth century.[60] But referring to the U.S. as a "melting pot" became commonplace after a play by the same name was produced in 1908. *The Melting Pot,* by Israel Zangwill,[61] centered on Russian Jews in the U.S. cutting ties with their roots. Though a commercial and popular success, the play was criticized by some for its characters' willingness to give up Jewish traditions. Similarly, Kushner takes his broad palate of characters and assimilates them into a new version of the U.S. imagined community. In so doing, he opens space for new members of the nation, but some critics question assimilation as a properly radical strategy for change. *Angels in America* does this "melting pot" work by "pinklisting" the historical figure Roy Cohn;[62] by refusing the character Joe assimilation even though he is gay; and by allowing the character Hannah assimilation despite her heterosexuality. To understand *Angels in America*'s political work one must examine this assimilation carefully, noting how it occurs and to whom.

In one of the play's most oft-quoted lines, Roy Cohn describes himself as "a heterosexual man ... who fucks around with guys."[63] With this line, Kushner provides the audience with the information that *Angels in America*'s representation of Roy Cohn has sex with men, a contention often suggested about the historical person the character represents. Kushner provides a disclaimer prefacing the published play stating that while Cohn was "all too real," Kushner's Cohn "is a work of dramatic fiction; his words are [Kushner's] inventions, and liberties have been taken."[64] But, despite this caveat, unavailable to an audience watching the Broadway production, the play takes a historically right-wing figure and folds him into the LGBT community. In fact, the play's most outspoken left-wing character, Louis, sings Kaddish after Cohn's death. In that moment, Belize, who, as a gay black man, represents everything Cohn fought against, says, "[Cohn] was a terrible person. He died a hard death. So maybe ... A queen can forgive her vanquished foe."[65] The play reshaped one of the most conservative men from the twentieth century into a member of the gay community. Since Cohn was already accepted as "American," his pinklisting by *Angels in America* expanded the imagined community of the U.S. to include this historical man, even though, according to the play, he was "gay."

Joe Pitt, another conservative gay character, receives the opposite treatment. He ultimately fails to assimilate into the society represented by the play's final scene. But since Joe is entirely Kushner's creation, paying close attention to this failure reveals the necessary behavior for assimilation in *Angels in America*. Joe begins the play recently transplanted from Salt Lake City to New York City, unhappily married, closeted, and an ambitious Republican lawyer with ties to Cohn. Cohn wants Joe to go to D.C. and be "his boy" in the Justice Department. Joe's wife, the bitterly unhappy Harper, opposes the move. As Joe struggles with this choice, he meets Louis, who works in Joe's office, and the two of them begin an affair. As this continues, Joe's ties to his wife and mother disintegrate. When Louis confronts Joe about involvement with Cohn and writing conservative legal briefs enshrining homophobia, Joe beats up Louis. The bruises become the wounds Prior wants to see on Louis to show true repentance. Hence, Joe becomes Louis' punishment for leaving Prior in his illness, and this penitence allows Louis to return to Prior as a platonic friend by the play's end. Joe, however, does not see a problem with the legal briefs he wrote and does not apologize to Louis or any other character for his actions. He ends the play abandoned by his mother, his lover, and his wife. To Harper, Joe says, "Call or ... Call. You have to." To which Harper responds, "No. Probably never again. That's how bad."[66] Joe is not part of the epilogue's community, even though his mother and ex-lover are. Thus, unlike Cohn, Joe is not forgiven. Joe could only be allowed into the epilogue's constructed family if he changed his politics. Hannah's inclusion in the final scene and her assimilation shows how this is so.

While not queer, Hannah experiences a complete assimilation; she is rewarded for it by the play's end. Most important about Hannah's acceptance in the epilogue is what it tells about the "proper" assimilation espoused by the play's text. After receiving a "coming out" phone call from Joe, Hannah sells her Salt Lake City house and moves to New York City. Hannah at first hates New York City but volunteers at the Mormon visiting center and functions far better than Harper. Although Hannah cannot save her son's marriage, she ultimately, through a series of coincidences, cares for Prior, convincing him that not all conservatives will judge him as he expects. When Prior expresses disgust at her beliefs, Hannah responds, "You can't. Imagine. The things in my head. You don't make assumptions about me, mister; I won't make them about you."[67] She also helps him understand his visions by saying, "An angel is just a belief, with wings and arms that can carry you. It's naught to be afraid of. If it lets you down, reject it. Seek for something new."[68] This, and a shared visitation from an Angel, bring the pair together. By the epilogue, Hannah has deserted her son and daughter-in-law and is reading the *New York Times* in Central Park with Prior, Louis, and Belize. Since she alone from the Pitt family remains, the text suggests that proper assimilation is from provincial to urbane, conservative to liberal, and biological family to constructed. There could have been other endings. Louis could have decided he loved Joe despite divergent politics. Hannah could have remained with Harper as her supportive mother-in-law. But the epilogue describes a different journey of success: that of an unworldly Salt Lake City widow to that of a cosmopolitan New Yorker. And while Hannah's journey may epitomize successful assimilation, women in general fare poorly in this play.

Women's Clipped Wings

Women occupy an ambivalent place within *Angels in America*: one in which female actors[69] play male characters, but male actors never play female characters. Instead, when male actors wear women's clothes, they depict male characters in "drag." In the world of the play, then, women in male clothes become "men" while men in female clothes become "queer." The dichotomy of representation codifies a type of sacrosanct and stable masculinity that cannot be undone despite dress, whereas the female gender is so precarious it can be undone by a suit. This begins in the first scene in which the actor playing Hannah represents a male rabbi[70] and continues with the same actor playing a male doctor.[71] Similarly, the actor playing Harper plays Roy Cohn's male colleague.[72] A generous reading of the cross-gender casting suggests that placing women actors in male parts demonstrates the ambivalence of gender, that showing a female playing a male embodies the deconstruction of gender binaries. But because cross-casting in *Angels in America* is unidirectional—female to male—it ultimately suggests a stability of the male gender. It depicts an ambiguous femininity, a sense that under every woman rests a man *in potentia*. But it does not create the same ambiguity for its male characters, even when cross-dressed.

Although Belize proclaims himself an ex-drag queen,[73] Prior is the only male character portrayed onstage in women's clothes, and it is when he is in drag.[74] Belize no longer does drag because, in his words, it is "politically incorrect."[75] Part of the debate about drag's suitability in the 1980s hinged on men in women's clothes perpetuating sexualized female gender norms, the idea that drag was a sexist depiction of male sexualization of women rather than a radical escape of heterosexual norms.[76] While Judith Butler and a host of feminist and queer scholars have wrestled with the politics of drag,[77] *Angels in America* does not allow its women characters drag. Instead, it uses their bodies to portray men and allocates drag solely to male bodies. Thus *Angels in America* plays with drag, but it is to reinscribe female heterosexuality and male stability even when cross-dressed.

The only moment in which a female character possibly engages in a queer act is when the Angel, played by a woman, kisses Hannah and produces "an enormous orgasm."[78] However, this metaphysical kiss hardly makes Hannah queer. As an interaction with an angel, the instance is more about religious ecstasy than worldly sex. Hannah's sexuality, as a widow with a grown son, is never investigated. The only exploration of a woman character's sexuality is that of the most sexually frustrated and misused character: Harper, Joe's wife.

One can here return to the connection between *Angels in America* and the Clinton campaign, noting how Hillary Clinton was pilloried by misogynists during her husband's 1992 Presidential campaign. Harper's representation is unfortunately in line with that misogynist rhetoric. Harper is often represented talking to herself, hallucinating, and later falling apart when her gay husband leaves her. She more closely resembles Blanche DuBois than a capable woman of 1993. The representation of Harper is one way in which *Angels in America* did not challenge the dominant ideology. Instead, *Angels in America* uses the dominant ideology's sexism for comic effect. In her first scene, Harper hallucinates a travel agent named Mr. Lies who promises to take her away from her loveless marriage.[79] This scene is played lightly for comedy, but examined seriously it is a disturbing image of a mentally ill woman left to her own devices. In her next scene, Harper argues against moving to Washington. Just as Hillary Clinton was beginning her own journey convincing the country that she, and other women, had the mental fortitude to lead the nation, *Angels in America* portrayed an incompetent woman uninterested in leading a new life in Washington. Harper states she cannot leave because she has to finish painting the apartment's bedroom. She has been working on it for over a year because she is scared to go in the room without Joe. That is, she is scared to do a simple task without a man's presence. Later in the scene, Harper suggests giving Joe oral sex because she heard from Dr. Ruth on the radio how to do so. Again, this moment is played for laughs, but it suggests a sexual naivety on Harper's part that no other character in the play suffers. Of course, not every character need be capable and mentally healthy, but Harper is the only heterosexual woman whose sexuality the play depicts. She is portrayed as childlike, powerless, and fragile. This is hardly a radical portrayal of a woman, and, since the misogyny of the 1990s was not challenged by this play, Harper's weakness might well have contributed to the play's palatability.

Even when Harper first leaves Joe, she does so based on fear rather than strength, her decision continuing to portray her as stereotypically weak and reactive. She leaves because she realizes the bogyman under the bed is Joe, exiting with Mr. Lies, her fantasy travel agent, signaling a break with sanity.[80] This is not an empowered slam of the door; this is losing touch with reality. Harper spends the next few scenes in "Antarctica," fantasizing about a loving Eskimo version of Joe and chewing "a pine tree down. With [her] teeth. Like a beaver" in order "to build … something, maybe a fire."[81] Harper was actually hallucinating and in Prospect Park the whole time. The tree came from the Botanical Gardens Arboretum.[82] This psychotic incident is presented humorously, with Hannah on the phone with the police saying, "She what? A pine tree? Why on earth would she chew a … Well you have no business laughing about it."[83] Once again Harper's mental illness—and only mental illness drives someone to chew trees in Prospect Park—is laughed away and seen simply as a silly character trait. When compared to Prior's hallucinations—which seem, by the end of the play, to be religious visions—Harper's mental state is the only one mocked. Prior receives concern, such as when Belize says, "You better fucking not flip out. This is not dementia. And this is not real. This is you, Prior, afraid of what's coming, afraid of time … I can handle anything but not this happening to you."[84] But Harper receives ridicule. The police laugh at her offstage, and Hannah dismisses her, saying "She's not insane, she's just peculiar."[85] Prior's illness, AIDS, is taken seriously, and the hallucinations or visions that attend it are frightening to him and his friends. Harper's illness, mental, is not taken seriously or even given a name—is she perhaps overcome with that time-honored trope of hysteria from lack of sex? As the play's only woman character with a sexual partner, it is hard to examine the play's gender politics without noting Harper's position as subordinate to a man, her ignored mental illness, and the way the text employs these traits for humor. Further, while Hannah gets to be part of the created family in the play's epilogue, Harper does not.

Harper ends the play on a plane heading west to San Francisco after leaving Joe for a final time. This could be seen as an act of independence were it not for the manner in which she departs. As she goes, she demands Joe's credit card, saying, "If I can get a job, or something, I'll cut the card to pieces."[86] Thus, she remains reliant on a man's income. Her statement "*if* I can get a job" (emphasis added) suggests she is not confident she can acquire employment. One could argue, perhaps, that she controls the situation, demanding Joe's credit card, and acting sensibly to ensure her immediate financial future. But her "sensible" behavior leaves her in the male-dominated world in which she has always lived, dependent on a man for money. Compare her to Nora in *Doll's House*, the quintessential stage image of leaving one's husband for independence. Nora leaves with no employment, security, or stability, in order to find herself. Perhaps Harper can find herself while living off her husband's credit card, but, because of the continued financial dependence and legal intertwining because there is no divorce, her departure resembles that of a child going to college more than a permanent break between romantic partners. Harper cannot live without Joe's support. The image of a woman depending on a man's financial support is another palatable conservative view of the world in this play. In fact, this hierarchy is even continued with the female Angel, who is depicted as weak compared to the male-gendered God.

As Prior states while relating his interactions with the Angel, "The sexual politics of this are *very* confusing,"[87] and so were the sexual politics of the early 1990s. However, Angels in America does little with its male/female relationships that might be seen as radical rather than palatably conservative. Prior states, "God ... is a man. Well, not a man, he's a flaming Hebrew letter, but a male flaming Hebrew letter."[88] Prior then describes female angels' subordination to the male God. Angels are, according to Prior, "basically incredibly powerful bureaucrats, they have no imagination, they can *do* anything but they can't invent, create, they're sort of fabulous and dull all at once."[89] Even more damning than angels' inability to "invent, create," which is the provenance of the male God alone, the primary angel character, played by a woman, says, "Made for His Pleasure, We can only ADORE."[90] This statement echoes the worst of misogynist ideology, that women are objects solely for sex, for "pleasure," and have no power beyond looking blindly up to their male leader, whom they "ADORE." While the sexual politics of the 1990s may have been complicated, the gender relations in *Angels in America* are clear, and women do not come out well in the play. Beyond representing women, angels are the closest to a representation of religion the play provides, but instead of demarking any particular "sins" or dogma, they continue the assimilationist trends of *Angels in America*.

In the *Journal of American Culture*, Amy Schindler expounds further on this subject of assimilation in her consideration of the symbolism of angels and their universalist theme. She contends "that angels reached new heights in popularity from 1990 through 1996 because an angel represents a spiritual but non-judgmental sign of divine intervention to help people deal with the AIDS crisis."[91] *Angels in America* reflects this notion, and its characters, whether Protestant, Mormon, or Jewish, all relate to angelic symbolism. Likewise, the play's spectators, who presumably spanned a variety of religions and sects, could grasp the symbolism of angels. This attention to non-denominational, universalist symbolism recalls Kushner's dream about an angel coming to his first friend to die of AIDS.[92] The dream is not about a friend's judgment based on a particular theology after death. It is about comfort and grace delivered by a "beautiful angel."[93] The angelic symbolism elides differences between faiths, but it also allows divergent characters, and—by extension—a variety of spectators, to relate to one another, to assimilate their beliefs into one. Angels are also represented as non-dogmatic healing creatures in the epilogue, which houses the play's most hopeful rhetoric.

Imagining New Citizens into the Nation

The essential optimism of the play, particularly in its epilogue, comes from its faith in America's teleology of progress, that is, the belief in an ever onwards and upwards movement of U.S. democracy throughout history. The play contends that every era sees a "more perfect union" and more equality. This is hardly a radical notion given the eighteenth-century origins of the phrase in the preamble to the U.S. Constitution. However, as the U.S. imaginary expands to include various minority groups, the effects of a "more perfect union" can have profound effects on the nation. And this movement to include a new minority—gay men—is seen in the imagined community displayed at the end of *Angels in America*.

Set in 1990, four years after the main action of the play, the epilogue depicts Prior, Louis, Belize, and Hannah sitting at Bethesda Fountain in New York's Central Park. The final images and words express a teleology similar to the winning rhetoric of the Clinton Campaign. The stage directions describe Hannah as "noticeably different—she looks like a New Yorker, and she is reading the *New York Times*"[94] Thus, Hannah's assimilation is complete. This mirrors Clinton's speech about giving "people a new choice, rooted in old values."[95] Hannah represents the traditional ideals of Mormon "family values" but now integrated into the "new choice" of the play's created family. She chose three gay men over her biological son and daughter-in-law, thus imagining that even conservatives can fit into this new vision of America.

The scene begins with Louis optimistically discussing world events—particularly the end of the Cold War—echoing the hope that Clinton's election would lead to sudden change. Louis says, "Remember back four years ago? The whole time we were feeling everything everywhere was stuck, while in Russia! Look! Perestroika! It's the end of the Cold War! The whole world is changing! Overnight!"[96] Recall that this play's opening night in California was on the eve of Clinton's election, and its Broadway premiere began near the time of Clinton's inauguration. The idea of leadership change leading to overnight "perestroika"—the Russian word for "restructuring"—would have rung in spectators' ears as the hoped-for change that Clinton promised. And one such pledge was inclusion of LGBT communities. The fact that in the play's final moments Prior states, "We will be citizens,"[97] lines *Angels in America* up exactly with the dominant ideology expressed by Clinton at the time. The play's optimism even extends to AIDS itself.

In the epilogue, Prior is still alive and utilizes the Bethesda Fountain as a metaphor for the end of the AIDS epidemic, allying the play with the hope that the Clinton Administration would take the epidemic seriously. The top of the fountain is a statue of an angel, continuing the non-judgmental spirituality of the 1990s, about which Prior says, "[Angels] commemorate death but they suggest world without dying."[98] This statuary, then, is both a memorial to AIDS dead, and a suggestion that in the future those dying will not exist. The four characters then tell the story of the angel Bethesda. During the Biblical time of the Second Temple, Bethesda descended from heaven, and a fountain sprang from where her foot touched down, and this water would heal any suffering, in body or soul. When the Romans destroyed the Temple, the spring ran dry. But it is said that when the Millennium comes, the waters "will flow again," and Hannah will "personally take [Prior] there to bathe. We will all bathe ourselves clean."[99] Finishing a play that began with "Millennium Approaches," *Angels in America* expressed the structure of feeling hoped for by a plurality of the U.S. that they were on the cusp of an ideological change regarding HIV/AIDS. And this turned out to be true. Clinton, among other government advances regarding the syndrome, increased AIDS funding by 43% in his first term.[100]

Prior's final lines lay bare the play's faith in progressive U.S. teleology, "We won't die secret deaths anymore. The world only spins forward. We will be citizens. The time has come. Bye now. You are fabulous creatures, each and every one. And I bless you: *More Life*. The Great Work Begins."[101] By rejecting secret deaths, such as the ones in *The Normal Heart*, *Angels in America* claims a public space for its gay characters. Even the tens of thousands of AIDS dead that came before Clinton are reclaimed in Harper's final monologue before the epilogue. She says, "Nothing's lost forever. In this world, there is a kind of painful progress. Longing for what we've left behind, and dreaming ahead."[102] This play, as it ends, repeatedly states its faith in progress, its belief in a utopian future, and, while more work is necessary, its conviction that Jill Dolan's utopian "better later" is just ahead.[103]

The play was able to do this assimilationist work for middle-class, white, gay men in particular in part because of its connection to the dominant ideology such as Clinton Campaign rhetoric. Its design, use of merchandise, assimilationist vision, and even its elision of race and misogynist treatment of women aligned it with the contemporaneous dominant ideology. The play was a major commercial success, at least in part because it was not radical. From its position in the culture industry, *Angels in America* managed to promote the emergent ideology of (some) gay men being part of the U.S. imagined community. This is not in spite of *Angels in America*'s position in the mainstream. It is *due* to *Angels*' place in the mainstream. It was able to imagine gay men (not women) into the nation. One can see that in its reception, particularly in its scholarship and reviews.

Scholarship on *Angels in America* came quickly, often linking the play's Angel to Walter Benjamin's description of progress in "Theses on the Philosophy of History." This elided Kushner's personal experience—his dream mentioned in the program note—and instead aligned the play with established scholarship, a move towards canonization. Academics report that while reading Benjamin's essay, Kushner was struck by the philosopher's understanding of history. That is, as "a chain of events ... one single catastrophe ... this storm [that] irresistibly propels [the angel] into the future to which his back is turned, while the pile of debris before him grows skyward. This storm is what we call progress."[104] In *Modern Drama*, Charles McNulty notes that *Angels in America* embodies Benjamin's theory of history, that the catastrophe of HIV/AIDS blows the play's characters backwards towards a new future. McNulty further claims that AIDS created potential for radical social change by placing gay men, people previously on the periphery of U.S. history, in the center.[105] But *Angels in America* was not canonized because of a relationship to a mid-century German theorist, nor due solely to its discussion of HIV/AIDS. Its institutional support, from both the academy and the mainstream press, accounted for its canonization. This endeavor constituted a volley in the late-twentieth-century culture wars.

In the U.S. academy during the 1980s and 1990s, a major point of contention was representation in the literary canon, a proxy "war for hegemony."[106] While "the classroom may not be the only, or even the primary," site in which the struggle for a society's norms takes place, academics wrestled with syllabi under the assumption that students are "profoundly affected by the views of human potentiality and conceptions of justice embedded in the texts they are assigned to read."[107] In 1988 many wondered aloud with English professor Joe Weixlmann "why Americans tend to regard the experiences of straight white males as 'universal,' whereas the experiences of females, gay men, and males of color are more often thought of as 'different' or 'other.'"[108] But *Angels in America* on Broadway, five years after Weixlmann's article, created gay male characters that were received as "universal" and were instantly canonized. The writing of John Guillory, the foremost scholar on canonization, provides insight into this process.

For Guillory, canonization does not rest solely on a text conforming to a society's ideology, nor on the text's intrinsic worth. Instead, the text needs institutional support, financial backing, and reproduction, all of which can be analyzed in "the history of both the production and the reception of texts."[109] Examining *Angels in America*'s path to Broadway, one can see that it had clear institutional and financial support. Even before Broadway, it was reproduced in several pre-New York City productions. After Broadway, it was reproduced hundreds of times on stages across the world, as an opera, and as an HBO miniseries. Before these reproductions occurred, however, judgment was rendered on the play. Academia provided a superlative grade in the form of immediate scholarly discourse, and *Approaching the Millennium*, a book-length anthology of criticism edited by Deborah Geis and Steven Kruger, appeared only four years after the play's Broadway opening.[110] But prior to scholarship, another institution, more important to the war for hegemony, held forth on the play. That institution—cited by Benedict Anderson as exceptionally central for the "imagined community" that conceives the nation—was the press. And, by and large, the U.S. media explicitly described *Angels in America* as "universal." This production, happening on Broadway, the center of U.S. theatre's hegemonic mainstream, had its characters normalized through journalism. This media canonization allowed gay men into the imagined community of the U.S. nation.

While the reviews' tenor varies to some extent, there are four main categories: positive reviews that avoid politics;[111] reviews that claim the play as art not propaganda, and call for the play's canonization in U.S. theatre;[112] reviews that acknowledge the play's politics as a sign of hope but continue to approach the play chiefly as art;[113] and reviews that focus primarily on the play's politics.[114]

Half a dozen reviews assert that the production lives up to its hype and that seeing the play constitutes "a fun night out," further normalizing gay men by avoiding potentially controversial questions of sexuality. This implicitly forwards the idea that gay men are inoffensive and worthy of inclusion in mainstream culture industry entertainment, and hence the imagined community. In a representative example, Jeremy Gerard, writing for the glossy, popular magazine *Variety*, argues "in a world where heightened expectations—and with a record-breaking top ticket price of $60 they will be exceptionally high—are typically dashed, 'Angels in America' delivers the theatrical goods in spades."[115] Overlooking politically enlightening or contentious moments, such as the cross-gender casting, Gerard simply treats the play as amusing. He describes: "The actors play multiple roles, with the women ... also playing men, contributing to the fun—and it should never be forgotten how much fun 'Millennium Approaches' is."[116] No reviews in this category mention possibly offensive moments, such as simulated sex between two men. Articles like this in fashionable periodicals such as *Variety*, *USA Today*, and *Newsweek* hailed *Angels in America* as mainstream. Even if spectators were offended by the play, they would know that mainstream reviewers thought a play that argued for gay citizenship and that portrayed the Reagan era as one of selfishness was "fun." The reviews implicitly accept the play's politics since they do not object to gay men being, as the *Newsweek* title puts it, "Center Stage."

More common are reviews that actively hail the production as art—not propaganda. These reviewers propose that *Angels in America* deserves a place within the U.S. dramatic canon due to its "universal" artistic themes. By framing the play as "universal," these reviews reveal a critical acceptance of *Angels in America*'s discussion of gay men as citizens. The influential theatre critic Robert Brustein writes in the liberal *The New Republic* that "if you compare [*Angels in America*] with any recent entry on the same subject ... you will see how skillfully Kushner navigates between, say, the shrill accusations of Larry Kramer's *The Destiny of Me* and the soggy affirmations of William Finn's *Falsettos* ... [Kushner's] very literate play once again makes American drama readable literature."[117] With this description, Brustein explicitly removes Kushner's work from the category of polemics and securely places it into the category of "literature." Brustein goes on to call Kushner "a strong-voiced, clear-eyed dramatic artist capable of encapsulating our national nightmares into universal art."[118] By arguing that *Angels in America* is "universal," Brustein "canonizes the piece."[119]

In the Sunday *New York Times*, however, the most obvious canonization of *Angels in America* appears in a review that compares the play to an art form with a large amount of cultural capital: opera. In a column called "Classical View," Speight Jenkins takes leave of his normal duties as a classical music critic to consider *Angels in America*. Jenkins gushes that "the new Broadway sensation 'Angels in America' constantly suggests opera in its scope, its sweep and its intense but precisely controlled emotionalism."[120] Jenkins compares Kushner to composers of extremely high cultural acclaim: Wagner, Verdi, and Berlioz. In so doing, Jenkins' places *Angels in America* in the category of "major art" that "dramatizes an epic subject: man's inhumanity to man … [and that] need not be narrowly defined" as drama only about AIDS or gay men. The very title of the column, "Classical View," places *Angels in America* in the pantheon of "classical" art. Similarly, the fact that Jenkins chose to review a play instead of his usual musical selections marks *Angels in America* as particularly notable. All told, reviews that treated *Angels in America* as high art with much cultural capital erected a rhetorical frame of worth—similar to that described by sociologist Pierre Bourdieu in *Distinction*—and a discursive framework of canonical "universality" around *Angels in America*.[121] This process helped guide spectators' horizon of expectations and instructed them that gay men were constituents of "universal" themes that comprise the human experience.

Unlike reviews that approached the play as art, many gave primacy to the play's political implications. These reviews tend to lack the optimistic belief that *Angels in America* marked a new era in gay civil rights. Many suggest, instead, that the play brought difficult truths to light—such as the deadly effects of AIDS in the 1980s, the debate centered on gays in the military, and the continued prejudice endured by gay men—but that the play fails to offer any viable solution to these problems. A few critics go so far as to argue that most of the play's characters are not "normal." Such sentiments seemingly contradict the argument that *Angels in America* brought inclusion and acceptance for gay men. Yet, since even these critics accepted the play's artistic value, they implicitly worked to count gay men as worthy subjects of mainstream representation and, thus, as part of the nation's imagined community.

For instance, on the conservative end of the political spectrum, Edwin Wilson's *Wall Street Journal* review suggests that the lack of "normal" characters in *Angels in America* is cause for complaint.[122] Part of a small set of conservative reviews that accept the play's artistic merits but not its politics, Wilson' maintains that: "Mr. Kushner is unquestionably a talented writer" who "in terms of pure theatre … has much to offer."[123] Yet, despite this praise, Wilson finds fault with claiming "homosexuals" as "universal" subjects. "It is when we come to the second part of Mr. Kushner's subtitle—his claim that the play deals with 'national themes'—that the play has problems," Wilson explains.[124] "'Angels in America,'" he continues, "represents the closed universe of a homosexual world: There is hardly a straight person in it who is normal."[125] Does Wilson's understanding, therefore, negate the play's ability to support the inclusion of gay men in the U.S. imagined community? Was the play able to redefine normalcy for anyone who did not already find the characters in this play "normal"? The review in the conservative *Christian Science Monitor* helps resolve these questions.

The Christian Science Monitor critic argues that *Angels in America* is "a harsh, shattering drama about futile struggles for love and power … but its homosexual themes may eliminate it from some theatergoers' agendas."[126] Suggesting that the play's themes are so far from "universal" that they may drive spectators away, the review nevertheless points to *Angels in America*'s artistic quality. The review acknowledges that the text won the Pulitzer Prize, but criticizes the production for going "beyond what the script calls for in depicting sexual situations and nudity for their shock value."[127] Objecting to representations of gay acts on Broadway, the *Christian Science Monitor* acknowledges the art of Kushner's text while objecting to mainstream representations of queer bodies. This review—like the one in the *Wall Street Journal*—nevertheless informs its readers about a mainstream play on Broadway that considers the concerns of "homosexuals" to be part of "national themes." Thus, the reviews in the *Wall Street Journal* and the *Christian Science Monitor* carry *Angels in America*'s ideology outside the theatre. The idea that gay men's lives were considered mainstream enough to warrant a successful Broadway play and a Pulitzer Prize was brought to readers who might not otherwise hear such ideas. By accepting *Angels in America* as worthwhile art, these reviews made it known that the emergent ideology of including gay men in the U.S. imagined community was acceptable to a large, mainstream audience.

Interestingly, reviews in liberal journals such as *The Village Voice* did less to further the play's ideology than did those in conservative journals such as *The Wall Street Journal* and *The Christian Science Monitor*. For Alisa Solomon, who already supported LGBT civil rights in her writing for the liberal *Village Voice,* the mainstream success of *Angels in America* was disagreeable. While the play made the emergent ideology of LGBT civil rights more palatable to the mainstream, it rendered the ideology less radical, and, thus, less valuable in her eyes. She writes that, "*Angels* doesn't plead for acceptance. It doesn't dramatize how we're just like mainstream America. In fact, it offers a lot of compelling reasons for why we wouldn't want to be just like mainstream America."[128] Here, Solomon explicitly disagrees that the gay characters in *Angels in America* are universal. She is one of the very few reviewers to articulate this position. Her column suggests discomfort with the idea that queerness is "just like mainstream America." It would seem that for Solomon, then, *Angels in America* is fundamentally dissatisfying because it fails to forward a sufficiently radical platform; hence, this antagonistic article did not further *Angels in America*'s assimilationist ideology, though it still accepted the play as art.

The one critic who refused to recognize *Angels in America*'s artistic value and who panned its political message was Yale Kramer. In a long article written for the conservative monthly magazine *American Spectator* and excerpted for the then equally conservative daily newspaper *Newsday*, Yale Kramer laments the play's politics and art. The *Newsday* excerpt, "Clipping the Wings of 'Angels,'" drives to the heart of his critique and argues that

"*Angels in America* lacks the prerequisite for greatness—the transformation of universal experience into art—and what it substitutes for universal experience is messages. It is a propaganda play, and likely to become as dated as Odets."[129] In *American Spectator* Yale Kramer expands his message: "Although the play is not profound, it is understandable that audiences find it dazzling. It was meant to leave the audience bewildered, to make us feel, at the end of it, like dumb hicks—straight, three-piece-suited, permanent-waved goyim."[130] Though no other reviewer mentions finding the play confusing, Yale Kramer continues, "Contributing to the confusion is the gratuitous and unexplained androgyny,"[131] by which he means the cross-gender casting. For Yale Kramer, this was neither fun nor politically interesting. In his description of an incident in Greenwich Village, Yale Kramer reveals the rationale behind some of his reactions:

> On the evening of Good Friday, a few steps from the Perry Street Theatre in Greenwich Village where *The Night Larry Kramer Kissed Me* is playing, you could see in the window of a gay sex shop a male mannequin wearing a pair of bulging jockey shorts and holding in one hand a couple of carrots and in the other a tube of K-Y jelly and a box of condoms. The sign above him read: 'Happy Easter. Be Bad. But be safe.' In front of the theater itself a sign announced: "Thursday night is singles night. Yes I'm available. Maybe, let's talk. Sorry, I'm taken. Ask for your 'signal tag' at the ticket booth." Next to each choice on the sign was a colored circular adhesive "signal tag"—green for "Yes," yellow for "Maybe," red for "Sorry." It was as though life and art had become indistinguishable.[132]

This passage is surprising for it appears at first glance to have little to do with *Angels in America*. What it reveals about Yale Kramer's relationship to *Angels in America*, though, is his fear concerning "homosexuality." The fact that he finds "life and art" becoming "indistinguishable" outside a gay theatre distasteful suggests that for Yale Kramer "homosexuals" are tolerable onstage but not off. This is not surprising given his definition of gay men. Yale Kramer states: "Despite the popular view of male homosexuality, sexual orientation is not the only socially relevant issue, or perhaps even the most important one. 'Badness' is—or rather transgression."[133] By defining male "homosexuality" as "transgression," Yale Kramer suggests that "badness" is acceptable onstage but not in everyday life. He ultimately dismisses *Angels in America*: "[Kushner] rejects as unacceptable the view that it is possible for gays and straights to live together peacefully if gays exercise more self-restraint and straights exercise more tolerance."[134] Yale Kramer wants gays to stay in the closet, that is, socially invisible.

The reasons for analyzing Yale Kramer's article on *Angels in America* in such detail are twofold. First, it is the only review that rejects the play both artistically and politically. Second, it juxtaposes nicely against reviews that accept the play's artistic merits but reject its politics. Contrasting the reviews of the *Wall Street Journal* and the *Christian Science Monitor* to Yale Kramer's piece, one gains a greater understanding of how the former two implicitly accepted gay men into the mainstream. Yale Kramer's piece argues that gays who refuse to be closeted do not deserve a place in mainstream society, unlike the *Wall Street Journal* and the *Christian Science Monitor* reviews that carve a niche for gay men's social visibility in the U.S. culture industry based on the artistic realm. If Geertz is right that art represents ideas in the material world,[135] then creating a representation onstage of gay men helps make openly gay men's existence in society more thinkable,[136] and conservative reviews like those in the *Wall Street Journal* and the *Christian Science Monitor* spread that emergent ideology in a way Yale Kramer's review did not.

With the exception of Yale Kramer's, though, the reviews of the Broadway premiere declared *Angels in America* "art." In so doing, most canonized the play's depiction of gay men as "universal." Implicitly or explicitly hailing *Angels in America* as universal included gay men in the U.S. imagined community. While some reviews resisted a play that imagined gay men as citizens (e.g., the *Wall Street Journal*, the *Christian Science Monitor*, and the *Daily News*), almost every review agreed that the play was "art." In so doing, the Broadway premiere of *Angels in America* rhetorically and symbolically shifted who was included in the nation's "imagined community." This is more of an assimilationist tactic then a radical one, but, nevertheless, the play challenged the imagined community of the United States to include gay men as universal, mainstream figures. One might argue that the Broadway premiere simply preached to the converted, a common dismissal of theatre's potential political impact, but that is not true. Reviews of the play report a variety of reactions from standing ovations[137] to "boos."[138] The reviews suggest that the play's politics were to blame for the mixed reactions, which implies a politically heterogeneous audience, not an auditorium of the "converted." Likewise, the national media coverage brought the play's themes to a varied readership. Whether spectators and readers liked it or not, there was a mainstream play on Broadway about gay men, and it was nearly instantaneously canonized by the press as "universal." It, thus, assimilated gay men into the U.S. imagined community.

Epilogue

The political work of the Broadway premiere of *Angels in America* was done from a position of extreme commercial and cultural success. Its record-high ticket prices, for-profit merchandise, prizes, and reviews that framed it as "art" rather than "propaganda" all contributed to its cultural position. This position probably did not produce many activists. Perhaps if the text's Brechtian elements had been exploited or if the play made mention of class in its identity politics, it could have been more of an "activist" or "Marxist" play. These aspects can and have been justifiably criticized.[139] Likewise, its treatment of women characters can hardly be called feminist. But these conservative qualities helped make the play "palatable" to the mainstream, and that helped reviewers see the play as art rather than propaganda. Because reviewers received the production as art, it was framed as "universal" in its themes. This "universality" included gay men—sometimes implicitly, sometimes explicitly—in the imagined community of the United States. Through its performance text, its central position in the culture industry, and the mainstream media discourse surrounding it in the form of reviews, *Angels in America: A Gay Fantasia on National Themes* imagined its characters—particularly its gay men—into the nation's conception of itself. Thus, the production supported gay civil rights not in spite of *Angels in America*'s position in the culture industry but rather because of it.

Notes

1. "The Angel Has Landed: *Perestroika* Hits Mark," *New York Observer*, December 6 1993, 26.
2. *Angels in America: A Gay Fantasia on National Themes, Part Two: Perestroika* (New York: Theatre Communications Group, 1993), 146.
3. Ibid.
4. Michael Paller, "Larry Kramer and Gay Theater," in *We Must Love One Another or Die: The Life and Legacies of Larry Kramer*, ed. Lawrence Mass (London: Cassell, 1997), 235.
5. Benedict R. Anderson, *Imagined Communities: Reflections on the Origin and Spread of Nationalism* (New York: Verso, 1991), 6.
6. J. Robert Cox, "Performing Memory/Speech: Aesthetic Boundaries" and "the Other" in *Ghetto* and *the Normal Heart, Text and Performance Quarterly* 12, no. 4 (1992); Joseph Roach, "Normal Heartlands," ibid.
7. Raymond Williams, *Marxism and Literature*, Marxist Introductions (Oxford: Oxford UP, 1977), 131.
8. "November 1, 1992: AIDS/*Angels in America*," in *Approaching the Millennium: Essays on Angels in America*, ed. Deborah R. Geis and Steven F. Kruger (Ann Arbor: U of Michigan P, 1997), 46.
9. David Román, "November 1, 1992: AIDS/*Angels in America*," in *Approaching the Millennium: Essays on Angels in America*, ed. Deborah R. Geis and Steven F. Kruger (Ann Arbor: U of Michigan P, 1997), 53.
10. Ibid.
11. *Utopia in Performance: Finding Hope at the Theater* (U.S.A.: U of Michigan P, 2005), 7.
12. *Perestroika*, 146.
13. The play's epilogue is set in 1990, but it is one brief scene and does not refer to President George H.W. Bush or his administration.
14. Roy Cohn was a lawyer famous for taking part in U.S. Senator Joseph McCarthy's infamous political witch hunt supposedly investigating Communist Party activity in the United States from 1950 to 1956. Cohn was also a part of the prosecution team for U.S. Department of Justice in the trial of Julius and Ethel Rosenberg who were executed in 1953 for providing information

regarding the atomic bomb to the Soviet Union. In 2008, another person implicated in the espionage trial admitted that Julius Rosenberg spied for the U.S.S.R., but that Ethel Rosenberg did not.
15. "Sex, Lies ... And Us," *The Advocate (The National Gay & Lesbian Newsmagazine)* 771 (1998).
16. William A. Henry III, "*Time:* May 17, 1993, Angels in America," in *New York Theatre Critics' Reviews* (New York: Critics' Theatre Reviews Inc., 1993), 212.
17. Anonymous, "The Queer Nation Manifesto," http://www.historyisaweapon.com/defcon1/queernation.html.
18. The play won two Fund for New American Plays/American Express Awards; the 1991 National Arts Club's Joseph Kesselring Award; the Bay Area Drama Critics Award for the Best Play of 1991; the London Evening Standard Award; the London Drama Critics Award; the Olivier Award for Best Play; and, on the eve of Broadway's first preview performance, *Millennium Approaches* was awarded the Pulitzer Prize. James Fisher, "Book Review: Approaching the Millennium: Essays on Angels in America," *Theatre Journal* 50, no. 4 (1998): 60; Edwin Wilson, "*The Wall Street Journal:* May 6, 1993, Tony Kushner's Gay Fantasia Arrives on Broadway," in *New York Theatre Critics' Reviews* (New York: Critics' Theatre Reviews Inc., 1993), 213.
19. With one exception: Yale Kramer's review for *American Spectator* Yale Kramer, "Angels on Broadway," *The American Spectator* 26, no. 7 (1993).
20. "On Theater: *Angles in America:* Tony Kushner's *Angels in America* Actually Deserves All—or Almost All—the Hype," *The New Republic* 208, no. 21 (1993): 29.
21. Jeremy Gerard, "Review: Angels in America: Millennium Approaches," *Variety*, May 10 1993. Though tickets were expensive, Kushner insisted Wednesday matinee and day-of tickets should be sold at a reduced price. Brustein, "*Angels in America*," 28.
22. Jeremy Gerard, "Two 'Angels'; One Soars," *Variety*, December 6 1993, 34.
23. For example, Jeremy Gerard, in *Variety,* begins his review, "Believe the hype" "*Variety*: May 10, 1993, Angels in America," in *New York Theatre Critics' Reviews* (New York: Critics' Theatre Reviews Inc., 1993), 243. Similarly, Linda Winer writes in *New York Newsday* that the production "has not been crushed by the hype and acclaim" Linda Winer, "*New York Newsday*: May 5, 1993, Pulitzer-Winning 'Angels' Emerges from the Wings," ibid., 209.
24. "*New York Newsday*: May 5, 1993, Pulitzer-Winning 'Angels' Emerges from the Wings," 210.
25. "*Angels in America*," 29.
26. Robin Pogrebin, "Wolfe Is Leaving Public Theatre," *Times*, February 12 2004, E5.
27. Dolan, *Utopia*, 7.
28. *Angels in America: A Gay Fantasia on National Themes, Part One: Millennium Approaches* (New York: Theatre Communications Group, 1993), 75.
29. *Perestroika*, 146.
30. Susan Bennett, *Theatre Audiences: A Theory of Production and Reception*, Second ed. (New York: Routledge, 1997), 48–52.
31. "Angels in America Advertisement," *New York Times*, May 16 1993.
32. For more on spectacle, politics, and nineteenth-century U.S. theatre, see: Amy E. Hughes, *Spectacles of Reform: Theater and Activism in Nineteenth-Century America* (Ann Arbor: U of Michigan P, 2012).

33. Haun, Harry. "Of Angst and Angels." Program of *Angels in America* from the Broadway premiere 1993, Call Number: *T-PRG Angels in America, The New York Public Library for the Performing Arts.
34. Ibid.
35. Ibid.
36. In 1990, the so-called NEA Four—Karen Finley, Tim Miller, John Fleck, and Holly Hughes—were denied grants for artistic projects on LGBT themes even though the projects were approved by a peer review process. In 1993, the same year as *Angels in America*'s Broadway premiere, the artists won a court case for funds equal to the proposed grants. While unrelated to the NEA grant received for the development of *Angels in America* in the late-1980s, spectators for the Broadway premiere may well have had this context in mind while they read the program note.
37. Haun, "Of Angst and Angels," 10, 14.
38. Botto, Louis. "Happy Birthday Broadway." Program of *Angels in America* from the Broadway premiere 1993, Call Number: *T-PRG Angels in America, The New York Public Library for the Performing Arts.
39. "Embracing All Possibilities in Art and Life," *New York Times*, May 5 1993, C16.
40. "Notes on *Angels in America* as American Epic Theater," in *Approaching the Millennium: Essays on Angels in America*, ed. Deborah R. Geis and Steven F. Kruger (Ann Arbor: U of Michigan P, 1997), 239.
41. Winer, "*New York Newsday*: May 5, 1993, Pulitzer-Winning 'Angels' Emerges from the Wings," 210.
42. "Notes on *Angels in America* as American Epic Theater," 238.
43. L.C. Cole, "Apocalypse, American-Style," *New York Native*, May 31 1993; Gerard, "Millennium; John Heilpern, "Angels in America: Indeed, the Millennium Approaches," *New York Observer*, May 10 1993; "*Perestroika*; Jack Kroll, "Mourning Becomes Electrifying," *Newsweek*, May 17 1993; John Lahr, "Curtain Up! Angels on Broadway Tony Kushner's Play May Be a Landmark in America Theatre," *The New Yorker* LXIX, no. 15 (1993); Ward Morehouse III, " 'Angels in America' Remains Earthbound," *Christian Science Monitor*, May 17 1993; Rich, "Embracing; "Following an Angel for a Healing Vision of Heaven on Earth," *New York Times*, November 24 1993; David Richards, "An Epic, All Right, but It's the Details and Future That Count," ibid., May 16; David Sheward, "Review: Angels in America: Millennium Approaches," *Backstage*, May 7 1993; John Simon, "*New York*: May 17, 1993, Angels in America (Rev)," in *New York Theatre Critics' Reviews* (New York: Critics' Reviews Inc., 1993); Doug Watt, "*Daily News*: May 14, 1993," ibid. (Critics' Theatre Reviews Inc.); Linda Winer, "*New York Newsday*: May 5, 1993, Pulitzer-Winning 'Angels' Emerges from the Wings," ibid.
44. Baz Kershaw, *The Radical in Performance: Between Brecht and Baudrillard* (London: Routledge, 1999), 47.
45. Bennett, *Theatre Audiences*, 118.
46. David Savran, *A Queer Sort of Materialism: Recontextualizing American Theater* (Ann Arbor: U of Michigan P, 2003), 129. Sedgwick used this phrase during the question period that followed a lecture at Brown University, 1 October 1992.
47. Savran, *A Queer Sort of Materialism*, x.
48. Ronald Reagan, "The Nine Most Terrifying Words in the English Language," http://www.youtube.com/watch?v=xhYJS80MgYA.

49. Bill Clinton, "Bill Clinton, New Democrat," *Blueprint Magazine*, http://www.dlc.org/ndol_ci.cfm?kaid=127&subid=173&contentid=252794.
50. Ibid.
51. Ibid.
52. Ibid.
53. Ibid.
54. ibid.
55. Kushner, *Millennium Approaches*, 16.
56. Kushner, *Millennium Approaches*, 95–99.
57. Kushner, *Millennium Approaches*, 98.
58. *Perestroika*, 108–09.
59. *Perestroika*, 109.
60. See: J. Hector St. John De Crevecoeur, *Letters from an American Farmer* (New York: Duffield, 1904).
61. Israel Zangwill, *The Melting-Pot* (Baltimore, MD: Macmillan, 1909).
62. Michael Cadden defines the term "pinklisting" as a "celebratory" and "speculative" practice of labeling historical figures as gay and lesbian in a way that "sees itself as providing role models and suggests, however problematically, the continuity of a gay and lesbian presence (and usually struggle) across the borderlines of time and place." Michael Cadden, "Strange Angel: The Pinklisting of Roy Cohn," in *Approaching the Millennium: Essays on Angels in America*, ed. Deborah R. Geis and Steven F. Kruger (Ann Arbor: U of Michigan P, 1997), 79. The fact that *Angels in America* assimilates an arch conservative like Roy Cohn is more complicated than, say, claiming Michelangelo as a role model. But questions about Cohn's sexuality swirled around him during his lifetime, and much of what Kushner writes in *Angels in America* is part of the public record. Hence, Kushner's "pinklisting" of Cohn is not pure invention, as Cadden explicates in detail.
63. Kushner, *Millennium Approaches*, 52.
64. Kushner, *Millennium Approaches*, 11.
65. *Perestroika*, 124.
66. *Perestroika*, 139.
67. *Perestroika*, 102.
68. *Perestroika*, 103.
69. In a paragraph about gender, it may be necessary to point out that the gender-neutral term "actor" is preferable to separating "actor" and "actress." After all, modern English no longer separates "poet" and "poetess," though that was common usage in the nineteenth century.
70. *Perestroika*, 103.
71. Kushner, *Millennium Approaches*, 48.
72. Kushner, *Millennium Approaches*, 69.
73. Kushner, *Millennium Approaches*, 67.
74. Kushner, *Millennium Approaches*, 36.
75. Kushner, *Millennium Approaches*, 67.
76. Charlotte Coles, "The Question of Power and Authirity in Gender Performance: Judith Butler's Drag Strategy," *eSharp*, no. 9 (2007).
77. Judith Butler, *Gender Trouble: Feminism and the Subversion of Identity*, Thinking Gender (New York: Routledge, 1990).
78. *Perestroika*, 118.

79. Kushner, *Millennium Approaches*, 24.
80. Kushner, *Millennium Approaches*, 86.
81. *Perestroika*, 16.
82. *Perestroika*, 18.
83. Ibid.
84. *Perestroika*, 47.
85. *Perestroika*, 18.
86. *Perestroika*, 139.
87. *Perestroika*, 41.
88. Ibid.
89. Ibid.
90. Ibid.
91. Amy Schindler, "Angels and the AIDS Epidemic: The Resurgent Popularity of Angel Imagery in the United States of America," *The Journal of American Culture* 22, no. 3 (1999): 49.
92. Haun, "Of Angst and Angels," 8.
93. Ibid.
94. *Perestroika*, 143.
95. Clinton, "Bill Clinton, New Democrat."
96. *Perestroika*, 143.
97. *Perestroika*, 146.
98. Ibid.
99. Ibid.
100. Robert A. Rankin and Angie Cannon, "Clinton's Promises."
101. Kushner, *Perestroika*, 147.
102. *Perestroika*, 140.
103. Dolan, *Utopia*, xx.
104. Walter Benjamin, "Theses on the Philosophy of History," in *Illuminations*, ed. Hannah Arendt (New York: Schocken Books, 1968), 257–58.
105. Charles McNulty, "Angels in America: Tony Kushner's Theses on the Philosophy of History," *Modern Drama* 39, no. 1 (1996): 13.
106. Barbara Foley, "What's at Stake in the Culture Wars," *The New England Quarterly* 68, no. 3 (1995): 478.
107. Ibid.
108. "Opinion: Dealing with the Demands of an Expanding Literary Canon," *College English* 50, no. 3 (1988): 277.
109. "Canon," in *Critical Terms for Literary Study*, ed. Frank Lentricchia and Thomas McLaughlin (Chicago: U of Chicago Press, 1990), 238.
110. Deborah R. Geis and Steven F. Kruger, eds., *Approaching the Millennium: Essays on Angels in America*, Theater—Theory/Text/Performance (Ann Arbor: U of Michigan P, 1997).
111. Gerard, "Millennium; "Two 'Angels'; Heilpern, "*Perestroika*; Kroll, "Mourning; Rich, "Healing; David Richards, "'Angels' Finds a Poignant Note of Hope," *New York Times (Sunday)*, November 28 1993; Simon, "*New York*: May 17, 1993, Angels in America (Rev); David Patrick Stearns, "Soaring 'Angels in America': Ethereal Epic Dissolution Takes Flight on Broadway," *USA Today*, May 5 1993; Watt, "*Daily News*: May 14, 1993; Linda Winer, "*New York Newsday*: May 5, 1993, Pulitzer-Winning 'Angels' Emerges from the Wings," ibid.

112. Clive Barnes, "*New York Post:* May 5, 1993, Angelically Gay About Our Decay," ibid. (Critics' Theatre Reviews Inc.); Gerard, "Millennium; Henry III, "*Time:* May 17, 1993, Angels in America; Lahr, "Curtain Up! Angels on Broadway Tony Kushner's Play May Be a Landmark in America Theatre; Rich, "Embracing."
113. Heilpern, "Millennium Approaches; Anna Quindlen, "Happy and Gay," *New York Times,* April 6 1994.
114. Frank DeCaro, "The Night Tony Kushner Kissed Me," *Newsday,* May 11 1993; Michael Feingold, "*The Village Voice*: May 18, 1993, Building the Monolith," in *New York Theatre Critics' Reviews* (New York: Critics Theatre Reviews Inc., 1993); David Hinckly, "'Angels' in Mainstream America," *Daily News,* June 8 1993; "Evaluating 'Perestroika's' Epic Proportions," *Daily News,* November 30 1993; Kramer, "Angels on Broadway; Ward Morehouse III, "*Christian Science Monitor*: May 17, 1993, 'Angels in America' Remains Earthbound," in *New York Theatre Critics' Reviews* (New York: Critics' Theatre Reviews Inc., 1993); Michael Musto, "Untitled," *Village Voice,* December 14 1993; Alisa Solomon, "Whose Tommy?," ibid., July 13; Wilson, "*The Wall Street Journal*: May 6, 1993, Tony Kushner's Gay Fantasia Arrives on Broadway."
115. Gerard, "Millennium," 211.
116. Ibid.
117. "*Angels in America,*" 29.
118. Ibid.
119. For explorations of canon formation and its relation to the concept of "universal" art, see: Guillory, *Cultural Capital: The Problem of Literary Canon Formation* (Chicago: University of Chicago Press, 1993).
120. "The Operatic Overtones of 'Angels in America'," *New York Times (Sunday),* June 27 1993, 2: 25.
121. Pierre Bourdieu, *Distinction: A Social Critique of the Judgement of Taste* (Cambridge, MA: Harvard UP, 1984).
122. "*The Wall Street Journal*: May 6, 1993, Tony Kushner's Gay Fantasia Arrives on Broadway," 213.
123. "*The Wall Street Journal*: May 6, 1993, Tony Kushner's Gay Fantasia Arrives on Broadway," 213, 14.
124. "*The Wall Street Journal*: May 6, 1993, Tony Kushner's Gay Fantasia Arrives on Broadway," 214.
125. Ibid.
126. Ward Morehouse III, "*Christian Science Monitor*: May 17, 1993, 'Angels in America' Remains Earthbound," ibid., 215.
127. Ibid.
128. "Whose Tommy?," 89.
129. "Clipping the Wigs of 'Angels'," *Newsday,* June 24 1993, 102.
130. "Angels on Broadway," 2.
131. Ibid.
132. "Angels on Broadway," 23.
133. "Angels on Broadway," 24.
134. ibid.
135. Clifford Geertz, *Local Knowledge: Further Essays in Interpretive Anthropology* (New York: Basic Books, 1983).

136. I write "openly gay men" because *Angels in America* contains no openly gay women.
137. Lahr, "Curtain Up! Angels on Broadway Tony Kushner's Play May Be a Landmark in America Theatre."
138. Winer, "*New York Newsday*: May 5, 1993, Pulitzer-Winning 'Angels' Emerges from the Wings."
139. Reinelt, "Notes on *Angels in America* as American Epic Theater; David Savran, "Ambivalence, Utopia, and a Queer Sort of Materialism: How *Angels in America* Reconstructs the Nation," in *Approaching the Millennium: Essays on Angels in America*, ed. Deborah R. Geis and Steven F. Kruger (Ann Arbor: U of Michigan P, 1997).

Bibliography

Anderson, Benedict R. *Imagined Communities: Reflections on the Origin and Spread of Nationalism*. New York: Verso, 1991.

"Angels in America Advertisement." *New York Times*, May 16 1993.

Anonymous. "The Queer Nation Manifesto." http://www.historyisaweapon.com/defcon1/queernation.html.

Barnes, Clive. "*New York Post*: May 5, 1993, Angelically Gay about Our Decay." In *New York Theatre Critics' Reviews*, 210. Critics' Theatre Reviews Inc., 1993.

Benjamin, Walter. "Theses on the Philosophy of History." In *Illuminations*, edited by Hannah Arendt, 253–64. New York: Schocken Books, 1968.

Bennett, Susan. *Theatre Audiences: A Theory of Production and Reception*. Second ed. New York: Routledge, 1997.

Botto, Louis. "Happy Birthday Broadway." Program of *Angels in America* from the Broadway premiere 1993, Call Number: *T-PRG Angels in America, The New York Public Library for the Performing Arts.

Bourdieu, Pierre. *Distinction: A Social Critique of the Judgement of Taste*. Cambridge, MA: Harvard UP, 1984.

Brustein, Robert. "On Theater: *Angles in America*: Tony Kushner's *Angels in America* Actually Deserves All—or Almost All—the Hype." *The New Republic* 208, no. 21 (1993): 29.

Butler, Judith. *Gender Trouble: Feminism and the Subversion of Identity*. Thinking Gender. New York: Routledge, 1990.

Cadden, Michael. "Strange Angel: The Pinklisting of Roy Cohn." In *Approaching the Millennium: Essays on Angels in America*, edited by Deborah R. Geis and Steven F. Kruger, 78–89. Ann Arbor: U of Michigan P, 1997.

Clinton, Bill. "Bill Clinton, New Democrat." Blueprint Magazine, http://www.dlc.org/ndol_ci.cfm?kaid=127&subid=173&contentid=252794.

Cole, L.C. "Apocalypse, American-Style." *New York Native*, May 31 1993, 28.

Coles, Charlotte. "The Question of Power and Authirity in Gender Performance: Judith Butler's Drag Strategy." *eSharp*, no. 9 (Spring 2007): 1–18.

Cox, J. Robert. "Performing Memory/Speech: Aesthetic Boundaries and "the Other" in *Ghetto* and *the Normal Heart*." *Text and Performance Quarterly* 12, no. 4 (1992): 385–90.

Crevecoeur, J. Hector St. John De. *Letters from an American Farmer*. New York: Duffield, 1904.

DeCaro, Frank. "The Night Tony Kushner Kissed Me." *Newsday*, May 11 1993, 44.

Dolan, Jill. *Utopia in Performance: Finding Hope at the Theater*. Ann Arbor, MI: U of Michigan P, 2005.

Feingold, Michael. "*The Village Voice*: May 18, 1993, Building the Monolith." In *New York Theatre Critics' Reviews*, 218–19. New York: Critics Theatre Reviews Inc., 1993.

Fisher, James. "Book Review: Approaching the Millennium: Essays on Angels in America." *Theatre Journal* 50, no. 4 (1998): 550.

Foley, Barbara. "What's at Stake in the Culture Wars." *The New England Quarterly* 68, no. 3 (September 1995): 458–79.

Geertz, Clifford. *Local Knowledge: Further Essays in Interpretive Anthropology*. New York: Basic Books, 1983.

Geis, Deborah R., and Steven F. Kruger, eds. *Approaching the Millennium: Essays on Angels in America*, Theater—Theory/Text/Performance. Ann Arbor: U of Michigan P, 1997.

Gerard, Jeremy. "Two 'Angels'; One Soars." *Variety*, December 6 1993, 33, 34, 58.

———. "Review: Angels in America: Millennium Approaches." *Variety*, May 10 1993, 243–44.

———. "*Variety*: May 10, 1993, *Angels in America*." In *New York Theatre Critics' Reviews*, 211–12. New York: Critics' Theatre Reviews Inc., 1993.

Guillory, John. "Canon." In *Critical Terms for Literary Study*, edited by Frank Lentricchia and Thomas McLaughlin, 233–49. Chicago: U of Chicago Press, 1990.

———. *Cultural Capital: The Problem of Literary Canon Formation*. Chicago: University of Chicago Press, 1993.

Haun, Harry. "Of Angst and Angels." Program of *Angels in America* from the Broadway premiere 1993, Call Number: *T-PRG Angels in America, The New York Public Library for the Performing Arts.

Heilpern, John. "The Angel Has Landed: *Perestroika* Hits Mark." *New York Observer*, December 6 1993, 1, 34.

———. "Angels in America: Indeed, the Millennium Approaches." *New York Observer*, May 10 1993, 26.

Henry III, William A. "*Time*: May 17, 1993, Angels in America." In *New York Theatre Critics' Reviews*, 212. New York: Critics' Theatre Reviews Inc., 1993.

Hinckly, David. "'Angels' in Mainstream America." *Daily News*, June 8 1993, 53.

———. "Evaluating 'Perestroika's' Epic Proportions." *Daily News*, November 30 1993, 47.

Hughes, Amy E. *Spectacles of Reform: Theater and Activism in Nineteenth-Century America* Ann Arbor: U of Michigan P, 2012.

Jenkins, Speight. "The Operatic Overtones of 'Angels in America'." *New York Times (Sunday)*, June 27 1993, 25.

Kershaw, Baz. *The Radical in Performance: Between Brecht and Baudrillard*. London: Routledge, 1999.

Kramer, Yale. "Angels on Broadway." *The American Spectator* 26, no. 7 (1993): 18–26.

———. "Clipping the Wigs of 'Angels'." *Newsday*, June 24 1993, 102.

Kroll, Jack. "Mourning Becomes Electrifying." *Newswek*, May 17 1993.

Kushner, Tony. *Angels in America: A Gay Fantasia on National Themes, Part One: Millennium Approaches*. New York: Theatre Communications Group, 1993.

———. *Angels in America: A Gay Fantasia on National Themes, Part Two: Perestroika*. New York: Theatre Communications Group, 1993.

Lahr, John. "Curtain Up! Angels on Broadway Tony Kushner's Play May Be a Landmark in America Theatre." *The New Yorker* LXIX, no. 15 (1993): 137.
McNulty, Charles. "*Angels in America*: Tony Kushner's Theses on the Philosophy of History." *Modern Drama* 39, no. 1 (1996): 13.
Morehouse III, Ward. "*'Angels in America'* Remains Earthbound." *Christian Science Monitor*, May 17 1993.
———. "*Christian Science Monitor*: May 17, 1993, 'Angels in America' Remains Earthbound." In *New York Theatre Critics' Reviews*, 215–16. New York: Critics' Theatre Reviews Inc., 1993.
Musto, Michael. "Untitled." *Village Voice*, December 14 1993, 46.
Paller, Michael. "Larry Kramer and Gay Theater." In *We Must Love One Another or Die: The Life and Legacies of Larry Kramer*, edited by Lawrence Mass, 235–55. London: Cassell, 1997.
Pogrebin, Robin. "Wolfe Is Leaving Public Theatre." *Times*, February 12 2004, E5.
Quindlen, Anna. "Happy and Gay." *New York Times*, April 6 1994, A21.
Rankin, Robert A., and Angie Cannon. "Clinton's Promises—President Did as He Said: 66% of Campaign Vows Met." *Seattle Times*, August 18 1996.
Reagan, Ronald. "The Nine Most Terrifying Words in the English Language." http://www.youtube.com/watch?v=xhYJS80MgYA.
Reinelt, Janelle. "Notes on *Angels in America* as American Epic Theater." In *Approaching the Millennium: Essays on Angels in America*, edited by Deborah R. Geis and Steven F. Kruger, 234–44. Ann Arbor: U of Michigan P, 1997.
Rich, Frank. "Embracing All Possibilities in Art and Life." *New York Times*, May 5 1993, C15-C16.
———. "Following an Angel for a Healing Vision of Heaven on Earth." *New York Times*, November 24 1993, C20.
Richards, David. "'Angels' Finds a Poignant Note of Hope." *New York Times (Sunday)*, November 28 1993, 1, 27.
———. "An Epic, All Right, but It's the Details and Future That Count." *New York Times*, May 16 1993, 1.
Roach, Joseph. "Normal Heartlands." *Text and Performance Quarterly* 12 (October 1992): 377–84.
Román, David. "November 1, 1992: AIDS/*Angels in America*." In *Approaching the Millennium: Essays on Angels in America*, edited by Deborah R. Geis and Steven F. Kruger, 40–55. Ann Arbor: U of Michigan P, 1997.
Savran, David. "Ambivalence, Utopia, and a Queer Sort of Materialism: How *Angels in America* Reconstructs the Nation." In *Approaching the Millennium: Essays on Angels in America*, edited by Deborah R. Geis and Steven F. Kruger, 13–39. Ann Arbor: U of Michigan P, 1997.
———. *A Queer Sort of Materialism: Recontextualizing American Theater*. Ann Arbor: U of Michigan P, 2003.
Schindler, Amy. "Angels and the AIDS Epidemic: The Resurgent Popularity of Angel Imagery in the United States of America." *The Journal of American Culture* 22, no. 3 (1999): 49–61.
Sheward, David. "Review: Angels in America: Millennium Approaches." *Backstage*, May 7 1993, 44.
Simon, John. "*New York*: May 17, 1993, Angels in America (Rev)." In *New York Theatre Critics' Reviews*, 207. New York: Critics' Reviews Inc., 1993.
Solomon, Alisa. "Whose Tommy?" *Village Voice*, July 13 1993, 89.

Stearns, David Patrick. "Soaring 'Angels in America': Ethereal Epic Dissolution Takes Flight on Broadway." *USA Today*, May 5 1993.

Sullivan, Andrew. "Sex, Lies ... And Us." *The Advocate (The National Gay & Lesbian Newsmagazine)* 771 (October 27 1998).

Watt, Doug. "*Daily News*: May 14, 1993." In *New York Theatre Critics' Reviews*, 220. New York: Critics' Theatre Reviews Inc., 1993.

Weixlmann, Joe. "Opinion: Dealing with the Demands of an Expanding Literary Canon." *College English* 50, no. 3 (March 1988): 273–83.

Williams, Raymond. *Marxism and Literature*. Marxist Introductions. Oxford: Oxford UP, 1977.

Wilson, Edwin. "*The Wall Street Journal*: May 6, 1993, Tony Kushner's Gay Fantasia Arrives on Broadway." In *New York Theatre Critics' Reviews*, 213–14. New York: Critics' Theatre Reviews Inc., 1993.

Winer, Linda. "*New York Newsday*: May 5, 1993, Pulitzer-Winning 'Angels' Emerges from the Wings." In *New York Theatre Critics' Reviews*, 209–10. New York: Critics' Theatre Reviews Inc., 1993.

Zangwill, Israel. *The Melting-Pot*. Baltimore, MD: Macmillan, 1909.

4 Commercialization
Rent

Prologue

Jonathan Larson collapsed clutching his heart during the last technical rehearsal of *Rent* on January 21, 1996, at the New York Theatre Workshop. But he did not die—yet. He thought he was having a heart attack and was rushed to Cabrini Medical Center. Doctors at Cabrini diagnosed him with food poisoning, pumped his stomach, and sent him home. Two days later, the chest pain returned and Larson went to St. Vincent's Hospital, which also sent him home, attributing his chest pain to stress and improper self-care during the run-up to his most important New York City production to date. On Larson's last night alive, he enjoyed watching a final dress rehearsal of *Rent*, which received a standing ovation from a friendly, capacity crowd made up of the production's backers and artists who called the New York Theatre Workshop home. Larson then went back to his apartment. There, he put a pot of water on the stove for tea, and his heart's aorta ripped open, allowing blood to pour into his chest, likely causing unconsciousness in approximately 15 seconds and death in under five minutes. If either Cabrini Medical Center or St. Vincent's Hospital had diagnosed Larson correctly with a congenital weakness in his aorta, Larson's chances of recovery would have been 80 to 90 percent. The New York Department of Health "fined Cabrini and St. Vincent's for their misdiagnosis and mistreatment."[1] This horrible misfortune framed every review of *Rent*'s premiere at the New York Theatre Workshop and its Broadway transfer. But, rather than seeing Larson's death as an accident, a mishap without meaning, reviewers provided a narrative structure for Larson's death and co-mingled his real-life death with the significance of his play. Critics heard *Rent*'s anthems of characters wanting to achieve greatness before impending death as "prescient" songs written by a man about to die himself.[2] These critics made it seem as if Larson knew he had a fatal illness, like HIV/AIDS patients did in the 1980s and 1990s, and, thus, that he had a limited time to create art. In actuality, Larson had a completely unknown heart condition and expected to live a typical lifespan.

By making Larson's score "prescient," however, the press presented Larson's death as tragic rather than accidental. Reporting on a manufactured real-life "tragedy," the media activated and underscored the production's already melodramatic tendencies. Since nearly every review led with Larson's death, and most at some point mentioned the "tragic" loss to U.S. musical theatre, Larson's untimely end became collapsed with the plot of the premiere of *Rent*. To paraphrase Rebecca Schneider writing in a different context, the live actors onstage in *Rent* became living surrogates for the actually dead author, making it possible for spectators to meet the eyes of one on the other side.[3] This excess connotation and the production's glowing reviews made *Rent* the hottest ticket in town and set up the conditions to successfully sell AIDS and bohemian poverty to mainstream theatre-goers. This commercial packaging of 1990s counter-culture found a safe home in *Rent,* which made it possible for the musical to transfer from its original downtown location to the newly Disney-fied Times Square. *Rent* became a Broadway theme-park-like simulacrum of Greenwich Village. Its popularity spawned a Broadway cast recording and two national tours within a year of its New York City opening. Scholars have noted *Rent*'s appropriation of 1990s counterculture, particularly LGBT issues, but, because *Rent* was such an economic powerhouse, it was able to support the emergent ideology of gay civil rights. In fact, it directly produced electoral change in the Deep South town of Charlotte, North Carolina. But, more prominently, previously radical LGBT ideologies were made visible on the national platform that supported *Rent*, the most successful new musical of the 1990s.

(Un)Contested Authenticity

The premiere of *Rent* made several claims to authenticity. It contended to accurately portray its AIDS-stricken bohemian characters of New York City's East Village; to be an anthem for the U.S. 1990s counterculture as represented by Larson's "starving artist" lifestyle; and to be a successful merger of edgy rock and musical theatre styles. Despite obvious ways one might contest these assertions, the press received *Rent* nearly without exception as wholly authentic in these respects. This authenticity, then, was the horizon of expectation given to audience members through media, location, *mise-en-scène*, and Larson's death.

The plot of *Rent* loosely takes three nineteenth-century sources and transplants them into the East Village of New York City in the 1990s. The sources are Henri Murger's novel *Scènes de la Vie de Bohème*; Giacomo Puccini's opera *La Bohème* adapted from Murger; and, most closely, Rugerro Leoncavallo's opera also adapted from Murger and titled *La Bohème*. From these sources, Larson created a series of scenes and songs focusing on artists, intellectuals, and the poor, most of whom are also HIV positive. The play's protagonists, both straight white men, are Roger and Mark, an aspiring songwriter and video artist respectively, who share an abandoned loft. In the derelict building's next room is a Latina heroine-addicted S&M dancer, Mimi, whose on again, off again relationship with Roger is a major plot point. Mark begins the play single because his ex-lover, the performance artist Maureen, left him for a female African American attorney, Joanne. They are all friends with Collins, an African American professor at NYU, who takes up with the Latino cross-dresser, Angel. The building in which Mark, Roger, and Mimi live, and the vacant lot next door in which Maureen performs, are owned by Benny, an African American yuppie who used to consider himself friends with Mark and Roger. Benny used to let Mark and Roger squat in the building for free, but he now demands the titular rent. Mimi, Roger, Angel, and Collins are all HIV positive. A chorus supplemented the main characters, made up, in the premiere, of two white men, two African American men, one white woman, one Asian American woman, and one African American woman. The chorus transforms from homeless people to members of an AIDS support group and other minor roles. The five-piece band—made up of white men playing drums, bass, guitar, and keyboards—is also onstage. The sprawling plot follows the various couples struggling to maintain successful relationships in the face of poverty and illness. In the end, Angel and Mimi both succumb to AIDS—though Mimi awakens from the dead, sent back to earth by Angel who tells her to return because of the love in a song that Roger has written for her. The entire cast then stands in a line at the edge of the stage singing directly to the audience a song that ends with the refrain, "No day but today" six times.

This complicated story, while having its roots in nineteenth-century art, was marketed and reviewed as updated and true to life in New York City's East Village based on Larson's experiences. Critics loved and repeatedly rehearsed the narrative of *Rent*'s *La Bohème* foundation, ignoring or, more likely, not knowing other potential sources. First, Lynn Thomson, the dramaturg of *Rent,* sued the Larson estate claiming to be the co-author of the text. This case went to court in 1997 and was thrown out in 1998, but likely would have been unknown to journalists during *Rent*'s 1996 opening. However, author and activist, Sarah Schulman, published a novel in 1990 called *People in Trouble* that has many plot similarities to *Rent*.[4] In Schulman's 1998 book, *Stagestruck: Theater, AIDS, and the Marketing of Gay America*,[5] she delineates the similarities between her novel and Larson's musical and portrays confronting Larson's estate. Though she ultimately decided not to sue for copyright infringement, Schulman uses *Stagestruck* to argue that *Rent* commodifies LGBT life at the expense of actually representing the oppression to which these groups were subjected. In her claim about *Rent*'s copyright infringement, the most striking similarity between the play and novel is a love triangle between two women and a straight man. But this relationship is portrayed in *Rent* with an important difference from that in *People in Trouble*. As Schulman points out in a 2005 interview, Larson "made the straight man the protagonist, whereas in [Schulman's] version he was the secondary character. … It's the issue of taking authentic material made by people who don't have rights, twisting it so they are secondary in their own life story, and thereby bringing it center stage in a mainstream piece that does not advocate for them."[6] The cultural appropriation of minority art by the dominant culture is a prevalent practice in the U.S., and certainly shifting a play's protagonist from a lesbian to a straight white man qualifies. But, given the dearth of canonical plays with lesbian protagonists, Larson's putting straight white men front and center likely gave *Rent* more mainstream appeal. While some critics may have been familiar with Schulman, none mentioned her work, and, thus, the authenticity of Larson's update of *La Bohème* was not challenged in the premiere's press.

Thomson and Schulman's claims about their influence on *Rent*'s plot may not have been known by the press, but critics should have known that *Rent* did not represent Larson's real life, as many claimed.[7] Even as a one-to-one relationship between Larson's life and the situation of *Rent*'s characters was rehearsed, newspapers paradoxically recorded ways Larson's experience differed from that of his characters. For instance, of Larson's sexuality, New York's most prominent LGBT publication, *The Advocate*, wrote, "such is the degree of Larson's unqualified empathy for his gay and lesbian characters that it's hard to believe he wasn't gay himself (he wasn't)."[8] The paper, while noting Larson's sympathetic LGBT characters, needs to note—and emphasize—that Larson was not gay. Conflating Larson's poverty to that of his characters, Frank Rich, in 1996 a prominent op-ed columnist at *The New York Times*, wrote that "Mr. Larson had sacrificed his life to his work, waiting on tables for years."[9] This narrative of poverty persists through the reviews, but Larson's reported income was generally $20,000 to $25,000 a year,[10] which even in 1990s New York City was at least three times the 1996 U.S. government-defined poverty line of $7,763 earned per year.[11] Also complicating claims of Larson's poverty was his birth in White Plains, a comfortably middle-class suburb of New York City. In an interview after Larson's death, his father stated that one of his biggest regrets was not helping his son financially more than he did.[12] In that way, perhaps, Larson does resemble his characters, many of whom—particularly the protagonists Mark and Roger—have supportive, middle-class parents who seem willing to help their children financially. Like Larson, his characters Mark and Roger refuse help, choosing instead romantic poverty that could be undone easily with a phone call. But the critics reacting to *Rent* created a life for Larson that was that of a starving artist, not a comfortable, middle class man who chose to wait tables rather than take help from his parents or have a different day job while writing. Larson's musical upbringing also seems an unlikely source of an "authentic" rock opera.

Though called by most critics a successful fusion of contemporary rock music with the musical form, *Rent*'s score feels more in line with Larson's hero, Steven Sondheim, than 1990s rock. As a child, Larson was exposed to classical music, Pete Seeger, and opera.[13] In high school, his favorite musicians were Elton John and Billy Joel—hardly hard rock idols—and when he and friends went to New York City for day trips, Larson purchased tickets to musicals such as *Sweeny Todd* rather than rock concerts.[14] Reviewers of *Rent* write about the power of its rock music, "from the first screech of feedback"[15] to its finale of "a sophisticated version of basic bar-band blues, mixed with grunge."[16] But contrasted to mainstream rock of the early 1990s, *Rent* is tame.

It only takes a few comparisons to establish how family-friendly *Rent* was compared to mainstream 1990s rock. The ultimate 1990s breakup song, "You Oughta Know" (1995), from Alanis Morissette, includes lyrics such as, "Every time I scratch my nails down someone else's back, I hope you can feel it," and, "Are you thinking of me while you fuck her?" *Rent*'s breakup between Roger and Mimi has Roger singing, "All your words are nice Mimi / But love's not a three-way street / You'll never share real love / Until you love yourself—I should know."[17] Morissette's much more explicit lyrics and far more shrieking vocals are from the best-selling album of the 1990s.[18] Based on that fact, *Rent*'s trite break-up lyrics cannot be written off merely as a nod to commercial interests as Morissette's music was incredibly commercially successful. Instead, one needs to continue to compare *Rent* to popular music from the time to suggest what *Rent* was selling.

In particular, *Rent* was filled with lyrics that young people could feel rebellious listening to but parents would not find offensive. Note *Rent*'s attempts at lewd lyrics contrasted to contemporaneous pop songs. Compare *Rent*'s, "Touch! / Taste! / Deep! / Dark! / Kiss! / Beg! / Slap! / Fear!"[19] to Nine Inch Nails', "I want to fuck you like an animal / I want to feel you from the inside," from the song "Closer" (1994), which hit 41 on Billboard's Top 100 Chart. And Mimi's coy references to S&M, such as, "MIMI: Ow! / ROGER: Oh. The wax—it's— / MIMI: Dripping! I like it—between my— / ROGER: Fingers,"[20] do not hold a candle to Madonna's 1930's German bondage themed video from her 1992 single "Erotica," which ends on the lyric, "only the one who inflicts pain can take it away." Finally, nothing in the play's "angry" songs comes close to the rage, discordance, and feedback in the music of bands like Nirvana, Metallica, Guns 'N Roses, Bikini Kill, Sleater Kinney, or Hole. Instead, the musical's tame lyrics and musical styles are far less "authentically" of the hard-edge 1990s traditions, but are, instead, a part of the late 1990s Disney-fication of Broadway. *Rent* was the theme park version of a 1990s rock concert. But, of the 33 reviews focusing on *Rent*'s premiere, 24 find the musical a successful melding of rock's hard edge and musical theatre's storytelling.[21]

The media's contentions about the authenticity of *Rent* were not limited to the production's music. They continued into the play's depictions of urban poverty, youth, and death. Reviews made much of the New York Theatre Workshop's East Village location, with the *Wall Street Journal* describing "limousines and taxies snak[ing] through East Fourth Street, a strip of tenements and bodegas,"[22] and a *New York Times* critic stating that she saw onstage "privilege side by side with poverty" and that "one of the nicest things about seeing 'Rent' on East Fourth Street is that when you leave (Café La Mama is right across the street), you feel a genuine link between theater and life."[23] What critics rehearsed, here, was a sense that the poverty depicted in *Rent* was completely in line with the New York Theatre Workshop's neighborhood. And, while there was poverty in the East Village at that time, the 1990s mainly saw a wave of gentrification sweeping through the area. Though not what critics meant, a great connection did, in fact, exist between the production and its neighborhood because *Rent*'s poverty primarily consists of artists choosing faux destitution and to live in an abandoned "rent free" building rather than to take money from their parents. This chosen deprivation connects to the production's East Village neighborhood because in the 1990s La Mama and the New York Theatre Workshop were artistic urban pioneers that would ultimately contribute to the gentrification of the area. Both the play's characters and the production's location seemed more "dangerous" to those in limousines than they actually were. This geographical titillation partially explains *Rent*'s popularity. Even once *Rent* moved to the intentionally distressed Nederlander Theatre on Broadway, *Newsday* described the location as "a shunned house considered to be on the 'wrong' side of 42nd Street."[24] It is hard to imagine exactly what the "wrong" side of Times Square meant in the late-1990s when the Broadway district was made a thoroughly safe tourist destination free of pornography and poverty. Mark Sussman wrote in *TDR*'s Spring 1998 issue that, "The Times Square Business Improvement District (BID) is one of at least six major regulatory interests in the neighborhood, not counting the developers and private corporations that will actually build on and inhabit the land."[25] He noted that a BID tour highlighted, "The pace of change in Times Square has accelerated rapidly since 1996 ... [with] long, hard looks at the Virgin Megastore, the spanking new clone of Little Italy's Ferrara's, the new zipper signs on the Morgan Stanley building that give 'real time' information from Wall Street, and the AT&T fiber-optic sign that hangs on the facade of Marriot Marquis Hotel."[26] John Bell, writing on the Disneyfication of Times Square, highlighted its communal aspects: "In that network live theatre will serve, like theme-park performance, as a place where Disney consumers can participate in (consume) a Disney event with other Disney customers, helping to establish in person a temporary Disney consumer community."[27] Similarly, consuming *Rent* allowed its spectators to feel part of a bohemian counterculture in the safety of Broadway. After all, not only was BID remodeling the architecture of Times Square, it was also "using six million dollars in annual assessments on local merchants, [to create] an autonomous security zone, with its own police, trash collection, pink plastic-garbage can liners, and 'homeless outreach teams'" that made sure homeless would not reach out to Broadway-bound tourists.[28] Nevertheless, even when *Rent* played on Broadway, critics tended to consider the authenticity of *Rent*'s portrayal of urban poverty synonymous with its location.

The set and costumes of *Rent* continued the expensive simulacrum of urban poverty. The set, with an exposed upstage wall of the theatre, a white paper lantern moon, an abstracted Christmas tree made of metal pipes and lights, an industrial catwalk, and a few props such as some folding chairs and tables, was designed with intentional minimalism. This created an atmosphere that seemed "rough" rather than "polished," "makeshift" rather than "refined," and, most importantly, "authentic" rather than "commercial." Of course, successfully creating a theatrical set that appears rough and makeshift, and yet still serves the production, is as difficult as creating a polished-looking set, and *Rent*'s successful "found space" set was a credit to designer Paul Clay. The set downtown at the New York Theatre Workshop was Clay's creation, and for the Broadway transfer, it was simply "scaled up."[29] For a similar "gritty," "found space" effect, the Nederlander Theatre, which was dark before *Rent* moved in, was adorned with urban murals, graffiti, distressed leopard-print carpeting, and "the sort of crockery mosaics that can be found on the bases of lamp posts on St. Mark's Place."[30] Thus, the exterior and lobby of the Nederlander continued the expression of authentic "urban decay," though it was merely a performance. The costumes, a mix of thrift-store-chic, fabulous drag, PVC-pants, and 1990s yuppie uniforms for the "straights" that inhabited the play, remained the same from the New York Theatre Workshop to the Nederlander as the cast did not change and Angela Wendt remained the designer. These modern dress costumes made it seem as if the young characters simply walked on stage from the street. But, again, much artistry is required to make costumes onstage appear as if they are "real" and "contemporary" rather than created. The set and costumes, therefore, continued the idea that this production showed an authentic, urban, edgy, artistic experience, and this was how the reviews reacted to the design elements of the production.

The press also found the play to be an accurate depiction of contemporaneous youth and counterculture, most frequently comparing it to a *Hair* for the 1990s.[31] *Hair*, of course, was the rock opera that opened off-Broadway in 1967 and transferred to Broadway in 1968 depicting 1960s counterculture youth deciding whether to dodge the draft for the Vietnam War. It coined the term "rock opera" and spawned the anthem "The Age of Aquarius." There are obvious comparisons to *Rent*: each began off-Broadway and transferred to Broadway as a commercial phenomenon; each depicted bohemian youth (and the youth in each are choosing bohemia, not forced into poverty, though that is rarely mentioned); each had characters under threat of death, whether from conscription to fight in Vietnam or from the AIDS epidemic; and each included a song depicting its epoch. For *Hair*, that was "The Age of Aquarius." For *Rent*, that was "Seasons of Love," about which Ben Brantley in *The New York Times* gushed, "And when the whole ensemble sings of making the most of limited time in 'Seasons of Love,' the heart still melts and the eyes still mist."[32] It is surprising that Brantley was so complimentary of this song because he wrote a few paragraphs earlier: "But let's not kid ourselves. This is the stuff of theater-as-theme park and the Nederlander has become East Village Land."[33] Brantley acknowledges the commercialization of the East Village in the faux-distressed Broadway theatre, the Nederlander, but he still ends his review proclaiming the affective authenticity of *Rent*'s big number. He goes so far as to describe a bodily reaction—"the eyes still mist"—to the powerful affect of *Rent*. And reporting on a particular bodily dysfunction—the death of Larson—was the most consistent and important way in which the press proclaimed *Rent* authentic.

Literally every review for *Rent*, both at the New York Theatre Workshop and on Broadway, informs the reader of Larson's death. And every review also includes a plot summary that includes not only descriptions of characters with HIV positive status, but also the death of characters due to AIDS. The descriptions of Larson and the characters collapse into a particular type of tragedy—the death of artists, too young. Because of the similarity, it is easy to confuse the cause of Larson's death and believe he died of AIDS rather than a congenital heart condition. Because Larson's death was real, however, it promoted the type of spectator bodily reaction to stage emotion described by Brantley and created the conditions for spectacle and melodrama.

Rent and Melodrama

Calling *Rent* melodramatic is not meant pejoratively. Rather, it links the musical to one of the strongest U.S. theatrical traditions. Melodrama's traces continue from its nineteenth-century roots into the twenty-first century, particularly in film. Often decried as mere escapism, theatre scholar Bruce McConachie writes in his foundational text on melodrama that "we need to understand not what audiences were escaping from, but what they escaped to, and what impact this willing suspension of disbelief may have had on their lives."[34] Analyzing *Rent* as a melodrama, as utilizing aspects of this U.S. theatrical tradition, allows one to ask what fantasy it allowed audience members to enact. Doing so in regards to the 1996 premiere of *Rent* at the New York Theatre Workshop and its transfer to the Nederlander Theater on Broadway shows that its audiences wanted a way to safely experience the danger of living a bohemian lifestyle all in a family-friendly theme-park style.

Judging from reviews and interviews, audiences of *Rent* found it fulfilled their desire to feel like young, endangered, starving artists. About the experience of seeing *Rent*, Gordon Edelstein, currently the artistic director of the Long Warf Theatre, remembers, "Even if you were no longer young, you remember[ed] when you were. And even if you never lived on the edge, you fantasized about living that way."[35] It is the fantasy of being young, of living on the edge, of being in danger, that *Rent* allowed audiences to experience. Evidence suggests that most audience members at *Rent* were neither imperiled nor living in poverty; thus, this "authentic" production created for them a lively illusion. Frank Rich reports that "few theatergoers in the house demographically matched the castoffs on stage,"[36] and a photograph of a standing ovation after the show at the New York Theatre Workshop depicts many white people with grey hair in nice suits and skirts.[37] With tickets priced at $67.50 on Broadway, it is unlikely many people "living on the edge" made their way in to the Nederlander. Even the discounted $20 tickets given to the first rows required the price of several meals, as well as the ability to wait in line for "a full twenty-four hours" before the show.[38] This would likely rule out anyone truly "on the edge."

Yet this fictional experience of youthful peril and bohemia was built on a real death—Larson's. The excess signification created by the author's heart attack, the lyrics about death, and the media coverage of the production all collapsed Larson's death and his characters into one event that allowed for a particularly melodramatic experience. Other scholars have explored *Rent*'s connection to past forms, particularly opera, and the production's commercialization of bohemia and AIDS—but none has connected its excess signification to melodrama. David Savran begins to implicitly discuss *Rent*'s connection to melodrama, noting that both Angel and Mimi are "updated tragic mulattas,"[39] a figure heavily used in nineteenth-century melodrama. But Savran's discussion goes no farther as he focuses on *Rent*'s cultural appropriation. Nevertheless, understanding *Rent*'s connection to melodrama is important and worth study, particularly given melodrama's extreme popularity in the United States. By utilizing Amy E. Hughes' work on spectacle in melodrama as a foundation, one can discern how *Rent* used the tropes of melodrama to commercialize the HIV/AIDS epidemic. Following McConachie's writing on melodrama in general, answering in detail what audiences escaped to while watching *Rent* provides more evidence that audiences were engrossed by feelings of a supposedly authentic, youthful, and urban experience.

When writing about the sensational in melodrama's spectacle, Hughes invokes the necessity of "a virtual/actual body experiencing fictional/factual peril."[40] This particular type of danger was experienced by spectators of *Rent* because of how Larson's death was folded into the vulnerability faced by his characters. To make her point, Hughes invokes Baz Kershaw discussing the radical potential of spectacle in Buster Keaton's film *Steamboat Willie* (1928). In that film, a wall falls, and Keaton is saved only because he stands where the opening of a window surrounds him. "The utter vulnerability on display is heightened because the distance between Keaton and his character collapses with the wall. ... In more general terms, human mortality immortalizes itself in the moment of spectacle, and the spectator sees this paradoxical process as it is happening."[41] Most reviews of *Rent*'s premiere report the experience of hearing songs, particularly "One Song Glory," as "eerily haunting and prescient ... about making a contribution before he dies."[42] The pronoun "he" that the author of the review utilizes is ambiguous. Does "he" refer to the character, Roger, faced with an HIV/AIDS death who wants to make an artistic contribution before he dies? Or does "he" refer to Larson, the young, ambitious artist who wrote *Rent* to make a contribution before he died? The framing of the production with

Larson's death collapsed the distance between the author and his characters, and "human mortality was immortalized" in this ballad, with spectators seeing, and reporting about, "this paradoxical process." In this way, the sensation—the perceived danger—in *Rent*'s spectacle was based in large part on Larson's death.

Meaning was then made from *Rent*'s sensational spectacle as the media framed Larson's death as a tragedy on par with his fictional creation rather than as a meaningless accident. When reviewers wrote statements such as, "'Rent' was supposed to be the promising beginning of Jonathan Larson's contribution to Broadway, however, and not a shrine. How tragic that we can't look forward to what he'll do next,"[43] the press canonized a particular speculation about Larson's potential. Larson's death is truly sad, but there is no way to know what his legacy to Broadway would have been had he not died. *Rent* could have been his *Citizen Kane* with no masterpiece follow-up as easily as it could have been the first in a long series of hits. Nor can one know what *Rent*'s reception would have been like without the lens of Larson's death through which to view the musical. The critics created the tragedy in Larson's death, and, like any good melodrama audience, reviewers reveled in its pathos.

Similar to how the death of Larson and his characters' peril were collapsed together, the distance between Larson as a straight, white man from the suburbs collapsed into agreement with his HIV-infected characters and minority-infused cast. This led one article in the *New York Times* to proclaim "that the show was motivated by [Larson's] need 'to respond in some way' to his friends coping with AIDS, and to celebrate the lives of people who have died young. He is now one of them."[44] Through the sensational aspects of *Rent*'s spectacle, the fictional HIV-infected songwriter Roger is conflated with *Rent*'s actually dead author, Larson. In the process, articles often imply a confusion between Larson's actual congenital heart disease and his characters' fictional HIV/AIDS infections. By stating that Larson is "now one of them," the article commingles Larson's real-life heart disease with his characters' deaths and near deaths from HIV/AIDS. This conflation of a non-fictional birth defect and fictional HIV/AIDS cases creates an uncommon bond between the "blameless" death of a suburban son with the "shameful" urban death through AIDS that was, by 1996, a typical trope in U.S. drama. This unlikely combination of Larson's death and his characters allowed the so-called "shameful" death by HIV/AIDS to be whitewashed with Larson's blamelessness. Rather than a product of a "gay lifestyle," as AIDS was called by reviewers of *The Normal Heart*, or as a sacrificial mode by which gay men could be assimilated into the nation as in *Angels in America*, the confusion between Larson and his characters portrayed HIV/AIDS as a danger to a suburban, white, straight male. And because of Larson's death—even though not from AIDS—that danger unified his heart disease with the HIV epidemic. As the reviewer wrote, Larson was "now one of them." But the danger spectators of *Rent* perceived—the fictional danger of the characters' collapsed with Larson's actual death—was not factual in the sense that no one onstage or in the audience was in danger. This is the case with melodramatic stage tricks when an audience member feels a character/actor is in fictional/actual danger, and *Rent* presented a similar feeling.

This combination of character/actor and fictional/actual danger was the primary spectacle in *Rent*. Spectacle in the production was not chiefly made of special effects, but created by what Hughes calls intensity and excess. According to Hughes, intensity is a defining quality of spectacle, which, like scale, exists only in relation to norms. An event or experience is described as intense when it exceeds the expected or the routine.[45] Larson's death on opening night of *Rent* and its subsequent collapse into the production text of the play went beyond the routine expected on opening night. Larson's death was an "excess of potential" in two important ways.[46] First, there was the way in which reporters depicted Larson's talents and the loss thereof—a literal excess of potential outside the text of *Rent*. According to this narrative, the production was evidence that Larson's talent, cut down in its prime, had vast, now lost, potential. But, in a more abstract manner—and the manner in which Hughes uses the term—the production of *Rent* elicited an excess within its performance. After Larson's death, audiences listening to ballads such as "One Song Glory" heard them sung by the voice of a dead man. How could one not hear anthems about death with lyrics such as, "One song glory, one song before I go / Glory, one song to leave behind"[47] without being reminded that one was watching Larson's swan song? This *memento mori* produced an experience in the theatre beyond the norm, one that created a convergence of the fictional and non-fictional worlds into one rare, perhaps unique, viewing experience. And while special effects were not the main component of the spectacle of *Rent*, the production's visuals enhanced its intensity and excess.

The piece of visual spectacle mentioned most often in reviews is the ensemble coming downstage in a line and singing directly to the audience. This stage picture—like the evocation of Larson's death—blended the fictional and non-fictional worlds, the characters and actors. A representative example is the *New York Times* review of the New York Theatre Workshop production, "And when the whole ensemble stands at the edge of the stage, singing fervently about the ways of measuring borrowed time, the heart both breaks and soars."[48] Both acts ended with the stage picture of a line of actors singing to the auditorium. The first act ended with the song "La Vie Bohème B" including the lyrics, "To you, and you and you, you and you / To People living with, living with, living with / Not dying from disease / Let he among us without sin / Be the first to condemn / La Vie Bohème / La Vie Bohème / La Vie Bohème" and "The opposite of war / isn't peace / It's creation."[49] When the act one finale posits the acts of living and creating as the opposite to dying and war, it connects the life and creation of *Rent* by Larson to his death and his "war" to achieve recognition. In addition, during the first song of the second act, "Seasons of Love," the cast again sang straight to the audience, this time most precisely of "ways of measuring borrowed time." Forming a line on the apron of the stage, the company sings how many minutes make up a year, and soloists intone ways to count time other than in minutes, such as, "In truths that she learned / Or in times that he cried / In bridges he burned / Or the way that she died."[50] This song, about the limits of life, and these characters' painful awareness of life's finitude, made reviewers' hearts break and soar in part, at least, because it conflated their knowledge of Larson's finished life with these characters' concern about their own impending ends.

While a line of actors singing may not seem a comparable spectacle to that of a train rushing towards a victim tied to the tracks—the type of melodramatic spectacle Hughes holds up as most people's expectation—there is an important similarity. The moment in *Rent* when the actors stood at the lip of the stage and sang directly out to the audience conflated the actors and characters. Hughes suggests that this conflation of actor/character in light of perceived danger was fundamental to spectacle in nineteenth-century melodrama. The cast, singing about the finite nature of life, invoked Larson's real death, the characters' potential deaths, and, lastly, the perceived poverty and urban bohemia of the actual actors. It was in this last category that the actor/character conflation was most strong. When a character sang about being a starving artist, there was a horizon of expectations set up by the press that, in fact, these "unknowns" singing onstage really were starving artists, just as the press depicted Larson. And, as the cast was made up primarily of actors who were not already famous, audience members did not have past performances hindering the ability to conflate the actors/characters onstage. Indeed, many of the reviews and much of the publicity played on the "rags to riches" quality of the cast, depicting a story of actors living hand to mouth before becoming Broadway stars. The anonymity of the people onstage also made it easier for spectators to confuse the actors with characters. If, for example, the premiere of *Rent* had cast a known actor, such as Madonna, as Mimi, it would have been more difficult for spectators to see the character Mimi as "real" at the edge of the stage. Madonna would have had too many past performances "haunting" her presence, as Marvin Carlson would put it.[51] Spectators would have seen Madonna *playing* Mimi, instead of an actor whose life was coterminous with Mimi's circumstances. The "unknown" actors playing in the premiere of *Rent*, however, could easily be perceived by the audience as "authentic" representations of the play's characters. Thus, when the actors directly addressed the audience, spectators saw bohemians struggling to fulfill their artistic ambitions, the characters of *Rent* and the actors simultaneously singing seemingly truthfully to the audience. When actors broke the fourth wall in this way, they created spectacle exceeding the norms spectators expected. As the actors were not particularly haunted by past roles, and because the reviews and publicity conflated the situation of the author, cast, and characters, audiences saw the actors *as* their characters during this moment of direct address.

These several line-ups onstage also demonstrated the cast's diverse bodies and characters' diverse sexualities, providing contrast to perceived societal norms. Continuing to insist that spectacle is based on "relations rather than essentials," Hughes suggests that, "Our sense of the spectacular springs from the cultural norms that are jarred, destabilized, and exceeded in the process of representation," and points out that bodies are frequently at the center of spectacle.[52] The row of *Rent*'s cast at the lip of the stage is the most referred to tableau in the production's reviews, and the fact that this image stands out in the midst of this press avalanche regarding the production "reveals the unique pressures and politics of [its] historical moment."[53] This column of actors/characters represented racial difference, sexual difference, and class difference, all aspects of diversity with which the U.S. nation was coming to terms in the 1990s, particularly in relation to the AIDS epidemic. Through the past efforts of mainstream plays like *The Normal Heart* and *Angels in America,* gay people and AIDS victims were no longer invisible in the cultural landscape. However, *Rent* represented a more heterogeneous variety of skin tones and a more extensive representation of wealth than many AIDS plays before it. Its representation of people with HIV/AIDS was not just middle-class white gay men. This jarring of norms was part of what made *Rent* so powerful; the way it slipped into its incredibly mainstream commercial package hints at an emergent ideology that included more bodies and sexualities in the U.S. body politic. But the norms that were jolted by the line of material bodies onstage were somewhat resettled in the final moments of the play, particularly by Angel's death and Mimi's resurrection.

The line of bodies singing directly to the audience included bodies of color and characters with LGBT sexualities. Perhaps the most prominent example of both was Wilson Jermaine Heredia, who played Angel, the cross-dressing lover of Collins. Angel's death from HIV/AIDS and the portrayal of his death safely buried the character's radical sexuality and non-white skin tone. Angel's death occurs during the song "Contact," which is all about sex. Given that the play suggests Angel contracted HIV/AIDS through sex, perhaps portraying his death in a song about sex makes sense. On the other hand, no other character with HIV/AIDS who participates in the song "Contact" dies, with the possible exception of Mimi who has a resurrection. The lines Angel sings before he vanishes from stage, never to return, are, "Take me / Take me / Today for you / Tomorrow for me / Today me / Tomorrow you / Tomorrow you / Love / You / Love you / I love you / I love / You I love / You! / Take me / Take me / I love you."[54] "Take me" employs a double entendre highlighting the song's sexual nature but also asking someone to take Angel away from this life. Given Angel's religious name, it is hard not to hear this line as a call to be taken by God. And this double meaning, wavering between romantic and religious love, continues through the rest of Angel's final lines. It is as if Angel is being called home, to a place where he belongs, as a martyr, loving "you"—Collins? God?—as Angel leaves the world of *Rent* that is dominated by straight white male protagonists. In this moment, some of the radical possibility is drained from the line of multi-hued bodies and diverse character sexualities that sings directly to the audience. In fact, Angel will not be in the final tableau. Instead, Angel's death becomes a necessary part of the success of the straight protagonists.

The next time Angel is mentioned, it is to further the ambitions of the two straight, white, male protagonists. The scene begins with the reveal of a pastor telling Mark, Roger, Collins, and Benny to get off church property, just after Angel's funeral.[55] Collins, Angel's lover, has two lines, both about the inability to pay for the funeral. Rather than speak to Angel's death, their love, or the tragedy that has befallen them, Collins' two lines after the funeral are purely about finance. But not to worry, Benny will pay for the funeral—then he and Collins exit, leaving Mark and Roger alone on stage. At this point in the play, Mark and Roger—the straight white protagonists—both find the inspiration for their art. Mark decides to quit his paying job making news footage and return to his bohemian indie film project, singing, "Angel's voice is in my ear."[56] So Angel's death, while mourned to some extent, is much more important to the play's plot as the inspiration for Mark's film. Angel becomes a martyr for art and originality, allowing the surviving straight white man, Mark, to succeed and remain "authentic" rather than "sell out." In the same scene, just after Angel's funeral, Roger sings, "I see Mimi everywhere."[57] Much as Angel's death provides the necessary prodding for Mark to return to his artistic rather than corporate dreams, Angel's death helps Mark see Mimi's absence, which will ultimately lead to him writing her a love song. The two men finish the scene, singing together, "Dying in America / At the end of the millennium / We're dying in America / To come into our own / But when you're dying in America / At the end of the millennium / You're not alone / I'm not alone / I'm not alone."[58] These lyrics echo the millennial concerns of *Angels in America*, alongside its concern about being deathly ill and outside the dominant sexuality. However, the lyrics are sung by two straight, white men who are squarely in line with the dominant sexuality. While the final repeated lines, "I'm not alone" suggest the camaraderie of people dying from HIV/AIDS in the U.S. at the end of the 1990s, they simultaneously point to Angel whose death is the instigation of this song. And, because Angel's name suggests a metaphysical being, the song can be read as a statement that Mark and Roger are not alone because Angel is still, on some spiritual plane, with them. Instead of surviving and being part of the final scene speaking directly to the audience—as is Prior's role in *Angels in America*—Angel's role in *Rent* is to die in order to artistically inspire the straight, white men and to comfort them from beyond the grave: a true martyr. To continue this reading, during the scene of Mimi's resurrection, Angel plays the role of a heavenly force with power over life and death.

Mimi's death and resurrection suggests, in the vein of melodrama, that the love between her and Roger is too pure to succumb to death. But this logic implies that the love between Angel and Collins is somehow impure—literally disease-ridden to the point of destruction, though all four members of the couples are HIV-positive. Thus, while *Rent* put a relationship between a transgender character of color and a male character of color onstage, the play ultimately relied on the old trope of the death of the queer character to reinstate the straight couple at the top of the plot's hierarchy. Angel, the queer body of color, is sacrificed in order that the straight couple may succeed despite disease. Near the play's finale, Mimi returns to Roger's apartment, ill, shivering, and whispers "I love you" to Roger before she dies. If *Rent* were a literal adaptation of *La Bohème*, the play would end here with Roger calling out Mimi's name in anguish. But *Rent* is not an updated version of an opera. It is a melodrama in which (straight) love is triumphant. After Mimi's death, Roger plays a love song for her, and at the end of it, she awakens, like a princess in a 1990s AIDS fairy tale. When resuscitated she describes being "in a tunnel ... heading for this warm, white light," but before she could reach the light, "Angel was there—and she looked good. And she said, 'Turn around, girlfriend—and listen to that boy's song."[59] Angel, the dead queer character, serves as a heavenly influence that allows the straight white protagonist to successfully requite his love. In this moment, the end of *Rent* is similar to the final tableau of George Aiken's *Uncle Tom's Cabin*. Aiken's final image is that of the dead, white girl, Eva, clothed in heavenly robes, on the back of "a milk white dove, with expanded wings, as if just soaring upwards."[60] She is holding her arms out in benediction to the dead, black man, Uncle Tom, who kneels before her, recreating the hierarchy that *Uncle Tom's Cabin*, to some degree, challenges: white skin above black skin. Similarly, Angel's death in *Rent* and the report from Mimi that a heavenly version of Angel sends Mimi back to earth to experience Roger's love while Collins must do without Angel's love reinscribes the hierarchy that *Rent*, to some degree, challenges: straight sexuality above queer sexuality. Thus, in the end, *Rent* oscillates between showing radical bodies and sexualities onstage and reinscribing the hierarchies that the play sometimes seems to challenge. The ending of *Rent* also swings between McConachie's nineteenth-century melodrama categories: providential and materialist.

Rent undulates back and forth from a materialist, melodramatic retelling of *La Bohème* to a providential, melodramatic AIDS fairy tale set in a timeless land of illness and bohemianism where love can conquer all. McConachie divides melodramas roughly into these two categories:

> Providential melodramas use timeless, universal settings; autocratic institutions ensure order; natural innocence is glorified; God ensures a happy ending; and there is a return to a utopian paradise.
>
> Materialist melodramas use time-bound, historical settings; liberal, bourgeois institutions ensure order; social respectability is honored; chance puts happy endings at risk; and there is acceptance of the material status quo.[61]

At first glance, *Rent* appears to have a time-bound setting: 1990s New York City. However, there are also "timeless" aspects of the production on which reviews comment—for instance, the similarities to the nineteenth-century texts from which *Rent* was inspired, and the well-worn comparisons to the 1960s production of *Hair*. While decorated with 1990s fashion and cultural references, *Rent*'s conscious connection to previous depictions of bohemia suggests that urban artistry is somehow timeless in its essential fight against social conventions. Because of this, *Rent* was both time-bound and timeless. Similarly, while the play seemingly concerns itself with poverty, a trait of materialist melodrama, there are also ways that *Rent* glorifies "natural innocence"—a trait of providential melodrama. The characters may not seem innocent, as they are junkies, S&M dancers, and supposedly scarred by the ravages of poverty, but all are idealists who refuse to "sell out." Frank Rich in the *New York Times* describes *Rent*'s characters as "revel[ing] in their joy, their capacity for love, and, most importantly, their tenacity."[62] And while Angel dies as a martyr to this idealism, Mimi's return to life ensures a happy ending to the play with the cast once again lining the lip of the stage to sing the *carpe diem* chorus, "No day but today" directly to the audience.[63] Thus the play activated the tropes of poverty alongside a type of innocence not generally available to people who are as desperate as these characters are supposed to be. This fluctuation fulfilled competing desires from 1990s audiences for a materialist message alongside yearnings for happy endings. The fact that materialist messages and happy endings are often contradictory was part of the power of *Rent*. It was able to fulfill these opposing longings in audiences. In this way, *Rent* successfully combined traits of the providential and materialist melodramas that have proven extremely influential on U.S. mainstream entertainment.

The huge mainstream popularity of the production suggests that contemporaneous mainstream audiences found *Rent* appealing at least in part due to its presumption of an ahistorical, supranational connection between bohemian cultures. Part of this premise was the power of youthful innocence and its ability to survive and even thrive despite perceived tarnishing of that innocence by poverty, addiction, and disease. Ultimately, while the play created a false world of "authentic" artistic bohemia utilizing diverse bodies onstage and varied sexualities in characters, *Rent* managed a continuation of the old U.S. trope of a happy ending for the play's straight, white male protagonist thanks to the martyrdom of a black, queer "other." But this does not mean that *Rent*'s diverse cast and depiction of characters with a variety of sexualities had no liberal effects, particularly in regards to continued assimilation of LGBT characters into the U.S. national imaginary.

Selling AIDS and Bohemia

Despite *Rent*'s foundations in melodrama and regressive tropes, it nevertheless utilized its position as an incredibly successful piece of mainstream theatre to normalize LGBT civil rights issues, which is more than most preceding AIDS dramas were able to do, as they tended to concentrate on gay men. *Rent*'s success as a piece of mainstream entertainment can be measured in ticket sales, media visibility, peripheral sales, and touring productions. And while this success may have been based primarily on *Rent*'s palatability, there were some aspects of an emergent ideology of greater inclusivity imbedded in the text and its reception. The greater the success the play achieved, the greater the exposure of U.S. audiences to the play's radical elements. For instance, in Charlotte, North Carolina, *Rent*'s commercial appeal went head to head with its LGBT content, and electoral change occurred as a result. The politicians who found the play's themes too risqué were thrown out of office in favor of those who would accept profit over social conservatism, an example worth examining in detail. But *Rent*'s success, both in terms of finances and ideological work, began with its downtown production at the New York Theatre Workshop.

Rent's success came quickly. A month after *Rent*'s premiere at the New York Theatre Workshop and its subsequent rave reviews, the *Wall Street Journal* described crowds of affluent spectators making their way "toward the New Theatre Workshop [sic], where the new musical is the town's toast."[64] This vision of wealthy patrons making their way downtown to the now-famous but then remote theatrical outpost of the New York Theatre Workshop describes the flashbulb success of *Rent*. The venue was so unknown at the time that the *Wall Street Journal* did not even print its name correctly. *Rent* sold out its New York Theatre Workshop run, and tickets were some of the hardest to get in New York, making a Broadway transfer nearly inevitable. Once the Broadway version opened, the musical brought in approximately $500,000 a week with the New York Theatre Workshop receiving about $500,000 yearly from royalties.[65] Previously, the New York Theatre Workshop's annual budget had been $1.4 million, so *Rent* increased its income by over a third. But *Rent*'s influence in the mainstream theatre world was not solely financial. Through its press coverage and original cast soundtrack, *Rent* was also one of the most influential plays on the stage even for those who could not acquire or afford tickets to see it.

The media coverage of *Rent* was unprecedented for a U.S. play in the 1990s, with reportage in culture sections of national newspapers like the *New York Times*, in industry magazines such as *Rolling Stone* and *Time-Out*, and in popular entertainment magazines like *People*. About a month after the usual opening night review, the *New York Times* ran a three-story package with a full-color photograph of the entire cast above the fold of its culture section under the headline, "The Birth of a Theatrical Comet."[66] Following the headline, the front page had a short, anonymous introduction of the section's three articles. The first was "The Seven Year Odyssey That Led to *Rent*,"[67] which followed the by-then well-worn story of Larson's "starving artist" days through his untimely death before he could see his play's amazing success. The fact that the section headline heralded *Rent* as an instant success and the first article focused on its long trek to the stage was not a contradiction either reporter noted. The second article was a collection of brief biographies of all 15 members of the *Rent* cast alongside color headshots.[68] The third article was by classical music critic Bernard Holland evaluating the musical's connection to opera.[69] There was also a full-page advertisement for the production. It consisted simply of the title, *Rent*, in its unique "post no bills" font alongside box office information.[70] This font, taken from downtown building notices stapled to construction sites, continued the production's faux downtown experience. Of all this coverage, Robert Viagas in *Playbill* wrote, "No show in memory has gotten such a prominent multi-story boost in the paper's most widely-read arts section."[71] On top of this, there were fashion spreads in periodicals like *TimeOut New York*, *Rolling Stone, People,* and the *Daily News* that further promoted the musical.[72]

The fashion spreads featuring the cast of *Rent* showed even those who could not see the actual production the faux danger and excess that was so crucial to the production's spectacle. Like all the articles on *Rent*, the fashion spreads tended to mention Larson's death, and, in a continuation of mixing character and actor, the clothes in which the actors posed were cheap, often second-hand articles, or even their own clothes. Rather than captions marking the expensive, brand-name clothes and accessories that tend to outfit mainstream photo shoots, the fashion spreads featuring the cast of *Rent* boast captions such as, "Anthony sports a T-shirt, $18, by Jack Hammer," and "Adam matches his own tank top with vinyl pants, $25, from Smyloop and his own shoes," and "Gwen wears her own outfit."[73] The fact that the actors are denoted solely by their first names, and that their clothes are a mix of cheap items and their own possessions, creates several semiotic systems. First, utilizing inexpensive clothes as opposed to the normally exorbitantly priced clothes in fashion spreads continues *Rent*'s faux bohemianism. False because as this was a posed photo shoot, clothes from any number of designers could have been used, particularly with *Rent* being a major Broadway hit. Second, photographing the cast in cheap clothes continues the narrative that the actors are unchanged from their success and are all still starving artists. Photographing the actors in expensive clothes would have instead positioned the actors in the midst of their meteoric rise to fame. Finally, since the caption denotes some clothes as the actors' own, the photo shoot continues to conflate the actors with their characters. Though their characters are not named in the article, the play's denizens haunt the shoot—after all, it is a photograph of the cast of *Rent*—and, thus, the characters' and actors' clothes are conflated. For instance, the photograph of Daphne Rubin-Vega, who played Mimi, is not that of a woman modestly dressed. Instead, she wears a tight, hip, sexy outfit that does not contradict her character's job as an S&M club dancer. Therefore, even without entering the theatre to see *Rent*, readers of these magazines' fashion spreads could enjoy the same types of excess and perceived danger—the cast's "poverty" mixed with Larson's death—that created the melodrama onstage.

All this coverage created a nearly instantaneous demand for the ability to enjoy *Rent* outside the confines of New York City, so a Broadway cast soundtrack and touring productions were quickly commissioned. The soundtrack was released on Geffen Records on August 27, 1996, only seven months after the play's opening at the New York Theatre Workshop. It debuted at #19 on the Billboard chart. Touring productions began as early as November 1996, less than a year after the New York Theatre Workshop premiere. These nationwide extensions of *Rent* brought its story and ideology to the nation at large, and its popularity remained undampened by the show's politics.

There was only one city in the United States that rejected *Rent* on its tour: Charlotte, North Carolina, where politicians found *Rent* too salacious to award public funding. As the exception, Charlotte becomes an interesting case study to demonstrate what politics existed in *Rent* and how its economics actually effected electoral change in this one town in the Deep South. The story begins with Charlotte's earlier production of *Angels in America* that proved controversial to the town's government who held the local art funding's purse strings.

Despite the Broadway success of *Angels in America*, regional versions of the production were not nearly as popular as the touring productions of *Rent*, and *Angels in America* had nothing comparable to a soundtrack near the top of the Billboard charts. This made *Rent* more prominent, more mainstream, and more commercial than *Angels in America* ever was. To some degree, the six-hour length of *Angels* made producing it prohibitive, but its politics also made it a difficult sell in the 1990s. This was the case still in 1997 when *Rent* was making a splash nationally. Charles Isherwood addressed this issue head on in *The Advocate*. He wrote,

> But as *Rent* hits the road, the proverbial question remains: Will it play in Peoria? With characters that include a drag queen and his boyfriend, a lesbian couple, and HIV sufferers of various genders and sexual stripes, the musical looks like a tough sell in the South and Midwest, where it will be teamed in 'best of Broadway' subscription series with such innocuous fare as *The King and I* and *Smokey Joe's Cafe*.[74]

To this doubt, however, Jeffrey Seller, the producer of *Rent* both on Broadway and on the road, replied, "*Rent* is no *Angels in America*. ... Its political manifesto isn't as prominent as in *Angels in America*, though it's there. The first thing you think about with *Angels* is the urgency of its politics. With *Rent* the first things you think of are its wonderful characters and its music."[75] Seller, then, promotes *Rent*'s commercial potential by directly comparing it to *Angels*, and by stating that *Rent*'s politics, while existent, are secondary. Seller's predictions that the production would sell nationwide proved correct. Except in Charlotte, North Carolina.

In Charlotte, *Rent* and *Angels in America* remained intertwined, for a scandal involving a previous production of *Angels in America* made the president of the city's Blumenthal Center for the Performing Arts pass on producing *Rent*. In 1996, Charlotte Repertory Theatre produced *Angels in America* and *Six Degrees of Separation*—another play with prominent gay characters—and faced a financial backlash, though not from lack of spectators. Charlotte Rep did not suffer a lack of ticket sales for these two productions. Instead, the Mecklenburg County Commission voted to remove $2.5 million of funding to the county's Arts and Science Council, a major supporter of the theatre. In explanation of the cut, Commissioner Hoyle Martin spelled out its connection to the production of plays with LGBT content: "I don't think [such plays] project the kind of values and ideas that most people in our community feel comfortable with ... As an elected official responsible for determining how funds are spent, I have to make those judgments."[76] After this, the president of the Blumenthal Center seemed hesitant to face similar budgetary consequences. She stated that programing material with similar content to *Angels in America* and *Six Degrees of Separation* would be "too risky on a subscription series that's only four years old."[77] What she feared, though, was political fallout more than lack of audience. Commissioner Martin asserted the rectitude of the decision to not fund theatre with LGBT content,

> I did not enter into this lightly ... I sat down with 48 members of the gay and lesbian community because I think you always have to listen to the other side, but in the end it only reaffirmed what I believe. There are many gay and lesbian people in Charlotte who are responsible citizens—they're living in sin, of course, but we're all responsible to God for that—and who I have no problem with. But I have a problem when some of them shove it in my face. I don't shove myself in their face.[78]

Much as Yale Kramer's singular completely negative review of *Angels in America* suggested that gay people are fine as long as they are in the closet, Martin's comment suggests that he, too, would like gay people—who, to him, are inherently "living in sin"—to be socially invisible. Carroll Gray, then president of Charlotte's Chamber of Commerce, had a very different opinion.

Gray, as the president of the Chamber of Commerce, felt that such open bigotry could hurt the city's bottom line. Gray argued that, "This sends the wrong message to the community and the world. ... For the past couple of decades, Charlotte has made a case for itself as an open, inclusive city. I think it will be manifest at the next election that [Martin's] opinion is in the minority."[79] It is interesting that instead of an arts or civil rights organization defending *Rent*, it was the Chamber of Commerce. This shows that the play was a commodity that some in the government of Charlotte felt would be a loss not to capitalize on. And Gray was right about the effects of these financial decisions "at the next election." In 1998—one year after refusing

Rent—only one of the five Mecklenburg County Commissioners who voted down funding the county's Arts and Science Council was reelected.[80] In a "Where Are They Now?" piece in *Charlotte Magazine* from 2010, the author remembers that, "The controversy generated venomous rhetoric on both sides and garnered national attention for Charlotte, which had been burnishing its reputation as a progressive New South city" and blames this damage to the city's reputation on the Commissioners' inability to get reelected.[81] Thus, the commercial potential of *Rent* was such that losing the possibility of hosting its touring production was enough for the citizens of Charlotte to want a government able to stomach LGBT representation in the theatre, at least in the name of profit.

From the unique example of Charlotte refusing *Rent*, and from the play's simultaneous touring productions, and from the hundreds of millions of dollars earned by *Rent*, one can see that commercialism, more than any type of political idealism or even artistic consideration, was the spoonful of sugar that helped the aspects of *Rent*'s emergent ideology get swallowed. *Rent*'s most obvious emergent ideology aspects were devoted same-sex relationships, a transgender or transvestite character (the script is vague), and HIV/AIDS not being solely a disease of gay men. While plays before *Rent* had these aspects, none had *Rent*'s amazing, national—and eventually international—reach. While same-sex relationships had been portrayed on Broadway before, *Rent*'s same-sex love songs were so remarkable that *The Advocate*—New York's premiere LGBT newspaper—wrote that it was during *Rent*'s two same-sex love duets, "I'll Cover You" and "Take Me or Leave Me," "that gays and lesbians will get the biggest surge from *Rent*—seeing same-sex couples unabashedly declaring their love for each other on the musical stage is truly a thrilling sight."[82] The next line in the review is about the sadness the reviewer feels about Larson's death and the thrill of seeing same-sex love duets on Broadway is the impetus for that sadness. These duets would not have "Played Peoria," as Isherwood put it, without the overt and successful commercialism of the production overcoming whatever ideological prejudices producers had.

Similar to *Rent*'s gay characters, transvestite characters had been seen on Broadway before *Rent*'s Angel, but Angel was particularly popular and also sometimes seen as transgender, making a previously "deviant" sexuality acceptable for audiences around the nation. In fact, with his name and martyrdom, Angel became a pivotal fulcrum on which the play's fairy tale happy ending rested. Since Angel's post-death role of sending Mimi back to the world of the living is similar to the final tableau in Aiken's *Uncle Tom's Cabin*, it follows that Hughes' description of Uncle Tom relates to Angel: "This vignette emphasizes the courage and moral purpose of a protagonist from an allegedly inferior race."[83] If a spectator in New York or one of the cities to which the production toured viewed a trans character as "inferior," the play nevertheless emphasized his "courage and moral purpose," not only in life, but also in death. In this way, similar to Uncle Tom, audiences that might otherwise have found Angel lesser found him a compelling and heroic martyr.

A final way in which *Rent* challenged the dominant ideology across the country was by portraying HIV/AIDS as a disease that infected characters who were not solely gay men. Again, while *Rent* was not the first or only play to do so, its reach was unprecedented, and, hence, its message that HIV/AIDS affected all manner of people stretched beyond what other pieces of theatre could. Not only that: the disease, because it infected most of the characters, was not stigmatized. HIV/AIDS was shown to be non-discriminating. Further, the infected characters, from the straight, white, male protagonists, to the straight, female love interest, to the trans martyr of color, were all portrayed sympathetically. They were, literally, the heroes of the play, the characters for whom the audience was supposed to root. While the characters of *Rent* are sequestered into a marginal area of New York City, it was because they wished to lead a bohemian life, not because of external prejudice such as the kind characters faced in *The Normal Heart*. Likewise, while depicting a romanticized version of HIV/AIDS and bohemia—which allowed for the play's commercial success—*Rent* nevertheless portrayed same-sex love unabashedly, a transvestite character heroically, and HIV/AIDS as infecting/affecting nearly everyone onstage. That is, in the world of *Rent*, simply being straight or in any other way privileged did not protect anyone from HIV/AIDS. This message could be tolerated because the play made tremendous amounts of money, and that profit was the sun that allowed *Rent* to thrive in even conservative U.S. theatre ecologies.

Also notable in this production's conditions of reception, its politics are not the topic of abhorrence in *any* of the reviews and articles about *Rent*'s New York Premiere. In the 32 articles about the productions of *Rent* in New York City during 1996, none of them questions the sexual politics of the play.[84] From the positive reviews that love the play, to the negative reviews that question the play's musical qualities or production values, not a single journalist in any way questions the unabashedly in-love same-sex couples, the heroic transvestite/transgender character, or the all-encompassing specter of HIV/AIDS. If these aspects are commented on at all, it is positively, but more commonly they are simply noted while describing the plot or characters. Most of the reviews are glowing; many mention the play's support of the emergent ideology of LGBT civil rights alongside extremely positive comments about the play. This is doubly notable as plays such as *The Normal Heart* and *Angels in America* prompted at least some negative political comments and also because *Rent* was focusing not merely on gay civil rights, but on a cast of more-encompassing LGBT characters and their needs. Because the New York productions, the tours, and the soundtrack were all so popular, one can see that the general enjoyment of the production was not merely by the critics. Hence, an acceptance of LGBT civil rights passed from radical venues into the commercial powerhouse of *Rent*.

These reactions in the press and in commercial returns are quantifiably different from those of *The Normal Heart*, *Angels in America*, and the dozens of plays to take HIV/AIDS as their topic in the 1980s and 1990s. Thus, the response to *Rent* from critics and fans shows how dramatic the change in ideology over time was from 1985 to 1996. Remember, after all, that *Rent* premiered barely 11 years after *The Normal Heart* was excoriated in the mainstream press as a gay screed. But without its commercial success, *Rent*'s political effects would not have been possible. Charlotte's political establishment was thrown out over financial concerns, not over unease about LGBT civil rights. In this way, *Rent* and its commercial popularity demonstrated an ability to portray LGBT civil rights issues across the country and even to change leadership of a community that would not succumb to its profit-making apparatus.

Epilogue

Making the radical palatable often involves a complicated walking of the line between the "kinda hegemonic, kinda subversive,"[85] but there is no denying that there were subversive elements within the extremely commercial, extremely mainstream, productions of *Rent* in New York City in 1996. While critics have often focused on its commercial aspects as a problem politically, without *Rent*'s mainstream success, including its national tours and popular soundtrack, its elements of a more inclusive emergent ideology would not have reached such a wide cross-section of the U.S. nation. Similarly, scholars have naturally examined *Rent* in relation to its stated influence, *La Bohème*, but *Rent*'s success can be more accurately attributed to its relation to one of the most popular genres ever to grace the U.S. stage: melodrama. By creating a contemporary melodramatic fairy tale, Larson tied *Rent* to extremely regressive tropes of race and gender, but doing so allowed his script to include a more complete LGBT representation onstage, and these representations corresponded to catchy songs that an entire generation of musical theatre-makers and fans would carry in their heads for life. In this way, *Rent* was able to support the emergent ideology of LGBT civil rights in the 1990s.

Notes

1. Jonathan Larson et al., *Rent* (New York: HarperEntertainment, 1997), 52.
2. Frank Rich, "East Village Story," *The New York Times*, March 2, 1996; Linda Winer, "The Prize-Winning 'Rent' Moves to Broadway," *Newsday*, April 30, 1996.
3. Rebecca Schneider, *Performing Remains: Art and War in Times of Theatrical Reenactment* (Abingdon, Oxon; New York: Routledge, 2011), 109.
4. June Thomas, "Sarah Schulman: The Lesbian Writer *Rent* Ripped Off," *Slate* (2005).
5. Sarah Schulman, *Stagestruck: Theater, AIDS, and the Marketing of Gay America* (Durham, NC: Duke UP, 1998).
6. Thomas, "Schulman."

120   *Commercialization*

7. Ben Brantley, "Rock Opera À La 'Bohème' and 'Hair'," *New York Times*, February 14, 1996; "Enter Singing: Young, Hopeful and Taking on the Big Time," *The New York Times*, April 30, 1996; Michael Feingold, "Long-Term Lease," *Village Voice*, February 20, 1996; Peter Galvin, "New Bohemians," *The Advocate*, April 30, 1996; Jeremy Gerard, "Rent," *Variety*, May 6, 1996; Eric Grode, "Rent," *Back Stage*, February 23, 1996; John Heilpern, "Rent: Glorious Last Testament Shakes up the American Musical," *The New York Observer*, February 26, 1996; Margo Jefferson, "'Rent' Is Brilliant and Messy All at Once," *New York Times (Sunday)*, February 25, 1996; Leighton Kerner, "Downtown Arias: Assessing the Opera in *Rent*," *Village Voice*, March 19, 1996; Ken Mandelbaum, "Rent," *Theater Week*, March 4, 1996; Rich, "East;" Winer, "Rent."
8. Galvin, "New Bohemians," 58.
9. Rich, "East," 19.
10. Larson et al., *Rent*, 14.
11. United States Census Bureau, "Poverty Thresholds 1995," https://www.census.gov/hhes/www/poverty/data/threshld/thresh95.html.
12. Larson et al., *Rent*, 11.
13. Larson et al., *Rent*, 8.
14. Larson et al., *Rent*, 10.
15. Grode, "Rent," 48.
16. Justin Davidson, "Passions and Puccini: 'Rent' Invokes 'Boheme,' but It Seizes Realism," *Newsday*, April 30, 1996, B3.
17. Larson et al., *Rent*, 120.
18. Rock Music Timeline, "1990s Decade Overview," http://www.rockmusictimeline.com/1990s.html.
19. Larson et al., *Rent*, 116.
20. Larson et al., *Rent*, 83.
21. Clive Barnes, "Puccini Meets the E. Village," *New York Post*, February 14, 1996; Brantley, "Rock Opera;" "Enter Singing;" Davidson, "Passions;" Feingold, "Long-Term;" Jeremy Gerard, "Rent," *Variety*, February 19, 1996; ibid., May 6; Grode, "Rent;" Heilpern, "Rent;" Jefferson, "Brilliant and Messy;" Kerner, "Downtown;" D.L. Lepidus, "Rent," *The Westsider*, February 22–28, 1996; Mandelbaum, "Rent;" Rich, "East;" Winer, "Rent."
22. Donald Lyons, "'Rent,' New Musical Is Deserved Hit," *The Wall Street Journal*, March 6, 1996.
23. Jefferson, "Brilliant and Messy."
24. Winer, "Rent."
25. Mark Sussman, "New York's Facelift," *TDR: The Drama Review* 42, no. 1 (1998): 34.
26. Sussman, "New York's Facelift," 35.
27. John Bell, "Disney's Times Square: The New American Community Theatre," ibid.: 27.
28. Sussman, "New York's Facelift," 34.
29. Brantley, "Enter Singing," C16.
30. Ibid.
31. Barnes, "Puccini;" Brantley, "Rock Opera;" "Enter Singing;" Jim Farber, "Entertaining 'Rent' No New Lease on Rock Opera Genre," *Daily News*, February 22, 1996; Feingold, "Long-Term;" Gerard, "Rent;" Heilpern, "Rent;" Jefferson, "Brilliant and Messy;" Lepidus, "Rent;" Lyons, "Rent;" Mandelbaum, "Rent;" Rich, "East;" Winer, "Rent."

32. Brantley, "Enter Singing," C16.
33. Ibid.
34. Bruce A. McConachie, *Melodramatic Formations: American Theatre and Society, 1820–1870*, 1st ed. (Iowa City: U of Iowa P, 1992), x.
35. Larson et al., *Rent*, 142.
36. Rich, "East."
37. Larson et al., *Rent*, 54.
38. Larson et al., *Rent*, 133.
39. Savran, *A Queer Sort of Materialism*, 40.
40. Amy E. Hughes, *Spectacles of Reform: Theater and Activism in Nineteenth-Century America* (Ann Arbor: U of Michigan P, 2012), 32.
41. Baz Kershaw, *Theatre Ecology: Environments and Performance Events* (Cambridge: Cambridge UP, 2007), 218.
42. Winer, "Rent."
43. Ibid.
44. Anthony Tommasini, "The Seven-Year Odyssey That Led to 'Rent'," *New York Times*, March 17, 1996.
45. Hughes, *Spectacles of Reform: Theater and Activism in Nineteenth-Century America*, 16.
46. Hughes, *Spectacles of Reform: Theater and Activism in Nineteenth-Century America*, 23.
47. Larson et al., *Rent*, 81.
48. Brantley, "Rock Opera," C18.
49. Larson et al., *Rent*, 106.
50. Larson et al., *Rent*, 109.
51. Marvin A. Carlson, *The Haunted Stage: The Theatre as Memory Machine* (Ann Arbor: U of Michigan P, 2001).
52. Hughes, *Spectacles of Reform: Theater and Activism in Nineteenth-Century America*, 14.
53. Ibid.
54. Larson et al., *Rent*, 116.
55. Larson et al., *Rent*, 121.
56. Ibid.
57. Ibid.
58. Larson et al., *Rent*, 122.
59. Larson et al., *Rent*, 128.
60. George Aiken, "Uncle Tom's Cabin," in *Staging the Nation: Plays from the American Theater, 1787–1909*, ed. Don B. Wilmeth (Boston, MA: Bedford Books, 1998), 327.
61. McConachie, *Melodramatic*, 257.
62. Rich, "East."
63. Larson et al., *Rent*, 129.
64. Henry Grunwald, "Crossover: 'Rent' and 'La Boheme'," *The Wall Street Journal*, May 2, 1996.
65. Greg Evans, "Judge Takes Larson Side in *Rent* Suit," Variety, http://variety.com/1997/biz/news/judge-takes-larson-side-in-rent-suit-1116676287/.
66. Anonymous, "Birth of a Theatrical Comet," *New York Times*, 17 March, 1996.
67. Anthony Tommasini, "The Seven-Year Odyssey That Led to 'Rent'," ibid., March 17.
68. Peter Marks, "The Young Voices of *Rent*," ibid., 17 March.

69. Bernard Holland, "Classical View: Flaws Aside, 'Rent' Lives and Breathes," *New York Times (Sunday)*, March 17, 1996.
70. "Rent Advertisement," *New York Times*, March 17, 1996, H3.
71. Robert Viagas, "Rent," *Playbill* (1996).
72. Gig Kourlas, "How They Play the Rent," *Daily News* (1996); Anne Marie O'Neill, "Talent for Rent," *People* (1996); Patti O'Brien, "Rent Strikes," *Rolling Stone* (1996); Gigi Guerra, "Bohemian Rhapsody," *TimeOut New York* (1996).
73. Guerra, "Bohemian Rhapsody."
74. Charles Isherwood, "Rent Control," *The Advocate*, May 27, 1997, 75.
75. Isherwood, "Rent Control," *The Advocate*, May 27 1997, 75–76.
76. Isherwood, "Rent Control," 76.
77. Ibid.
78. Ibid.
79. Ibid.
80. Anonymous, "Where Are They Now?: The Gang of Five," Charlotte Magazine, http://www.charlottemagazine.com/Charlotte-Magazine/August-2010/Where-are-They-Now/The-Gang-of-Five/.
81. Ibid.
82. Galvin, "New Bohemians."
83. Hughes, *Spectacles of Reform: Theater and Activism in Nineteenth-Century America* 37.
84. Barnes, "Puccini;" Brantley," "Rock Opera;" "Enter Singing;" Robert Brustein, "The New Bohemians," *The New Republic*, April 22 1996; Davidson, "Passions;" Evans, "Larson;" Farber, "Entertaining 'Rent';" Feingold, "Long-Term; Galvin, "New Bohemians; Gerard, "Rent; ibid., May 6; Grode, "Rent;" Grunwald, "Crossover;" Guerra, "Bohemian Rhapsody;" Heilpern, "Rent;" Holland, "Flaws Aside;" Margo Jefferson, "'Rent' Is Brilliant and Messy All at Once," ibid., February 25; "Rent," *The New York Times*, May 5 1996; Kerner, "Downtown;" Kourlas, "How They Play the Rent;" Larson et al., *Rent*; ibid; Lepidus, "Rent;" Lyons, "Rent;" Mandelbaum, "Rent;" O'Brien, "Rent Strikes;" O'Neill, "Talent for Rent;" Rich, "East;" "Bring in the Funk," ibid., November 20; Tommasini, "The Seven-Year Odyssey That Led to 'Rent';" Viagas, "Rent;" Winer, "Rent;" Isherwood, "Rent Control."
85. Savran, *Queer Materialism*, 129.

Bibliography

Aiken, George. "Uncle Tom's Cabin." In *Staging the Nation: Plays from the American Theater, 1787–1909*, edited by Don B. Wilmeth, xi, 574. Boston, MA: Bedford Books, 1998.

Anonymous. "Birth of a Theatrical Comet." *New York Times*, 17 March 1996, H1.

Anonymous. "Where Are They Now?: The Gang of Five." Charlotte Magazine, http://www.charlottemagazine.com/Charlotte-Magazine/August-2010/Where-are-They-Now/The-Gang-of-Five/.

Barnes, Clive. "Puccini Meets the E. Village." *New York Post*, February 14 1996, 40.

Bell, John. "Disney's Times Square: The New American Community Theatre." *TDR: The Drama Review* 42, no. 1 (Spring 1998): 26–33.

Brantley, Ben. "Enter Singing: Young, Hopeful and Taking on the Big Time." *The New York Times*, April 30 1996, C13, C16.

———. "Rock Opera À La 'Bohème' and 'Hair'." *New York Times*, February 14 1996, C11, C18.
Brustein, Robert. "The New Bohemians." *The New Republic*, April 22 1996, 29–30.
Bureau, United States Census. "Poverty Thresholds 1995." https://http://www.census.gov/hhes/www/poverty/data/threshld/thresh95.html.
Carlson, Marvin A. *The Haunted Stage: The Theatre as Memory Machine.* Ann Arbor: U of Michigan P, 2001. Print.
Davidson, Justin. "Passions and Puccini: 'Rent' Invokes 'Boheme,' but It Seizes Realism." *Newsday*, April 30 1996, B2-B3.
Evans, Greg. "Judge Takes Larson Side in *Rent* Suit." Variety, http://variety.com/1997/biz/news/judge-takes-larson-side-in-rent-suit-1116676287/.
Farber, Jim. "Entertaining 'Rent' No New Lease on Rock Opera Genre." *Daily News*, February 22 1996, 41.
Feingold, Michael. "Long-Term Lease." *Village Voice*, February 20 1996, 71.
Galvin, Peter. "New Bohemians." *The Advocate*, April 30 1996, 58–59.
Gerard, Jeremy. "Rent." *Variety*, February 19 1996, 56.
———. "Rent." *Variety*, May 6 1996, 210.
Grode, Eric. "Rent." *Back Stage*, February 23 1996, 1.
Grunwald, Henry. "Crossover: 'Rent' and 'La Boheme'." *The Wall Street Journal*, May 2 1996, A13.
Guerra, Gigi. "Bohemian Rhapsody." *TimeOut New York* (April 24–May 1 1996): 14–17.
Heilpern, John. "Rent: Glorious Last Testament Shakes up the American Musical." *The New York Observer*, February 26 1996, 20.
Holland, Bernard. "Classical View: Flaws Aside, 'Rent' Lives and Breathes." *New York Times (Sunday)*, March 17 1996, Section 2, p. 31.
Hughes, Amy E. *Spectacles of Reform: Theater and Activism in Nineteenth-Century America* Ann Arbor: U of Michigan P, 2012.
Isherwood, Charles. "Rent Control." *The Advocate*, May 27 1997, 75–76.
Jefferson, Margo. "Rent." *The New York Times*, May 5 1996, 20.
———. "'Rent' Is Brilliant and Messy All at Once." *New York Times (Sunday)*, February 25 1996, Section 2, p. 5, p. 22.
Kerner, Leighton. "Downtown Arias: Assessing the Opera in *Rent*." *Village Voice*, March 19 1996, 59–60.
Kershaw, Baz. *Theatre Ecology: Environments and Performance Events.* Cambridge: Cambridge UP, 2007.
Kourlas, Gig. "How They Play the Rent." *Daily News* (June 16 1996).
Larson, Jonathan, Evelyn McDonnell, Kathy Silberger, Larry Fink, Stewart Ferebee, and Kate Giel. *Rent*. New York: HarperEntertainment, 1997.
Lepidus, D.L. "Rent." *The Westsider*, February 22–28 1996, 12.
Lyons, Donald. "'Rent,' New Musical Is Deserved Hit." *The Wall Street Journal*, March 6 1996, A18.
Mandelbaum, Ken. "Rent." *Theater Week*, March 4 1996, 6–7.
Marks, Peter. "The Young Voices of *Rent*." *New York Times*, 17 March 1996, H7.
McConachie, Bruce A. *Melodramatic Formations: American Theatre and Society, 1820–1870.* 1st ed. Iowa City: U of Iowa P, 1992.
New York Theatre Workshop. "Rent Advertisement." *New York Times*, March 17, 1996.
O'Brien, Patti. "Rent Strikes." *Rolling Stone* (May 16, 1996): 54–58.

O'Neill, Anne Marie. "Talent for Rent." *People* (July 1, 1996).
Rich, Frank. "Bring in the Funk." *The New York Times*, November 20, 1996, A25.
———. "East Village Story." *The New York Times*, March 2, 1996, 19.
Rock Music Timeline. "1990s Decade Overview." http://www.rockmusictimeline.com/1990s.html.
Savran, David. *A Queer Sort of Materialism: Recontextualizing American Theater*. Ann Arbor: U of Michigan P, 2003.
Schneider, Rebecca. *Performing Remains: Art and War in Times of Theatrical Reenactment*. Abingdon, Oxon ; New York: Routledge, 2011.
Schulman, Sarah. *Stagestruck: Theater, AIDS, and the Marketing of Gay America*. Durham, NC: Duke UP, 1998.
Sussman, Mark. "New York's Facelift." *TDR: The Drama Review* 42, no. 1 (Spring 1998): 34–42.
Thomas, June. "Sarah Schulman: The Lesbian Writer *Rent* Ripped Off." *Slate* (November 23, 2005).
Tommasini, Anthony. "The Seven-Year Odyssey That Led to 'Rent'." *New York Times*, March 17, 1996.
Viagas, Robert. "Rent." *Playbill* (March 19, 1996).
Winer, Linda. "The Prize-Winning 'Rent' Moves to Broadway." *Newsday*, April 30, 1996, B3.

5 Normalization
The Laramie Project

Prologue

In 1995, 24-year-old Jonathan T. Schmitz from the small Michigan town of Orion appeared on a daytime television tabloid, *The Jenny Jones Show*, to meet a secret admirer. When Schmitz came onstage, he saw a woman who lived in his apartment complex sitting in a chair. Assuming she was his secret admirer, he gave her a kiss before the show's host told Schmitz that his aficionado was actually about to walk onstage. To Schmitz's confusion, Scott Amedure emerged from the television studio's wings. The episode was about men who had secret crushes on other men. Three days later, Schmitz withdrew money from the bank, bought a shotgun, shot Amedure twice in the chest, and then called the police to turn himself in for the killing.[1] Despite the clear-cut case, the prosecution failed to win its first-degree murder charge because Schmitz's lawyers utilized the so-called "gay panic" defense. This legal argument posits that "the reasonable and ordinary person provoked by a homosexual advance kills because the solicitation itself causes an understandable loss of normal self control ... this argument casts the ordinary, fallible human being as not only heterosexual but also one sufficiently homophobic to kill queers."[2] Based on this assumption of what a "normal" man was like, a U.S. jury in 1995 found Schmitz guilty only of second-degree murder. Four years later, in a small town in Wyoming, the gay panic defense no longer worked, indicating a shift in the dominant ideology's view of a "normal" reaction to gay citizens.

No one who grew up, or was an adult, during the 1990s needs to be reminded of the details of 21-year-old Matthew Shepard's murder. On October 6, 1998, Shepard was driven to the outskirts of the small town Laramie, Wyoming, tied to a fence, tortured, and left for dead by Aaron McKinney and Russell Henderson. Shepard became a *cause célèbre*, and literally thousands of articles were written about him, his murder, and his place in the emerging discourse of gay civil rights. In particular, his death fomented debate in the contemporaneous deliberation about adding sexual orientation to already existing hate crime legislation. Though by 1998 federal hate crime legislation covered religion, gender, and race, it was not until 2009 that the U.S. passed a more comprehensive hate crime law that included protection for LGBTQ individuals. Congress named that legislation in part for Matthew Shepard.

As Casey Charles writes in *Law and Literature*, the resistance to including sexuality in hate crimes legislation during the 1990s was ironic "in light of the existence of an extant legal doctrine[—the gay panic defense—]that *mitigate[d]* penalties for those who attack gays and lesbians."[3] The press for legal changes that would offer equal protection to LGBT citizens under the law was led by President Bill Clinton, beginning in earnest in 1997, but a host of previous activists and scholars gave him the language and political cover to do so. In 1990, queer theorist Eve Kosofsky Sedgwick pointed out that "the widespread acceptance of [the gay panic defense] seems to show … that hatred of homosexuals is even more public, more typical, hence harder to find any leverage against than hatred of other disadvantaged groups. 'Race panic' or 'gender panic,' for instance, is not accepted as a defense for violence against people of color or against women."[4] Though it may have been hard to find leverage to advocate for equal protection under the law for LGBT citizens in the early 1990s, McKinney's 1999 trial for Shepard's murder galvanized the U.S. under the rhetoric that no matter whether or not Shepard made sexual advances towards two straight men, he did not deserve torture and death. While this may seem commonsensical, one must remember that only a few years earlier, during the trial for Amedure's murder, the gay panic defense was successful. The failure of McKinney's lawyers during his trial demonstrated the weakening of the gay panic defense. The play *The Laramie Project* by Moisés Kaufman and the Tectonic Theater Project augmented and disseminated the new normal that killing a gay man was unacceptable regardless of whether or not he made a pass at a straight man.

Made up of over 200 interviews conducted and edited by Kaufman and his theatre company, The Tectonic Theater Project, *The Laramie Project* was less about the murder of Matthew Shepard and more about the town's reaction to the crime and subsequent events. The docudrama portrayed 66 characters utilizing eight actors and a bare-bones production aesthetic. Though edited and shaped by Kaufman who presented a point of view that supported LGBT civil rights, the play was received as objective, factual reportage, and as much about the U.S. nation as about one small town. These horizons of expectation gave the play a particularly effective ability to change minds regarding how LGBT citizens should be treated. This ability was not theoretically proven by theatre scholars doing close-readings of the text—in fact, academics often found *The Laramie Project* unsatisfying.[5] Instead, quantitative studies executed by psychologists repeatedly pointed to *The Laramie Project*'s ability to promote acceptance of LGBT citizens.[6] This is the normalization to which the title of this chapter refers. Normalization is a more precise term than acceptance because some U.S. citizens would not "accept" LGBT citizens as equal in 2000. But, by refuting the "gay panic" defense, the dominant ideology established that LGBT citizens were "normal" and deserving of protection under the law, even if some residual ideologies still refused to acknowledge same sex couples as "acceptable."

Normalization, instead of acceptance, implies folding into the legal system, visibility instead of invisibility, and social status instead of social death. Similarly, while the play took Matthew Shepard's HIV-positive status into account—both through potential infection of another character and via what his positive diagnosis supposedly revealed about his moral fiber—the play did not make the disease the center of Shepard's narrative. Instead, *The Laramie Project* made Shepard's life normal, and his absence abnormal, focusing on the town and leaving a void where Shepard should have been. Unfortunately, it took Matthew Shepard's actual death for *The Laramie Project* to combat the type of symbolic death faced by LGBT citizens.

Synecdoche, Wyoming

In the 1990s, LGBT citizens were more visible than in the 1980s through exposure in mainstream culture, political activism, and celebrities coming out. Nevertheless, LGBT people living in the United States were particularly vulnerable to violence. In 1992, the *Columbia Law Review* reported data about LGBT citizens from surveys collected in eight major cities in the United States: of those interviewed, 86% had been attacked verbally; 44% had been threatened with violence; 27% had objects thrown at them; 18% were victims of property vandalism including arson; and 30% reported sexual harassment, many by members of their own families or by police.[7] It was because of this that President Bill Clinton sought legal help to make LGBT citizens less susceptible to violence. His attempts at including sexual orientation as a category for protection in hate crime legislation did not pass, but because the subject of violence against LGBT citizens was already in the public discourse, Matthew Shepard's murder and *The Laramie Project* made a strong impact in the cultural setting. Shepard's killing marked a turning point in the dominant ideology's understanding of anti-gay violence, and the Tectonic Theater Project was uniquely positioned to create a docudrama that could ideologically and aesthetically appeal to the U.S. mainstream. But Shepard and *The Laramie Project* would likely not have been taken up by people pushing for legal change regarding LGBT civil rights without the events of the year prior to his murder.

In 1997 there was a determined attempt to make hate crimes national news and produce new legal protection. In June, Clinton devoted his weekly radio address to hate crimes, citing violence against the LGBT community specifically. In November, there was a conference at the White House focusing on hate crimes; the conference included participants such as the President, the Vice President, the Attorney General, and hundreds of activists, including LGBT groups such as the Human Rights Campaign (HRC). A few days after the conference, Clinton proposed to the 105th United States Congress "The Hate Crimes Prevention Act," which would have protected LGBT individuals as federal laws already protected people on the basis of race, religion, and national origin. It would not pass.

Almost a year later, in early October 1998, Shepard was beaten and left to die, which he did in a Denver hospital on October 12. His death gave a face to the movement attempting to pass hate crimes legislation that would protect LGBT citizens. Two days after Shepard was found tied to a fence outside Laramie, Clinton took the time to make a speech in which he rhetorically went from Shepard in specific, to LGBT people in general, to the need to pass his legislation. In his much-reported speech, Clinton said that the murder of Shepard "strikes at the very heart of what it means to be an American and at the values that define us as a nation. We must all reaffirm that we will not tolerate this" and that "just this year there have been a number of recent tragedies across our country that involve hate crimes."[8] In the two months after Shepard's murder, hundreds of newspaper articles were published about the events and their meanings. The *New York Times* alone published 73 articles relating to Shepard between his death on October 12 and the New Year. Thousands of similar articles would be published in periodicals across the country before *The Laramie Project* premiered in 2000. But a week after Clinton's speech in which he addressed Shepard's death, an editorial in the *New York Times* followed the Clinton rhetoric completely, using Shepard's murder as a specific horror, then as a general symbol, then finally as evidence for the necessity of legislative action.[9] The editorial stated that Shepard's "death has brought home to the American public as nothing else ever has the menace and hatred that homosexuals still face in being honest in the United States" and that "the Southern Poverty Law Center, after studying F.B.I. statistics, has calculated that gay men and lesbians are six times as likely to be physically attacked as Jews or Hispanics in America, and twice as likely as African-Americans."[10] The *New York Times*' conclusion from Shepard's death and the Southern Poverty Law Center's statistics is that, "The need for hate-crime laws is obvious."[11] In these ways, Shepard's murder in specific and violence against LGBT individuals in general were linked from the beginning in public discourse. Even a year after the murder, it was a topic of great currency in the press.

Frank Rich, writing for *The New York Times* in 1999, argued that the cultural output of the summer was partly a repercussion of Shepard's killing. He wrote that the summer of 1999 marked "a shift in the mainstream depiction of gay people away from the cuddly, guppie-next-door coming-out phase exemplified by ABC's canceled *Ellen*. However inadvertently (and heavy-handedly), *Summer of Sam* and *Bash* do take on the pathology of anti-gay violence—a mass-audience subject in the wake of the murder of Matthew Shepard much as AIDS became in the aftermath of Rock Hudson."[12] Rich ties Shepard's death to the HIV/AIDS crisis, suggesting that the social invisibility that led to tens of thousands of gay men's deaths from AIDS is similar to the lack of full protection under law that led to gay men's frequent murders. And while Rich picked two largely seen pieces of mainstream culture to use as examples, there were more he could have cited, such as the extremely popular and critically lauded film *Boys Don't Cry* that was released in February of 1999 and exemplified both anti-gay violence and small-town American life in a way that resonated with Shepard's murder.

Shepard's murder was hardly unique—that was the whole point of this press coverage. Amy I. Tigner in *Modern Drama* begins her writing about *The Laramie Project* with 17 names, followed by the dates when these people were murdered because of their sexual orientation.[13] She asks why Shepard became a national figure instead of the many other victims of hate crimes. She points to his race, class, and age, but, ultimately, to his position in a "Western pastoral"—a fascinating view, and one that gives insight into the play *The Laramie Project*.[14] However, if what made Shepard's death so captivating to the U.S. public was the Western pastoral setting of Laramie, then earlier murders of gay men in Laramie should have had similar effects. They did not. For instance, Steve Heyman, a gay man who taught psychology at the University of Wyoming and was the faculty advisor of the university's LGBT student organization, was killed in 1993 when thrown from a moving car. Beth Loffredda, another professor at the University of Wyoming, wrote about the many similarities between the crimes in her moving account of the aftermath of Shepard's death.[15] So why did Shepard become a national symbol and not Heyman or the scores of other victims of anti-LGBT violence?

Three factors made Shepard the face representing LGBT hate crimes violence: he embodied the ideal victim; he was portrayed as a boy rather than a man; and he was often compared to Jesus Christ. Romaine Patterson, a friend of Shepard's who is portrayed as a main character in *The Laramie Project*, reports in her autobiography that when she told her mother of Shepard's death, her mother replied, "You know, I always thought this sort of thing would happen to Matt" and that "in the days that followed [Patterson] would hear repeatedly by other people who had known him— that he was the embodiment of a victim."[16] Shepard's own mother said, "[Matt] had the posture of a victim ... he was the kind of person whom you just look at and know if you hurt him that he's going to take it—that there's nothing he can do about it, verbally or physically. When he walked down the street he had that victim walk."[17] This rhetoric was reported in the massive national press on Shepard.

Adding to the discourse that made Shepard a national symbol for anti-gay violence was his extremely small stature: only five feet, two inches tall and 105 pounds. His boyish, meek looks were captured in the few pictures released of him, in most of which he appeared younger than his actual age of 21. His mother's comment about his "victim posture" was printed on a picture of him in *Vanity Fair* in an oversize button up shirt looking directly into the camera eating at McDonald's. He looks like an adolescent son rather than an independent, sexually active adult. Such pictures led Andrew Sullivan, the popular gay writer, to rail against what he called the "marketing" of Shepard. Sullivan felt the photos that circulated repeatedly through press organs depicted Shepard "crouched sparrow-like on a waterfall, gazing cherubically into the distance. ... The point of this iconography is to divest

130 *Normalization*

Shepard of any maturity, any manhood, any adult sexuality."[18] Indeed, the *Vanity Fair* article in which the described photo appeared affirmed that,

> Parents throughout the country felt that Matthew could have been their son, an idea many had never contemplated before about a gay person. In part, this may have been a result of the fact that while he was described as gay, the press—in unwitting collusion with homophobia—did not portray Matthew as a sexual adult. He was depicted as having parents, rather than partners—loving, affluent, married American parents. He had an allowance; he wore braces. He was a member of the U.W. Episcopal Canterbury Club. He had a fragile, childlike look—a look of pale purity, the translucent beauty favored in religious art.[19]

While his HIV-positive status might have belied descriptions of his sexual "purity," it instead contributed to his victim status. After films like *Philadelphia* (1993), in which popular actor Tom Hanks played a suffering HIV-positive lawyer, and the play *Rent* (1996), in which characters like Angel were martyrs to the disease, Shepard's HIV status tended to contribute to his victim description rather than add a sense of sexual activity. This portrayal as a "perfect victim" without "any adult sexuality" and a "translucent beauty favored in religious art" led, almost inevitably, toward a comparison to Jesus Christ.

Shepard was quickly seen as a martyr for the LGBT civil rights movement that was pushing for hate crimes legislation, but a more specific connection to Jesus was made almost immediately. Matthew Shepard's name alone, with its undertones of a disciple and a metaphor often utilized for Jesus—a shepherd—no doubt led to some connection between Shepard and Christianity. But, at the vigil held in Laramie immediately after Shepard's attack, he was explicitly compared to Jesus, and that happened at many of the other vigils around the country.[20] He was tied to a wooden fence as he was tortured and beaten to death, and it was widely reported—inaccurately—that his arms were outstretched crucifixion style. The image of the empty wooden fence came to stand in for his murder, much as the wooden cross stands in for Jesus' death. Indeed, the *Vanity Fair* article with his diminutive picture is entitled, "The Crucifixion of Matthew Shepard," and compares the road on which the fence stood to Golgotha, the location of Jesus' cross.[21] But this was a highly constructed image. The fence was not in the middle of nowhere. A Super Wal-Mart marked the turnoff Henderson and McKinney took to get to the fence, and "Sherman Hills, one of the more upscale housing developments in Laramie, [was] within a half mile [and within sight] of the spot where Matt was tied (and where McKinney resided for a while as a child)."[22] But because quickly the press and public created and regurgitated the narrative of an innocent, childlike, martyred Shepard, the murder became a national phenomenon. One of the people whose attention the myth-making attracted was theatre-maker Moisés Kaufman who decided it was a "lightening rod" moment, a "moment in history when a particular event brings the various ideologies and beliefs prevailing in a culture into sharp focus."[23] Kaufman's own background likely reinforced his interest in Shepard's death and curiosity about how the town would react to Shepard's murder.

Kaufman had many intersecting identities that had rendered him an "outsider" in his own communities, which may have helped him identify with Shepard. The contemporaneous reviews of *The Laramie Project* and the scholarship written on the play tend to point out that Kaufman and his troupe were New Yorkers descending on Laramie as outsiders. But Kaufman was no native of New York City, and it is interesting that while most of the original production had the Tectonic Theater Project members playing themselves, John McAdams played Moisés Kaufman. McAdams' portrayal of Kaufman included an American Standard accent unlike Kaufman's actual Spanish-accented English. This depiction hid that Kaufman was not native to the U.S. and was as much an outsider to New York City as he was to Laramie. Kaufman's parents were Jewish Romanians who survived the Holocaust and, in the aftermath of WWII, immigrated to Caracas, Venezuela.[24] Born to Orthodox Jewish parents in South America, Kaufman was sent to Yeshiva, a type of schooling that provided both academic and religious instruction. While Kaufman reports valuing Talmudic scholarship's rigor and value of interpretations over answers,[25] Orthodox Judaism did not accept his sexuality as a gay man. Likewise, the culture of Catholic-dominated Venezuela created an environment that Kaufman describes as dominated by machismo and homophobia.[26] In 1987, while in a Caracas college, Kaufman joined the avant garde theatre Thespis headed by artistic director Fernando Ivosky whose name suggests a similar identity to Kaufman's. During this time, Venezuela was flush from an oil boom, and an international theatre festival brought luminaries such as Tadeusz Kantor, Jerzy Grotowski, and Peter Brook to Caracas. Kaufman was influenced by all of them, particularly Kantor's juxtaposition of all theatre's elements over a dictatorship of plot and language. At Thespis, the troupe did Grotowski-inspired exercises, but Kaufman reports not understanding their point. In order to understand better, he moved to New York City and enrolled in NYU where U.S. professors claimed to understand Grotowski's legacy. Kaufman says sardonically in an interview with Caridad Svich—another playwright living between many cultures—that in Venezuela he was a Jew and in New York he became a Latino.[27] Always the outsider, and at times feeling threatened—he states that it was unsafe to be gay in Venezuela[28]—Kaufman's influences and his work before *The Laramie Project* focused on those within a society who felt themselves outside the national imaginary.

These figures who influenced Kaufman's artistic process and those who became subjects of his pre-*Laramie* plays show that he had an early interest in people whose complex identities led them to suffering. Tadeusz Kantor was a Polish theatre auteur whose mixed Catholic/Jewish background was similar to Kaufman's, and the danger Kaufman felt as a gay man in Caracas was nothing compared to the danger Kantor experienced in Poland during the World Wars. Kantor created his first theatrical work in Nazi-occupied Kraków and continued to create non-state-sanctioned pieces throughout the twentieth century in Communist Poland. Jerzy Grotowski, by contrast, was a small child during WWII and a Communist Party member. However, his most famous theatre piece, *Akropolis*, which Kaufman saw in Caracas, was co-written and designed by an actual Auschwitz-Birkenau survivor, Polish Jew Józef Szajna, who is often uncredited in Anglophone Grotowski scholarship. But because Grotowski created exercises easily practiced by students and Kantor left no school behind, Kaufman practiced Grotowski training in Caracas and New York. However, the type of juxtaposition of text, image, sound, and movement Kaufman utilizes is more in line with Kantor's work than Grotowski's. After graduate school at NYU, Kaufman founded the Tectonic Theater Project, and their breakthrough production came in 1997 with *Gross Indecency: The Three Trials of Oscar Wilde*, which was the third most performed play in the U.S. during the 1998–99 season.[29] Similar to *The Laramie Project* in form with a few actors playing many characters and much direct address, *Gross Indecency* utilizes historical documents such as letters, court transcripts, and newspaper articles, to tell the story of Oscar Wilde's trials that would eventually imprison him based on his sexual attraction to men. Wilde, as a subject, married Kaufman's interests: Wilde was an Irish immigrant living in Britain, and was a man attracted to other men living in a society that legally disapproved of such relationships. Kaufman and his collaborators at the Tectonic Theater Project would use these influences and the success of *Gross Indecency* to begin work on *The Laramie Project* conjoining their artistic practices and Shepard's national media coverage.

After Shepard's murder, Kaufman had a "hunch" that traveling to Laramie with Tectonic company members and interviewing townspeople would lead to an important play that would "allow theatre to relate to current events."[30] In order to do so, the theatre used funds garnered from the many productions of *Gross Indecency* and was able to utilize the trending of Shepard in the national imagination to attract support from other theatre institutions. After the Tectonic Theater Project's first trip to Laramie in November 1998, four weeks after the murder, they returned to New York and put together a 90-minute workshop version of the play. That version was enough to gain support from Robert Redford's Sundance Theatre Institute and the New York Theatre Workshop. Both of these institutions provided funding, housing, and space for the long creation and rehearsal process that led to *The Laramie Project*'s final form. All told, the interviewing, writing, and creating took two years and required a high level of support. As Kaufman says, "It has become clear to me that it is impossible to create new theatrical forms using old methods. Neither *Gross Indecency* nor *The Laramie Project* could have been rehearsed for four weeks and then opened."[31] But when Kaufman or scholars of his work discuss these two plays as outside the mainstream because of their unusual process and form, it contradicts the fact that each play was more widely produced than most plays created utilizing the "old methods." This means that neither *Gross Indecency* nor *The Laramie Project* was avant-garde. They were both solidly mainstream in the sense that they were seen by many and reported on by national news outlets, made tremendous profits, and became part of the national discourse. In part, *The Laramie Project* became so popular because it was the production from the Tectonic Theater Project following the popular *Gross Indecency* and also because support from Sundance and the New York Theatre Workshop primed it for a mainstream release.

The Laramie Project had its first production in Denver, the nearest large city to Laramie, but quickly transferred to New York City's Union Square Theater on May 18, 2000. The intimate, 499-seat theatre located in a building in the storied Union Square first set the tone for the play's political activism. The park in Union Square has been historically the start and end for many political demonstrations, from the first Labor Day celebrations on September 5, 1885, to its 1997 designation as a Historical Landmark because of its significance to U.S. labor history. However, Union Square's radical past is belied, to some extent, by its late twentieth-century incarnation. While still a gathering place for protests, demonstrations, and rallies, it is also the site of New York City's first Business Improvement District (BID), a public/private partnership in which businesses within the district pay extra taxes to create redevelopment projects. Union Square companies primarily applied these funds to tourist-friendly renovations and security. Hence, the location for *The Laramie Project* was a clean, safe area for patrons to arrive, but held within it the flavor of activism. The production made use of this framing, primarily from *The Laramie Project*'s claims to objective documentary status about the nationally infamous murder of Shepard.

Actual Angels in America

The angels represented in *The Laramie Project* are actual. That is, they represent historical events. But in so doing, they combine documentary and spectacle and harken back implicitly and explicitly to Kushner's *Angels in America*, connecting *The Laramie Project* to prior AIDS plays and questions of gay citizenship. The text of *The Laramie Project* puts forward the town as the protagonist rather than an HIV-positive young man cut down too early. It shifts the audience's position from earlier AIDS plays, making *The Laramie Project* less voyeuristic and more participatory, as everyone in the audience had to react to Shepard's death, much the same way the residents portrayed onstage do. The major dramatic question the play asks, in fact, is how will the town react to Shepard's murder? The answer, representative of an emergent ideology in its historical moment, is that the town will accept the humanity and worth of Shepard's life. But any potential radicalism in the play is softened because of its grounding in sentiment, particularly Christian compassion and mercy, rather than in LGBT politics.

Documentary or ethnographic theatre, like *The Laramie Project*, provides a horizon of expectations for spectators with a higher truth content than fictional plays, regardless of the docudrama's actual veracity. While *The Laramie Project* uses Brechtian devices, such as a narrator, and Kantor-like juxtapositions of language, spectacle, and media, these techniques do not alienate spectators as much as highlight the non-fiction claims of the theatrical event. In its very first page, *The Laramie Project*'s narrator lays out the rules of the production: "On November 14, 1998, the members of Tectonic Theater Project traveled to Laramie, Wyoming, and conducted interviews with the people of the town. During the next year, we would return to Laramie several times and conduct over 200 interviews. The play you are about to see is edited from those interviews, as well as from journal entries by members of the company and other found texts."[32] Beyond the narrator, each of the characters is presented with his or her historical name. As ethnographers Jay Baglia and Elissa Foster put it, "By naming the people of Laramie in the script, we believe the [Tectonic Theater Project] appeals to the assumptions of positivism: that there is an objective truth that can be taken from *there* and brought *here*."[33] Regardless of whatever Brechtian devices are used to remind spectators that they are watching a piece of theatre, *The Laramie Project* always couches them in this documentary framing that makes claims to "objective truth."

The conflict in the play came primarily from contradiction rather than characters fighting to achieve goals. Kaufman relates Kantor's influence to the Tectonic Theater Project's work, summing up the Polish auteur's philosophy thus, "One goes to the theatre to see [theatrical] elements fighting each other to be the next 'text.'"[34] This type of formal clash is seen in what Kaufman calls "moment work." Kaufman explains, "Because you can have a Moment that deals only with lights, or a Moment that deals only with blocking or costumes, or sets, or music, or a combination of any of those. In doing that, we become very aware of the narrative potential of each theatrical element. And in doing so, reiterate their authority."[35] But rather than experiencing these Moments as formalistic and avant garde, as U.S. audiences did when Kantor's *Dead Class* came to New York in 1979, spectators of *The Laramie Project* in 2000 found the juxtapositions more like quick cuts between interviews in a film documentary.[36] Even when a particular Moment was about a different aspect of theatre from language, the audience understood the representation as documentary. For instance, when a line of actors turned their wooden chairs so the backs faced the audience, the audience understood these wooden chairs to be an aesthetic representation of the wooden fence to which Shepard had been tied. It may have been an abstract depiction, but, because spectators understood that the play depicted actual events, they understood the chairs as a "real" representation of "*the* fence." And when video was introduced, its juxtaposition with live actors onstage depicted the media invasion of Laramie after Shepard's murder. Actors carried cameras, microphones, and lights as monitors flew in from above the light grid "to create a kind of media cacophony."[37] This represented an actual event that happened in Laramie, not an alienating effect.

And while documentary in any form—film, theatre, television—is complicated by questions of truth and subjectivity, even a sophisticated spectator of a docudrama like *The Laramie Project* expects a different type of connection to historical events than what one gleans from watching fiction. A spectator does not, for instance, expect Kaufman to invent a line for a resident of the town—that would go against the verbatim rules set out by the Narrator's introduction. Thus, while Baglia and Foster are somewhat skeptical of the potential positivism in a production of *The Laramie Project*, they also admit that they could not "critique *The Laramie Project* for not representing reality better" without admitting that "some reality must, then, exist to be represented. What we wanted was a truth that transformed the meaning of Shepard's murder from one town's tragedy into an awakening of the nation's conscience."[38] Baglia and Foster are not the only critics who complain about *The Laramie Project*'s lack of literary qualities, but most miss the structure that gives the play exactly that.

The Laramie Project is structured very similarly to a narrative three-act play with the town as a protagonist and is organized like fiction, despite its documentary claims, with narrative drama's rising action and closure. Some contemporaneous critics, such as the influential Robert Brustein,[39] suggest that the play has no protagonist. If one uses the most narrow definition of protagonist—a character whose choices while pursuing a goal lead to the majority of a play's action—then *The Laramie Project* lacks a protagonist. But there is one entity whose choices are creating the play's action: the townspeople of Laramie. And spectators watch these characters react to Shepard's death in the same way audiences watch Hamlet react to his father's death, asking will Laramie choose revenge or forgiveness. But, it is easy to miss this structure because Shepard, the most obvious subject of the play, is absent. The title of the play points us to the subject, however. It is called *The Laramie Project* not *The Matthew Shepard Project*.

This shift to a polychoral protagonist that sometimes contradicts itself changes the position of the implied spectator and the moral order conveyed by the play's structure. Having the town as the protagonist rather than one character divides the potential subject positions for a sympathetic spectator. As Roger Freeman writes, "Staged oral history radically fragments the unitary subject and creates montages of voice that indicate a polyphonic subjectivity."[40] Providing more than one character as a protagonist allows a spectator an intersectional point of view. For instance, a liberal Christian raised in a rural setting who now lives in an urban environment could find voice for her multiple experiences in a variety of *The Laramie Project*'s characters.

Given Kaufman's own membership in multiple communities, perhaps this structure should come as no surprise. Utilizing a structure that fragments the unitary subject also demonstrates the Tectonic Theater Project's adherence to the dictates of performance anthropologist, Dwight Conquergood: "[G]ood performative ethnographers must continuously play the oppositions between Identity and Difference. Their stance towards this heuristically rich paradox of fieldwork (and performance) is both/and, yes/but, instead of either/or. They affirm cross-cultural accessibility without glossing over very real differences."[41] This both/and, yes/but dynamic is reached in part because the Tectonic Theater Project's members become characters themselves within the play, representing their own roles and prejudices alongside those of the townspeople. This creates the feeling of collaborative ethnography described in Diane E. Austin's article "Community-Based Collaborative Team Ethnography: A Community-University-Agency Partnership."[42] In the case of *The Laramie Project*, though, it would be a Theatre-University-Town Partnership—that is, a collaboration between the Tectonic Theater Project and the University of Wyoming faculty and staff who gave the first interviews and pointed to Laramie townspeople who would be willing to speak.

Putting the town instead of Shepard at the center of the narrative also shifts the protagonist from the HIV/AIDS victim to the survivors. By 2000 the AIDS play had become an established genre, and, while some might argue that *The Laramie Project* is not of that canon, it actually demonstrates a dramatic shift in how HIV/AIDS is represented onstage. Shepard's HIV-positive status is mentioned briefly late in the play, though his positive diagnosis does color how some Laramie residents see Shepard's morality. However, his HIV status as a plot point is most important to the straight, white, female police officer who is exposed to the virus while trying to save Shepard. Whether or not she contracts the disease and how her mother, husband, and children react to her potential infection is a major question throughout the play. Despite the play's absence of a young man with AIDS as a protagonist, there are strong structural similarities between *The Laramie Project* and earlier AIDS plays.

While Shepard didn't die from HIV/AIDS, he still functions, structurally, in the place of the HIV-positive youth cut down too early, a theatre trope by 2000. Instead of focusing on any one character's struggle to survive, or a romantic relationship threatened by HIV/AIDS, *The Laramie Project* presents a community struggling to give meaning to the loss of a young, gay, HIV-positive man. Given the rhetoric from Kramer, Kushner, and LGBT activists about the "murder" of gay men by the President Reagan and Bush Administrations for inaction regarding the HIV/AIDS epidemic, within *The Laramie Project* is buried a reaction not just to hate crimes, but also to the HIV/AIDS deaths in the U.S. during the 1980s and 1990s. When the play suggests that the town is to some degree culpable for Shepard's death because of inaction against anti-gay prejudice, *The Laramie Project* is also pointing out that the same prejudice allowed for 20 years of apathy by the U.S. government resulting in tens of thousands of HIV/AIDS deaths. Rather than focusing on a single protagonist, or on government officials, *The Laramie Project* turns the spotlight towards the survivors, some gay, some straight, some friends of Shepard's, some strangers—in short, the U.S. nation at large. *The Laramie Project* gave spectators the opportunity to not only come to terms with their feelings about the violence done to Shepard, but also that done to the U.S. gay community at large over the prior two decades.

The Laramie Project used this dual position, commenting both on Shepard's death and tens of thousands of deaths, to argue for a moral order of radical forgiveness. Commenting through its structure on needless death and the need for forgiveness over revenge is part of the power of the play. In a special issue of *Theatre Symposium* dedicated to the topic of "moral order," Steve Scott, of Chicago's Goodman Theatre, wrote an article entitled, "What Moral Order? A Report from the Trenches."[43] Essentially detailing the skepticism of his theatre colleagues on the very concept of a moral order, Scott explains,

> When I quoted from Lorca or Galsworthy, I was met with stares and in some cases sneers. These writers, I was told, were working in a society in which there existed some real moral order, some sort of prescribed set of moral and social standards that were generally accepted by a majority of people, even if a vocal minority rejected them. But that was then, and this is the twenty-first century, I was told—and in our world that kind of moral order no longer exists.[44]

In an age of postmodernism and supposed radical subjectivity, no sophisticated artist or scholar could still believe in a singular moral order; this was the refrain Scott heard again and again. However, narrative structure itself implies a moral order. "Narrative is the 'moral order,' the structure that conveys a meaning. It is also the 'moralizing order,'" writes theatre scholar Roger Freeman.[45] Therefore, the structure and context of a text presents a moral order—what Althusser would call an ideology. Because *The Laramie Project* was the second most produced play of 2000–2001, it seems the moral order/ideology it espoused was accepted by the dominant ideology. That moral order/ideology is that the community of the play must accept gay people as human citizens deserving of legal protection. The community in the play is that of Laramie, but the small Wyoming town functions as a synecdoche for the U.S. nation. Thus, *The Laramie Project* suggests that the nation must fold LGBT people into its conception of citizenship. However, that emergent ideology is tempered and made palatable to the dominant ideology by the fact that the characters in *The Laramie Project* include LGBT people in the national imaginary more through the lens of compassionate Christianity than through LGBT activism. One can see this throughout the text of the play.

Christian Angels in America

As the town of Laramie is the play's protagonist, and its reaction to Shepard's death is the action, the play's conflict comes not from a single character's goals and challenges, but, instead, from juxtaposition. In *A Journey through Other Spaces*, Kantor writes: "[The] totality [of a production] is achieved via the process of balancing the contrasts between diverse scenic elements, such as motion and sound, visual forms and motion, space and voice, word and motion of forms."[46] Kaufman's Moment work took Kantor's theory to heart and created a balancing act of juxtapositions throughout the play that fashioned the tension necessary to keep a spectator's attention. That tension was based around a single question: "How will the town, ultimately, react to Shepard's murder?"—a question to which there was a definite answer at the climax of the play. Thus, when interpreting *The Laramie Project*, one is not tracking characters' arcs *per se*, but instead juxtapositions. Tracing the many juxtapositions through the course of the production text demonstrates that *The Laramie Project* depicts Laramie forgiving Shepard's murderers on the basis of Christian mercy, ultimately accepting Shepard into the fold of the town's imagined community through Christian compassion. Because the town was seen as a synecdoche for the U.S. nation, its inclusion of Shepard within the imagined community supported an emergent ideology, but it did so based on the dominant ideology's religion rather than political rights. This use of religion as a basis for ideological work made the performance palatable to national audiences.

Looking at how compassion, Christian imagery, and children dying before their parents are juxtaposed throughout *The Laramie Project*'s three acts makes it easy to see how Moment work functions to deliver meaning to an audience. Early in Act I, one of the play's most prominent characters is introduced, police Officer Reggie Fluty, the woman who responded to the call when Shepard was found unconscious and tied to the fence. Fluty is depicted as a straight mom fighting for a symbolic gay son, Shepard. Fluty represents a protective, maternal presence absent in most of the mainstream AIDS plays of the 1980s and 1990s. She even risks contracting HIV herself to help save Shepard who is presented, structurally and through juxtaposition, as her child. Fluty describes finding Shepard and believing him to be "thirteen, fourteen years old because he was so tiny."[47] The audience is given the image of a protective female figure trying to save an adolescent boy with this line, even though this is not factually the case. Fluty also explains that the blood covering him made CPR difficult and that "the only place that he did not have any blood on him, on his face, was what appeared to be where he had been crying down his face."[48] This depiction of Shepard, tied to the wooden fence, with tears made visible and lasting, connects to the Christian imagery of statues of Jesus on the cross crying miraculous tears of blood. Fluty's description of finding what seemed to be a crying adolescent covered in his own blood is juxtaposed with the emergency room intake doctor's discussion of the severity of Shepard's injuries: "You expect these kind of injuries to come from a car going down a hill at eighty miles an hour ... but you don't expect to see that from someone doing this to another person."[49] His description allows the audience to picture the brutality of the torture that Shepard suffered. The doctor then defines Shepard as a "kid" for whom he "felt a great deal of compassion."[50] In that moment, treating Shepard, he thought, "We are all [God's] kids."[51] Because Fluty's monologue about Shepard at the end of Act I is immediately followed by the doctor's lines, her maternal care is juxtaposed with the doctor's thoughts about God's compassion, and, therefore, there is a sense that Fluty is Mary to Shepard's Jesus and the doctor's God.

This Christian subtext continues. In Act II, the audience learns that Fluty is the daughter of another major character, Marge Murray.[52] Fluty stoically relates her exposure to HIV via Shepard's blood, but Murray says, "I just hope [Fluty] doesn't go before me. I just couldn't handle that."[53] This, again, juxtaposes Fluty with maternal love and the premature death of a child. While Fluty is the child in danger referred to in Murray's line, the entire play revolves around a child—Shepard—who died before his parents. Of course, one of the most famous children to die before his mother is Jesus. Towards the end of the play, when Fluty learns she does not have HIV, her first thought is to "Thank God" and her mother recites, "Hail Marys."[54] Thus, one can see throughout the lines, images, and other characters to which Fluty is juxtaposed a subtext of Mary, Jesus, and God. Similarly, one can see the importance of Christian imagery in the play by tracking the use of angels within it.

Two characters in *The Laramie Project* have relationships with symbolic angels, and these associations show how Christian imagery and LGBT activism are linked throughout the play. The characters are Jedadiah Schultz and Romaine Patterson. The audience is introduced to Schultz talking about acting in a scene from Kushner's *Angels in America* in order to win a theatre scholarship to attend college. He does so despite his parents' disapproval of "homosexuality."[55] Schultz shares his parents' negative views on LGBT rights but is willing to play a gay person onstage to win a college scholarship. He and Patterson will be juxtaposed throughout the play.

Patterson is an out lesbian and the first of Shepard's friends introduced in the play. She describes his beaming smile, his ability to get along with people, and his desire to get into politics.[56] This description is juxtaposed with Shepard's academic advisor saying, "In retrospect—and I can only say this in retrospect of course—I think that's where he was heading, towards human rights. Which only adds to the irony and tragedy of this."[57] Thus, Patterson is from the first linked to the political aspects of Shepard and his killing. In Act II, Patterson's reaction upon learning about Shepard's murder on the news humanizes the tragedy. Her sympathy for a friend is juxtaposed with Schultz's heterosexist statement, "When you've been raised your whole life that [being gay is] wrong—and right now, I would say that I don't agree with it—yeah, that I don't agree with it but—maybe that's just because

I couldn't do it and speaking in religious terms—I don't think that's how God intended it to happen. But I don't hate homosexuals."[58] Later, Schultz will take back this comment, but Act II demonstrates his discomfort with the LGBT community expressed overtly in religious terms.

In Act III, these two characters make their most explicit connection to angels—Patterson through activism, and Schultz through theatre. At Shepard's funeral, the radical Kansas Baptist minister, Fred Phelps, is represented preaching his particular brand of hate: "This murder is different, because the fags are bringing us out here trying to make Matthew Shepard into a poster boy for the gay lifestyle."[59] The text then jumps six months forward to the trial of Russell Henderson. While the narrative chronology leapt, only a few seconds of performance time occurred—just enough for the narrator to state that Phelps returned for Henderson's trial, but so did Patterson. Patterson declares, "So our idea is to dress up like angels. And so we have designed an angel outfit—for our wings are huge—they're like big-ass wings—and there'll be ten to twenty of us that are angels—and what we're gonna do is we're gonna encircle Phelps … and because of our big wings—we are gonna com-pletely block him … And we're calling it 'Angel Action.' Yeah, this twenty-one-year-old little lesbian is ready to walk the line with him."[60] This moment often received applause from audiences.[61] The ovations are no surprise given the play's depiction of Phelps' despicable rhetoric towards Shepard[62]—the character represented in *The Laramie Project* as a boy, a martyr, a victim. Patterson's nondenominational, inclusive, and loving but nevertheless religious symbols of angels provided the audience with an opportunity to demonstrate support via applause championing a compassionate response to Shepard's death to contrast Phelps' hatred.

Connecting the "Angel Action" explicitly to the similar use of angel symbolism in *Angels in America* is a monologue from Schultz a few scenes later describing an argument with his parents about auditioning for the part of Prior in the University of Wyoming production. Schultz proudly relates his winning rhetoric: "The best thing that I knew I had them on is it was just after they had seen me in a performance of *Macbeth*, and onstage like I murdered like a little kid, and Lady Macduff and these two other guys and like and she goes, 'Well, you know homosexuality is a sin'—she kept saying that—and I go, 'Mom, I just played a murderer tonight. And you didn't seem to have a problem with that.'"[63] The obvious point of Schultz's rhetoric is that one can play a sinner onstage without being one. But underlying it is his description of Macbeth, who "murdered a little kid"—similar to how the play reported Shepard's death, the death of an innocent. Schultz seems to be asking his mother, and, by extension, the audience: Why is it okay for him to play the killer in Shepard's scenario but not the victim? Is Shepard truly worse than Henderson and McKinney just because of his choice of sex partners? The juxtaposition of Patterson's Angel Action and Schultz's rhetoric regarding portraying "sinners" onstage answer conclusively that, no, Shepard was not guilty for his own death because of his sexuality.

In the epilogue of the play, Schultz and Patterson are literally put side by side onstage. Schultz has come around entirely to believing in the equality of LGBT citizens, and Patterson is a budding LGBT activist. Schultz states, "I just can't believe I ever said that stuff about homosexuals, you know. How did I ever let that stuff make me think that you were different from me?"[64] Immediately following, Patterson says: "I just recently found out that I was gonna be honored in Washington, D.C., from the Anti-Defamation League. And whenever I think about the angels or any of the speaking that I've done, you know ... Matthew gave me—Matthew's like guiding this little path with his light for me to walk down."[65] These two juxtaposed speeches demonstrate the power of angels in this play: to change minds, to change lives, to fight hate with love. And while these two examples are fairly secular uses of a religious symbol—activism and theatre—they link to the play's exploration of religion.

While many religions are represented in *The Laramie Project,* a Christian theology ultimately informs the play's resolution. When asking how the town will react, seeking justice is a perfectly reasonable hope. An eye for an eye justice would be sentencing the killers to the death penalty, and, given the heinous nature of their actions, desiring such an outcome is understandable. The play, however, suggests that a different outcome is more advantageous: forgiveness, mercy, and respect for life. Stephen Wangh, one of Kaufman's professors at NYU and a co-writer of *The Laramie Project*, writes that, "In the end, it was this last influence (religion) that became a central character in our story, because Laramie, like many places in the United States, is a God-fearing town, a town in which the voices of Christianity speak with great authority."[66] Some of that religious influence is obvious, like its influence on Schultz and as represented in Phelps. But some is less so, such as the symbolism surrounding the fence where Shepard was killed, the compassion showed by the doctors in the play, and, ultimately, the decision to end the cycle of violence through forgiveness.

Towards the beginning of the play, the audience is given a lesson in the "sociology of religion in the West."[67] The sects represented are Baptist, Mormon, Unitarian, Catholic, and Muslim. While there may be more religious faiths in the actual town of Laramie, the play represents only these five, and, of them, only four have strong through lines. The Mormon faith becomes important for the arc of Russell Henderson because he is a member of that church. The Baptist religion, fairly or unfairly, comes to represent a hateful theology through the lines of Phelps and the town's unnamed Baptist minister. Islam is represented by a female, feminist University of Wyoming student whose views end up constituting the proper guilt the community should feel. But the Catholic faith ends up being the voice of wisdom presented in the play.

A Catholic priest, Father Schmit, provides the play's moral grounding, regarding both Shepard and the play's creation itself. He is introduced in the play during the "sociology lesson," and in contrast to the other religious leaders who discuss their churches' views on sexuality, Schmidt ignores

Shepard's sexual orientation altogether. Instead, the priest discusses organizing a vigil for Shepard: "We wanted to get other ministers involved and we called some of them, and they were not going to get involved. And it was like, 'We are gonna stand back and wait and see which way the wind is blowing.' And that angered me immensely. We are supposed to stand out as leaders."[68] In this speech, Schmit bypasses the Catholic Church's negative view on LGBT rights and instead focuses on the need for religious leadership, in this case for an interfaith vigil dedicated to Shepard's life and soul. At least this is how his character is represented in the play. Schmit's place in the play is even more memorable in Act II.

In the second act, during a scene called "Two Queers and a Catholic Priest," two gay members of the Tectonic Theater Project express trepidation at meeting with Laramie's Catholic priest. They are surprised when he states, "Matthew Shepard has served us well."[69] The idea of service speaks to the idea of martyrdom. In Catholic theology, a martyr dies in service to the larger community. With these words, instead of condemning Shepard or his sexuality, Schmit compares him to respected saints. How has Shepard's death served? It has revealed the latent violence in the community. This violence is not just physical, as Schmit points out: "You think violence is what they did to Matthew—they did do violence to Matthew—but you know, every time that you are called a fag, or you are called a you know, a lez or whatever ... Dyke, yeah, dyke. Do you realize that is violence? That is the seed of violence. And I would resent it immensely if you use anything I said, uh, you know, to—to somehow cultivate that kind of violence, even in its smallest form. I would resent it immensely. You need to know that."[70] In comparison to the obvious violence in Phelps' language, and the tacit violence in so many other characters' language, Schmit's request resonates deeply.

The scene ends with Schmit imploring the ethnographers "to say it correct," and this becomes the moral center of the play's creation. While Scott complains that it is unfashionable among the artists with whom he interacts in Chicago to believe in a "moral order," Schmit suggests that there is a "correct" way to make this piece of art. This is the opposite of relativism. Schmit's entreaty creates a Catholic ideology at the heart of the play's text, and never does the play give voice to Schmit's views on LGBT rights. It seems safe, then, to assume that Schmit does not go against the Catholic doctrine that same-sex intimacy is wrong. But what the play presents, instead, is Schmit's view that taking life and engaging in verbal violence are *more wrong*. The sin that concerns him is adding to the violence of society, not who is having sex with whom. Schmit's view, then, stands in stark contrast to the representation of the town's Baptist and Mormon leaders.

Unlike Schmit's imploration to not use his words for violence, the Baptist and Mormon leaders of Laramie are presented as extremely violent. The unnamed Baptist minister does verbal violence to Tectonic Theater Project member, Amanda Gronich, and he supports the death penalty for the killers.

The Mormon Church goes one step further and excommunicates Henderson, a kind of ultimate religious violence. Immediately after the play depicts Schmit saying verbiage can be violence, the Baptist minister has the lines: "Now, as for the victim, I know that that lifestyle is legal, but I will tell you one thing: I hope that Matthew Shepard as he was tied to that fence, that he had time to reflect on a moment when someone had spoken the word of the Lord to him—and that before he slipped into a coma he had a chance to reflect on his lifestyle."[71] These words, implying that Shepard is in hell unless he repented his sexuality, do the same violence to his interviewer Amanda Gronich that Schmit suggests calling someone a "fag" or a "dyke" does. The Baptist minister also supports retaliation in the form of physical violence, the death penalty, for the killers. As for the Mormon Church, after Henderson's hearing, "The church held a disciplinary council, and the result of that meeting was to excommunicate Russell from the Mormon Church. And what that means is that your name is taken off the records of the church, so you just disappear."[72] Thus, the violence done to Henderson by the Mormon Church ironically ends in the type of social death that threatened LGBT citizens in the 1980s and 1990s. Schmit is the only religious leader portrayed in the play who wants to keep the killers alive and in the fold of the imagined community.

Though the play does not mention Schmit's views on the death penalty, it does provide lines about what roles Schmit believes the killers should have in society. As he does not state otherwise, one can assume that Schmit follows Catholic dogma that is firmly against the death penalty. Instead of suggesting the killers should die, or be excommunicated, Schmit suggests that the role Henderson and McKinney must fill is that of teacher. "How did you learn? What did we as a society do to teach you that? See, I don't know if many people will let them be their teachers. I think it would be wonderful if the judge said, 'In addition to your sentence, you must tell your story, you must tell your story.'"[73] Schmit's view on the killers is not just valuing life in general, but valuing the killers' lives in particular to learn how to prevent more violence. The play juxtaposes Schmit's plea for the killers to tell their stories with a representation of McKinney's confession. In essence, the structure of the play follows Schmit's advice to let McKinney tell his story.

It is interesting that Kaufman chose Schmit as the moral center of the play and as the character whose comments seem, periodically, to control the goals of the script. Kaufman actively chose all of the edits of the 200 plus interviews, of course, but this decision is particularly notable since Schmit's request that they "tell it correct" is repeated at the end of the play giving a Catholic priest an authority unlikely for a play that is actively advocating for LGBT civil rights. And Kaufman had other options. A Unitarian minister who also planned Shepard's first vigil in Laramie was interviewed, but she did not become a character in the play.[74] Using a Catholic priest instead of a Unitarian minister accomplishes explicit and implicit rhetorics. Explicitly, Schmit preaches forgiveness and understanding. Implicitly, the Catholicism

Schmit practices finds Shepard's sexuality a sin. But for Schmit, and, hence, the "proper" Christianity depicted in the play, the need to do no violence outweighs the need to judge and condemn. The forgiveness and compassion of Christianity in this play overshadow the religion's vengeful and angry aspects, whether displayed by Patterson's angel wings covering Phelps' rage, or exhibited by Schmit's voice surpassing those of Laramie's Baptists and Mormons. Therefore, even those in the audience who might enter the theatre condemning LGBT citizens on religious grounds can find a way to accept Shepard into their imagined community because of the play's particular use of Christianity. This can also be seen in the play's religious imagery that is not character based.

The fence where Henderson and McKinney tied, tortured, and killed Shepard is a recurring symbol in the play. It is described as "a pilgrimage site,"[75] and a Laramie native describes taking visitors to the location. He describes it as "so stark and so empty" and that this isolation makes "the 'God, my God, why have you forsaken me' [come] to mind."[76] *The Laramie Project*'s direct allusion to Jesus' crucifixion and the stark Biblical location of Golgotha continues the *imitatio Christi* already taken up by two years of press coverage, despite the site's nearby Wal-Mart and housing development. Company members Greg Pierotti and Leigh Fondakowski, who later in the play are the "two queers" who interview Father Schmit, both describe their reactions to the fence in the same scene that it is named a pilgrimage site. Pierotti states, "I broke down the minute I touched it. I feel such a strong kinship with this young man" and Fondakowski reports, "Greg was crying on the way back. I couldn't bring myself to tears, but I feel the same way."[77] Touching the fence mirrors touching a holy site, finding connection with a past religious figure through bodily contact, knowing or believing that you both share the same space, and, hence, a connection. Pierotti's body undergoes change from this encounter, physically manifesting a "kinship" through tears. And while Fondakowski does not report touching the fence or crying, she sees the change in Pierotti and feels "the same," that is, a kinship, or compassion, for Shepard.

While compassion is not the sole provenance of religion, the decision of Laramie to show the killers compassion—which is the answer to the plot's major dramatic question—is depicted as Christian in *The Laramie Project*. At the end of Act I, the final moment is a monologue from the doctor in Laramie's emergency room who tended to both Shepard and McKinney. McKinney, after destroying Shepard and getting into another fight, was brought to the emergency room by his girlfriend. Hence, Dr. Cantway had the two men "two doors down" from one another in his hospital. He describes the experience, "Then two days later I found out the connection and I was … very … struck!!! They were two kids!!!!! They were both my patients and they were two kids. I took care of both of them … Of both their bodies. And … for a brief moment I wondered if this is how God feels when he looks down at us. How we are all his kids … Our bodies … Our souls … And

I felt a great deal of compassion ... For both of them ..."[78] *The Laramie Project*, by the end of Act I, foreshadowing the play's finale, expresses compassion for Shepard *and* his killers. The doctor does not describe an eye for an eye justice. He describes a turning the other cheek type of compassion, for both victim and victimizer.

Though Act II is when *The Laramie Project* introduces Schmit and his moral authority, Act III is when the Christian imagery of the play culminates and ultimately provides the play's resolution. If Shepard is represented as Jesus throughout the play and the media, then Dennis Shepard, his father, operates structurally in the place of God. Dennis Shepard's statement to the court after McKinney is found guilty of murder is the play's climax. In it, he seems to literally hold the power of life and death over his son's killer, and he shows forgiveness. His words are, "I give you life in the memory of one who no longer lives. May you have a long life, and may you thank Matthew every day for it."[79] This blessing, reminiscent of the Christian theology that one may have life based on the death of Jesus, continues the Christian rhetoric of the play. Dennis Shepard also proclaims that Matthew Shepard did not die alone tied to the fence. He lists the friends that were with his son: "the beautiful night sky and the same stars and moon that we used to see through a telescope ... the daylight and the sun to shine on him ... the scent of pine trees from the snowy range ... [and] the ever-present Wyoming wind."[80] But, most of all, "he had God" and Dennis Shepard felt better knowing that his son "wasn't alone."[81] This is the play's answer to the description of the fence as Golgotha in Act I when "God, my God, why have you forsaken me?" was invoked. Just as in the Christian belief about Jesus' crucifixion, while it may seem as if a son was alone during his death, he was not actually abandoned by God. And the forgiveness Dennis/God shows killers/sinners is, for *The Laramie Project*, the proper response to horrific, violent, hatred.

There is not a lot of psychological research on forgiveness,[82] but what exists suggests that, like Dennis Shepard as represented by the Tectonic Theater Project, to forgive, a person must confront what is lost and let it go. To forgive, one cannot hold on to the absent and one's own victim status. In particular, one must give up a desire for vengeance. Kaufman, in personal correspondence with *The Laramie Project* co-author Wangh, wrote, "At that moment, [Dennis Shepard] was letting go. And this was another big lesson about mercy, that somebody has to let go before [he or she] can really be merciful."[83] It stands to reason, then, that if mercy is about letting go, revenge—or, perhaps one might instead call it justice—is about holding on. Wangh writes, revenge "is a conjuring trick performed not by the living but by the dead, because revenge is performed in the name of—or as a proxy for—a deceased person or a past injury. Thus, the act of revenge serves to deny that the death has taken place, proclaiming that the dead person or the past event is still operative."[84] Psychiatrist Sandra Kiersky adds: "feelings of revenge not only ward off pain but also block recognition of our own contribution to the violence. They confirm that someone else is guilty and must be punished as evidence of this fact. As McKinney needed to believe that he was nothing like Shepard, we need to believe that we are nothing like McKinney. Recognizing ourselves in McKinney means acknowledging our own need to construct a sense of well-being at the expense of others."[85] Jill Dolan suggests that *The Laramie Project* should encourage "characters to be angry about what happened to Shepard," instead of practicing the type of letting go that Dennis Shepard's actions embody.[86] Choosing forgiveness over anger, or even over what Dolan no doubt sees as justice, is a difficult choice, but *The Laramie Project* suggests forgiveness is necessary in order to relate to the killers—to learn from them, in Schmit's terms—in order to build a society that does not "grow children like that."[87]

Whether Dennis Shepard forgave McKinney in real life, however, is questionable, and one can debate whether the play earns its climactic moment. In the New York premiere of *The Laramie Project*, it was important to Kaufman, as director, that the actor playing Dennis Shepard break down and cry during his court statement. This seems to stray from historical fact, however. Fondakowski, the head writer, remembers: "Dennis didn't break down at that moment. The reason Dennis Shepard asked for life imprisonment was that the defense team was going to bring up all kinds of unpleasant information about Matt Shepard during the penalty phase, and as part of the deal, McKinney agreed never to tell his side of the story. Besides, it was clear when Dennis said, 'May you have a long life and may you thank Matthew every day for it,' he believed that life in prison might be a more terrible punishment for McKinney than death."[88] So if scholars feel unsatisfied by the play's ending,[89] is it because the play took a shortcut to forgiveness? Is Dennis Shepard a "deus ex machina" as Alisa Solomon suggests?[90] Wangh considers this unlikely given that most audience members would not have access to the actual events *The Laramie Project* portrays. Instead, he suspects that there may be "a sense that the play is not clear about *who* needs to be forgiven."[91] He argues that the confession McKinney gives in the play is a start, but that *The Laramie Project* shies away from truly interviewing and giving voice to McKinney—ignoring his childhood molestation by an older boy, for instance.[92] The play also does not delve deeply into the backstories of Phelps, Laramie's unnamed Baptist minister, and other conservative religious figures, perhaps because the Tectonic Theater Project members "were not ready to confront [their] own prejudices against this society's holy protagonists."[93] Did the Tectonic Theater Project not heed Schmit's admonition, then, to learn from society's homophobes to understand what made them and how to build a more just society? Perhaps. But, again, one must note that *The Laramie Project* was the second most produced play of the 2000–2001 theatre season, and the critical reception, as opposed to the scholarly reception, was almost universally positive. For most audiences, then, Dennis Shepard's act of forgiveness was satisfying. But, perhaps for some spectators, seeing Dennis Shepard give up his victim status was a difficult undertaking with which to empathize.

Olga Botcharova, who led many conflict resolution programs in Bosnia, Croatia, and Yugoslavia, argues that giving up victimhood is particularly difficult because one must release the "anger [that] may have served as the only source of energy for a victim."[94] Dennis Shepard, as portrayed by *The Laramie Project*, is willing to give up the "righteousness which belongs to victimhood."[95] And, in so doing, he releases a righteous anger that the LGBT community has the justification to feel, not just for Shepard's death, but for all LGBT citizens who died due to violence, apathy, or social invisibility. *The Laramie Project*, promoting forgiveness over anger, championing letting go over justice, portrays a tectonic shift in LGBT representation onstage. By refusing a representation based in anger, victimhood, marginalization, or even justice, *The Laramie Project* forgives the systemic aspects of U.S. society that led to the tens of thousands of LGBT deaths in the 1980s and 1990s. Dolan finds this move away from anger objectionable, and the shift towards "a more religious than political discourse" problematic because it allows "systemic homophobia and bigotry ... off the hook."[96] But is forgiveness the same as letting a system off the hook? And need religious discourse be inherently of less worth than political discourse? As philosopher Hannah Arendt put it, "The fact that [Jesus] made [the 'discovery' of forgiveness] in a religious context and articulated it in religious language is no reason to take it any less seriously in a strictly secular sense."[97] And, in the year 2000, 82% of U.S. citizens self-reported as Christian,[98] so utilizing a religious rather than a political discourse may have helped lead to the play's popularity. Finally, regardless of its religiosity, which may have made the script palatable, the play does have politics running through it that supports an emergent ideology. Through its refutation of the gay panic defense, the play presents a shift of the legal status of Shepard, and, by extension, all LGBT people.

We Are Citizens

The gay panic defense, by suggesting that a "normal" reaction to being flirted with by a member of the same sex is lethal violence, implicitly suggests that a gay person should not receive the same legal protections as a straight person. By portraying the town of Laramie, and, by extension, the U.S. nation rejecting the gay panic defense, *The Laramie Project* folds LGBT citizens into legal protection from violence. That type of legal protection is an important step towards citizenship. One can follow the play's deconstruction of the gay panic defense by tracking juxtaposing views of Laramie residents and the degree to which they blame Shepard for his own death.

In the first act, a variety of characters describe the final time Shepard was seen in Laramie, at the Fireside bar. McKinney's girlfriend, Kristin Price, states, "A guy walked up to [McKinney] and said that he was gay, and wanted to get with Aaron and Russ."[99] Price continues that Henderson and McKinney decided to rob Shepard and beat him up "to teach him a lesson not to come on to straight people."[100] The bartender working that night refutes this account, contending Henderson and McKinney moved to the area in which Shepard sat, suggesting they approached him.[101] Patterson asserts that Shepard "would never not talk to someone for any reason,"[102] implying that even if approached by two hostile men, Shepard would have still interacted with them. This contradictory reconstruction of Shepard's final moments in public allows space for spectators to wonder who approached whom at the Fireside—and, crucially, puts forward the idea that the violence done to Shepard was to teach him "not to come on to straight people."[103] This back and forth is continued in Act II.

An Act II scene titled, "Live and Let Live" juxtaposes speech from homophobic Laramie residents against statements from the LGBT community of Laramie to refute the logic of the scene's title. It begins with Schultz's monologue about not understanding "homosexuality" and continues into a resident stating that, "This is what gay people do. This is what animals do."[104] That comparison of gay people to animals is juxtaposed with a seemingly more sympathetic view from a resident who states: "It doesn't bother anybody because most of 'em that are gay or lesbian they know damn well who to talk to. If you step out of line you're asking for it. Some people are saying he made a pass at them. You don't pick up regular people. I'm not excusing their actions, but it made me feel better because it was partially Matthew Shepard's fault and partially the guys who did it … you know, maybe it's fifty-fifty."[105] This statement, beginning with the idea that nobody in Laramie cares if one is gay, ends with the idea that Shepard's death is half his fault for being openly gay. That tortured logic is, of course, the engine of the gay panic defense. No wonder that monologue is juxtaposed with a female character saying, "Yes, as a lesbian I was more concerned for my safety … I think we all were. And I think it's because somewhere inside we know it could happen to us anytime."[106] The scene ends with an explicit repudiation of the "live and let live" rhetoric that in part allows the logic of the gay panic defense to function: "What it boils down to: If I don't tell you I'm a fag, you won't beat the crap out of me. I mean, what's so great about that? That's a great philosophy?"[107] In other words, in Laramie before Shepard's murder, one must hide one's sexual identity to survive, while the phrase "live and let live" is tossed around to obscure the homophobia and latent violence that threatens to erupt at any moment. That dormant physical aggression became overt when Henderson and McKinney killed Shepard, and the town's reaction to the "live and let live" philosophy comes to a head in the play's account of McKinney's trial.

Act III of *The Laramie Project* represents McKinney's trial and makes his use of the gay panic defense a referendum on that notion, ending with a jury finding it inadequate.[108] In court, McKinney's confession was played via tape recording as one continuous piece of evidence. However, *The Laramie Project* places several lines from other characters in the midst of McKinney's admission of guilt. The play interrupts McKinney's words after he says, "Well, [Shepard] put his hand on my leg, slid his hand like as if he was going to grab my balls" as explanation for the crime.[109] *The Laramie Project* interjects two important lines to comment on McKinney's confession. First, a lesbian character states, "When that defense team argued that McKinney did what he did because Matthew made a pass at him ... I just wanted to vomit, because that's like saying that it's okay" and, a second lesbian character adds, "I was really scared that in the trial they were going to try and say that it was a robbery, or it was about drugs. So when they used 'gay panic' as their defense, I felt, this is good, if nothing else the truth is going to be told ... the truth is coming out."[110] McKinney then continues his story of beating Shepard to death. The two interjected lines make explicit to spectators the logic of the gay panic defense: that, at heart, it suggests murdering a gay man is okay. The lines also suggest that McKinney's story is truthful, that through his confession in court, "the truth is coming out." This may not have been the case. McKinney's defense lawyers may have decided the gay panic defense was the most likely gambit to save their client. There was, after all, no question of his guilt, merely a question of whether he would be sentenced to first- or second-degree murder. Though not represented in *The Laramie Project*, the judge actually threw out the "gay panic" defense, writing, "Is it murder if a white supremacist kills a white man who jostles him in a crowd, but only manslaughter if he kills a black man who does the same?"[111] The judge's argument mirrors Sedgwick's view on the gay panic defense precisely,[112] except that, in rejecting it, the Wyoming court refused to allow that a "normal" man might react with homicidal violence to a gay sexual advance. Nevertheless, observers felt "that the gay panic defense continued to seep insidiously into the remainder of the trial."[113] Therefore, *The Laramie Project* may have been justified omitting the detail that the judge rejected the defense's first line of reasoning. Regardless, the play represents McKinney's trial as a referendum on the gay panic defense, and McKinney's guilty verdict shows the defense does not work, that the law did not believe killing Shepard was in any way justified even if he "slid his hand like as if he was going to grab [McKinney's] balls."[114] Therefore, the implication of the guilty verdict in the play is that Shepard was human and did not deserve to be beaten or killed. He was a citizen and had the protection of the state irrespective of whether he made a pass at a straight man.

The Laramie Project, then, portrays a movement from invisibility/social death/justified murder to visibility/social recognition/legal protection for Matthew Shepard explicitly, and implicitly for all LGBT citizens of the United States. While much of the play's rhetoric is religious in nature, *The Laramie Project* nevertheless clearly refutes the legal discourse of the gay panic defense. In so doing, it grants LGBT citizens more access to U.S. law. In the end, though, the climax of the play hinges on a Christian value of mercy and forgiveness, ebbing some of the righteous anger towards those in society who did violence to LGBT citizens, either directly or through decades of inaction. Perhaps because of its utopian vision of a truly equal United States and lack of condemnation of the guilty, *The Laramie Project* was extremely well received in the mainstream, calling for a new era of understanding between gay and straight communities rather than mutual recrimination.

This Is Our Town?

The reviews of *The Laramie Project* took to heart the deconstruction of the gay panic defense, demonstrated that the New York premiere instructed audiences to have compassion for a gay man, helped to produce a discourse of gay citizenship and legal protection, and legitimated a move towards a U.S. judiciary that did not discriminate against gay men. The play's press coverage did all this by furthering the production's own claims to factuality and by describing the Tectonic Theater Project's onstage Laramie as a synecdoche of the U.S. nation.

The reviews of the New York premiere frame *The Laramie Project* as factual, authentic, and a newly useful form of docudrama that is even more accurate than news media. Nearly every article specified that Kaufman and the other members of the Tectonic Theater Project conducted over 200 interviews to create this play, implicitly calling attention to the play's docudrama style, and several refer to the play as a new theatrical form of investigative journalism.[115] John Heilpern in the *New York Observer* states that there is a "shocking absence of anything approaching controversial television documentaries in the U.S., [and that] the theater has an effective role to play" in filling that lack.[116] For him, *The Laramie Project* provides the necessary detail and nuance to better understand Shepard's death and the politics that surrounded it. The New York *Post* calls the play "a new and firm step toward the documentary as a valid and even common theatrical form."[117] Indeed, though the reviewer feared upon entering the theatre that *The Laramie Project* might be little more than a peon to gay politics, he ultimately wrote that it was "a theatrically enthralling investigation into the background of the crime, and the waves of its aftershock."[118] Notable, beyond his compliment of the play, is the reviewer's description of *The Laramie Project* as an "investigation," again placing it in a documentary category. Similarly, Charles Isherwood writing in *Variety* states that in the play "the voices of Laramie are more varied than the media snapshots that emerged in the aftermath of the crime."[119] In other words, the play is more rich and full than the implicitly two-dimensional media coverage of Shepard's murder and its aftermath. The press reception highlighted and authenticated the play's claims to represent Laramie in the aftermath of Shepard's killing as fact, not fiction, through its surprisingly complex characters. One of the characters most mentioned was Father Schmit, and reviews often focus on him and the play's religious nature.

By highlighting the play's focus on religion, reviews further Shepard's martyr status, and foster the play's depiction of Schmit as the moral center of the play. Connecting to the prior two years of press about the Shepard murder, many of the reviews describe the play in Christian terms: the "crucifixion" of Shepard,[120] a "vision that changes lives,"[121] or "a mosaic as moving and important as any you will see on the walls of the churches of the world."[122] Many also discuss the character of Father Schmit, suggesting that he is the most sympathetic character because of his compassion for Shepard and his leadership in the community.[123] These explicit references to the play's religious framework helped provide spectators with a horizon of expectations that allowed for a political message regarding Shepard's death within a Christian context. The reviews also connected *The Laramie Project* to earlier AIDS plays.

The press surrounding the premiere of *The Laramie Project* linked the play to prior AIDS theatre in two primary ways: first, through reporting the HIV scare that the character Officer Reggie Fluty experiences, and second, via comparisons to *Angels in America*. Many of the reviews mention the plot point that Fluty is exposed to HIV through Shepard's blood,[124] and, in so doing, implicitly note that Shepard was HIV-positive when he died. Because of earlier plays that dealt with HIV/AIDS transmission, the press can sum up this plotline quickly: "There is, more privately, the female cop who may have been exposed to HIV in getting Matthew down from the fence because of cheap gloves; her later all-clear is a joyous moment."[125] The short-hand nature with which newspapers can elucidate this story arc demonstrates that it plays into a trope. The shift in that trope is that Shepard, the HIV-positive victim, is not concerned about transmitting the disease to a lover or being cared for by a male-dominated community. Instead, he receives maternal care at the hands of a "female cop" who is in that way exposed to the disease. This is a far cry from the reviews of *The Normal Heart* that discussed HIV/AIDS as a disease that was deserved due to the "homosexual lifestyle."[126] *The Laramie Project* is also compared to *Angels in America* in a number of reviews,[127] generally suggesting that they are both "portrait[s] of what America thought and felt at a particular moment."[128] That each play presents a portrait of the nation's views on LGBT citizens demonstrates the connections and distance between the two. While both represented young gay men in danger because of the country's negligent politics, *Angels in America* placed HIV/AIDS at the center of its representation of the gay community, while the disease is a side note in *The Laramie Project*'s discussion of hate crimes. Nevertheless, the media connection of the two plays shows this shift, and one sees in the coverage of *The Laramie Project* a dramatic change in the press reception of gay men with HIV/AIDS on the mainstream stage. *Angels in America*, however, was not the only U.S. canonical play to which *The Laramie Project* was often compared in its reviews.

Many of the reviews drew similarities between *The Laramie Project* and Thornton Wilder's *Our Town*, and this comparison between a depiction of a specific, western town to Wilder's fictional, "Everytown, USA," framed *The Laramie Project* as a synecdoche of the U.S. nation. In so doing, the reviews argued that *The Laramie Project* described the U.S. as a place where killing a gay man was not an anomaly—that the U.S. was, in fact, a place where people like Matthew Shepard were murdered regularly because of their sexuality. On the front page of the Entertainment section of the *New York Times*, Ben Brantley wrote that *The Laramie Project* "is *Our Town* with a question mark, as in 'Could this be our town?' There are repeated variations by the citizens of Laramie on the statement 'It can't happen here,' followed immediately by 'And yet it has.'"[129] Similarly, the *New York Post* reviewer states that, "What emerges [from *The Laramie Project*] is a small town, much like any other, one actually priding itself on what it perceives as its live-and-let-live tolerance,"[130] and the *Village Voice* review argues that Laramie "isn't a plague spot, only an average collection of human beings."[131] For these reviewers, *The Laramie Project* described a town like any other in the U.S., and that means this type of horrific anti-gay violence could occur in any U.S. town, as much as it might shock local sensibilities. In this way, the reviewers argued, perhaps unintentionally, that Laramie, as portrayed by the Tectonic Theatre Project, was a synecdoche of the U.S., as a town representative of the dominant ideology. The *New York Times* also specifically mentions a character described as a "feminist Muslim student" at Laramie's university who says that, "We are like this. We ARE like this. WE are LIKE this,"[132] emphasizing a connection to Shepard's killers rather than trying to create a distance from them. Finally, *Variety*'s review ends with the comment that "there is comfort to be found in the chorus of Laramie voices quietly mourning the loss of a boy they never knew, as well as the innocence of their town."[133] While this may sound specific to Laramie, the fact that the chorus of voices "never knew" Shepard though they are "quietly mourning" him is the same situation as that of the theatre spectator. So, too, then is the "loss of innocence" described in the review. While the play and reviews tend to directly address the topic of Laramie, they almost all explicitly or implicitly expand the *Our Town*-like qualities of *The Laramie Project* to the imagined community of the U.S. nation.

In fact, only two reviews resist this formulation. The most widely distributed was penned by the liberal John Heilpern in the *New York Observer*. He writes:

> So *The Laramie Project* is within the oral tradition that elicits the response, "I hear you!" Or as one of the more tolerant Laramie natives puts it: "As I always say, 'Do not fuck with a Wyoming queer.' Ah, those 'natives.' Bit of local color there, among the hicks and plain folk in *Our Town* cowboy country. Mr. Kaufman has made a tactical error, I think, in presenting the Laramie locals mostly in the guise of Thornton Wilder innocents and "characters." No doubt this is how they were pleased to present Laramie to him—"People are happy here." "A good place to live. Good people. Lots of space." "I love it here"—but was "our town" ever *Our Town* in the first place? This sentimental myth about community, caring and tolerance in middle America galls. It couldn't happen here? You bet it could. Laramie is just the sort of place the Shepard murder could happen. It did.[134]

This quote is particularly interesting because it resists the *Our Town* sentimentality embraced by the other reviews, but even more so because it completely misses an important line by the so-called "feminist Muslim student." She says of the candle vigil held in Laramie after Shepard's attack, "Someone got up there and said, 'C'mon, guys, let's show the world that Laramie is not this kind of a town.' But it is that kind of a town. If it wasn't this kind of a town, why did this happen here?"[135] In this line, one can see that the play directly contradicts Heilpern's suggestion of a naïve optimism about the goodness of the American Midwest.

As the reviews suggested that Laramie serves as a synecdoche for the nation as a whole, they also posited that the crime of killing Shepard had the power to expand the U.S. national imagination. They suggested that spectators *did* live in a country where this sort of crime could—and did—happen. But, with few exceptions, the reviews did not see the play as an attack on small-town America. In *USA Today*, Elysa Gardner opined, "There are surely some who expected *The Laramie Project* ... to be little more than an indictment of intolerant, narrow-minded values in small-town America. Those skeptics need only refer to a statement printed just below the cast list in the playbill, which dedicates the play to the people of Laramie as well as Shepard."[136] Gardner saw this dedication as a good-faith effort to present Laramie locals well, and, in so doing, she suggested that the Tectonic Theater Project defied expectations of urban theatregoers by including rural citizens of the U.S. in their cultural community. Gardner goes on to propose, "By presenting [Laramie's] residents as three-dimensional, usually well-intentioned folks who must suffer the consequences of the Shepard attack—most notably being cast as bigoted hicks by the reporters who descend on their town—Kaufman and company clearly seek to dispel the myth that people who live and talk a certain way are predisposed to the sort of prejudice and hatred manifest in such a vile act."[137] While Gardner explicitly indicated that *The Laramie Project* depicted supposed "hicks," her review implicitly argued that the rural characters and urban audiences were all citizens of the same nation where this sort of crime occurred. The spectators, in other words, like the residents of Laramie, had to deal with being a part of a U.S. where murderous hate crimes regularly happened, and the play's reviews represented the town and nation as conterminous.

Together these reviews worked to create a solidarity among the small-town residents of Laramie, the New York theatre-goers, and the national community of readers of the play's reviews, enveloping all of them into a new imagining of the U.S. community, one in which anti-gay violence had to be consciously admitted and addressed. The *New York Post* reported that the play represented "the puzzle of a crime that shocked even [Laramie's] most intolerant inhabitants."[138] That was certainly true, not just of Laramie, but of the residents of the United States who in editorials and political speeches stated again and again that no one—regardless of sexual orientation—deserved violence done against him or her. This was a moment when the emergent ideology that violence towards LGBT citizens was unacceptable was becoming part of the dominant ideology. The reviews of *The Laramie Project* in their historical context were a part of that ideological shift.

Epilogue

While *The Laramie Project* promoted the emergent ideology that LGBT citizens deserve the protection of law regardless of circumstances, and, in so doing, validated the humanity and citizenship of LGBT citizens, it did so utilizing the rhetoric of compassion. Compassion, tolerance, and mercy are the play's through lines, from its Christian undertones to Dennis Shepard's ultimate forgiveness of his son's killer. While this compassion validates Matthew Shepard's humanity and citizenship, it also "works to shore up relations of hierarchical power, between the bestower of compassion and the recipient, who must meet cultural designations of worthy suffering."[139] Thus, while Shepard—and his killers, for that matter—are represented as humans worthy of compassion in *The Laramie Project*, it is ultimately the accepted power structure that designates that worth: the judge, the law, and the straight, white, father figure who is also a stand-in for the Christian God. But compassion, while it can be used to strengthen the current dominant ideology, may also be used to challenge it. "Compassion across divides such as race and nation may upset these divisions and the social hierarchies they represent."[140] In this way, *The Laramie Project* worked towards shifting the dominant ideology in the United States away from the logic of the gay panic defense and towards a more equal representation for LGBT citizens under the law. Its use of compassionate rhetoric made it more palatable to a large, nation-wide audience. And it was effective at changing people's minds.

Unlike most pieces of political theatre, *The Laramie Project* has been demonstrated by psychologists and social scientists to have an effect on audiences. A longitudinal study performed at a public high school studied students' "homophobic attitudes" before and after a school production of *The Laramie Project* and an integrated curriculum in fine arts, humanities, science, and mathematics courses. It found that "a school-wide antihomophobia curriculum and performance of *The Laramie Project* provided measurable, sustained reductions in homophobic attitudes among students, even a year later, although girls attitudes changed sooner than boys."[141] Psychologists Anne Mulvey and Charlotte Mandell wrote an article on the efficacy of *The Laramie Project* simultaneously published in the *Journal of Gay & Lesbian Psychotherapy* and the anthology *Activism and LGBT Psychology*, edited by Judith M. Glassgold, and Jack Drescher, published by The Haworth Medical Press. This article, published in a medical context, argued that the play significantly reduced the "invisibility [that] occurs within heterosexist contexts and cultures that exclude, ridicule, or demonize individuals and groups based on alternative sexual identities or practices."[142] Finally, sociologists Anne René Elsbree and Penelope Wong utilized the play in a teacher-education curriculum and found a strong shift in self-reported attitudes towards LGBT citizens in the student teachers. In addition to a general increase in empathy and comfort addressing LGBT topics within the classroom, Elsbree and Wong reported that,

> In fact, students often commented about how unaware they were of the extent of homophobia in schools until after studying, reading, and discussing the issue. One secondary education student [teacher] noted: 'I often heard the terms 'faggot' and 'that's so gay' used when I was in high school, actually middle school, but I didn't think much about it because it didn't affect me. Now, after seeing the play and discussing this topic in class, I realize how serious the problem is and what I can do as a teacher to make the school climate safer for gay students.[143]

Studies like these demonstrated *The Laramie Project*'s ability in its contemporaneous moment to increase people's awareness of LGBT issues and to shift attitudes to a more compassionate place. While that compassion often came from a place of authority—teachers, in the last example—and reinforced a hierarchy because someone in power deigned LGBT people worthy of compassion, a teacher in middle school enforcing a ban on the word "faggot" in his or her classroom would nevertheless dramatically shift students away from heterosexist discourse.

This proven efficacy combined with the play's status of the second most produced play of the 2000–2001 season establishes that *The Laramie Project* was an important piece of culture for incorporating the emergent ideology of gay civil rights into the dominant ideology. It was mainstream, palatable, with an ability to change minds, and had an incredible reach. In fact, the play has remained in circulation well into its second decade of life. Its longevity and popularity are due in part to its minimal staging requirements and its popular 2002 HBO film adaptation. But *The Laramie Project*'s status as a successful mainstream play has given it the ability to continue to change minds, to help those in power, such as teachers, feel compassion for LGBT citizens and fight to prevent the type of heterosexism that led to Shepard's murder. While not radical in that the play does not push for a dismantling of contemporary society, the play is extremely successful in expanding the national imagined community to include LGBT citizens in a liberal, assimilationist sense. Therein lies its strength and the strength of the other case studies in *Making the Radical Palatable*.

Notes

1. Anonymous, "Fatal Shooting Follows Surprise on T.V. Talk Show," *New York Times*, 1 July, 1995.
2. Casey Charles, "Panic in *the Project*: Critical Queer Studies and the Matthew Shepard Murder," *Law and Literature* 18, no. 2 (2006): 234.
3. Ibid.

156   Normalization

4. Eve Kosofsky Sedgwick, *Epistemology of the Closet* (London: Harvester Wheatsheaf, 1991), 19.
5. Alisa Solomon, "Irony and Deeper Significance: Where Are the Plays?," *Theater* 31, no. 3 (2001); Roger Freeman, "Solving the *Laramie* Problem, or, Projecting onto *Laramie*," *Theatre Symposium* 15(2007); Stephen Wangh, "Revenge and Forgiveness in Laramie, Wyoming," *Psychoanalytic Dialogues* 15, no. 1 (2005); Jill Dolan, *Utopia in Performance: Finding Hope at the Theater* (Ann Arbor: U of Michigan P, 2005).
6. Elizabeth Saewyc and Sheila Marshall, "Reducing Homophobia in High School: The Effects of *the Laramie Project* Play and an Integrated Curriculum," *Journal of Adolescent Health* 48, no. 2 (2011); Anne Mulvey and Charlotte Mandell, "Using the Arts to Challenge Hate, Create Community: Laramie Lives in Lowell," *Journal of Gay & Lesbian Psychotherapy* 11, no. 3/4 (2007); Anne René Elsbree and Penelope Wong, "*The Laramie Project* as a Homophobic Disruption: How the Play Impacts Pre-Service Teachers' Preparation to Create Anti-Homophobic Schools," *Journal of Gay & Lesbian Issues in Education* 4, no. 4 (2007).
7. Kendall Thomas, "Beyond the Privacy Principle," *Columbia Law Review* 92, no. 6 (1992).
8. Bill Clinton, "Statement on the Attack on Matthew Shepard," Online from the Government Printing Office, www.gpo.gov.
9. "The Lesson of Matthew Shepard," *New York Times*, October 17 1998.
10. Ibid.
11. Ibid.
12. Frank Rich, "Summer of Mathew Shepard," ibid., July 3 1999.
13. Amy L. Tigner, "The Laramie Project: Western Pastoral," *Modern Drama* 45, no. 1 (2002): 138.
14. Ibid.
15. Beth Loffreda, *Losing Matt Shepard: Life and Politics in the Aftermath of Anti-Gay Murder* (New York: Columbia University Press, 2000), 14–15.
16. Romaine Patterson and Patrick Hinds, *The Whole World Was Watching: Living in the Light of Matthew Shepard*, 1st ed. (New York: Advocate Books, 2005), 146.
17. Melanie Thernstrom, "The Crucifixion of Matthew Shepard," *Vanity Fair*, March 1999.
18. Andrew Sullivan, "Afterlife," *New Republic* 6 (1999).
19. Thernstrom, "Crucifixion."
20. Loffreda, *Losing Matt Shepard: Life and Politics in the Aftermath of Anti-Gay Murder*, 26.
21. Thernstrom, "Crucifixion."
22. Loffreda, *Losing Matt Shepard: Life and Politics in the Aftermath of Anti-Gay Murder*, 34.
23. Moisés Kaufman, "Into the West: An Exploration in Form," *American Theatre* (2000): 17.
24. Linda Rapp and Claude J. Summers, "Moisés Kaufman (B. Ca 1964) GLBTQ: An Encyclopedia of Gay, Lesbian, Bisexual, Transgender, & Queer Culture.
25. Caridad Svich, "Moises Kaufman: 'Reconstructing History through Theatre'—an Interview," *Contemporary Theatre Review* 13, no. 3 (2003): 68.
26. "Moises Kaufman: 'Reconstructing History through Theatre'—an Interview," *Contemporary Theatre Review* 13, no. 3 (2003): 71.

27. "Moises Kaufman: 'Reconstructing History through Theatre'—an Interview," 72.
28. "Moises Kaufman: 'Reconstructing History through Theatre'—an Interview," 68.
29. "Moises Kaufman: 'Reconstructing History through Theatre'—an Interview," 71.
30. "Moises Kaufman: 'Reconstructing History through Theatre'—an Interview," 70.
31. Ibid.
32. Moisés Kaufman and Tectonic Theater Project., *The Laramie Project*, 1st Vintage Books ed. (New York: Vintage Books, 2001), 5.
33. Jay Baglia and Elissa Foster, "Performing the 'Really' Real: Cultural Criticism, Representation, and Commodification in *the Laramie Project*," *Journal of Dramatic Theory and Criticism* 19, no. 2 (2005): 133.
34. Rich Brown, "Moises Kaufman: The Copulation of Form and Content," *Theatre Topics* 15, no. 1 (2005): 54.
35. Ibid.
36. This similarity to film documentary would later lead to an easy adaptation of *The Laramie Project* from a play into an HBO film.
37. Kaufman and Tectonic Theater Project., *The Laramie Project*, 46.
38. Baglia and Foster, "Performing the 'Really' Real: Cultural Criticism, Representation, and Commodification in *the Laramie Project*," 136.
39. Robert Brustein, "The Staged Documentary," *The New Republic*, June 19 2000.
40. Freeman, "Solving Laramie," 107.
41. Dwight Conquergood, "Performing as a Moral Act: Ethical Dimensions of the Ethnography of Performance," *Text and Performance Quarterly* 5, no. 2 (1985): 9.
42. Diane Austin, "Community-Based Collaborative Team Ethnography: A Community-University-Agency Partnership," *Human Organization* 62, no. 2 (2003).
43. Steve Scott, "What Moral Order?: Observations from the Trenches," *Theatre Symposium* 15 (2007).
44. Scott, "What Moral Order?: Observations from the Trenches," 22.
45. Roger Freeman, "Solving the *Laramie* Problem, or, Projecting onto *Laramie*," ibid.: 110.
46. Tadeusz Kantor, *A Journey through Other Spaces: Essays and Manifestos, 1944–1990*, trans. Michal Kobialka (Berkeley: U of California P, 1993), 41.
47. Kaufman and Tectonic Theater Project., *The Laramie Project*, 36.
48. Ibid.
49. Ibid.
50. Kaufman and Tectonic, *The Laramie Project*, 37.
51. Kaufman and Tectonic, *The Laramie Project*, 38.
52. Kaufman and Tectonic, *The Laramie Project*, 53–54.
53. Kaufman and Tectonic, *The Laramie Project*, 55.
54. Kaufman and Tectonic, *The Laramie Project*, 86.
55. Kaufman and Tectonic, *The Laramie Project*, 12.
56. Kaufman and Tectonic, *The Laramie Project*, 19.
57. Kaufman and Tectonic, *The Laramie Project*, 20.
58. Kaufman and Tectonic, *The Laramie Project*, 57.
59. Kaufman and Tectonic, *The Laramie Project*, 78.
60. Kaufman and Tectonic, *The Laramie Project*, 79.
61. Wangh, "Revenge," 13.

62. The portrayal of Phelps and the Westboro Baptist Church is no worse than Phelps' own website. With the address of www.GodHatesFags.com, Phelps proclaimed an equal opportunity hatred. The site included a ticker tracking how many how many days Matthew Shepard had "been in hell," an account of the number of Jews "saved" during "these end days," and links to sister sites, such as www.JewsKilledJesus.com and www.PriestsRapeBoys.com.
63. Kaufman and Tectonic Theater Project., *The Laramie Project*, 85.
64. Kaufman and Tectonic, *The Laramie Project*, 98.
65. Kaufman and Tectonic, *The Laramie Project*, 98–99.
66. Wangh, "Revenge," 12.
67. Kaufman and Tectonic., *The Laramie Project*, 24.
68. Kaufman and Tectonic, *The Laramie Project*, 25.
69. Kaufman and Tectonic, *The Laramie Project*, 65.
70. Kaufman and Tectonic, *The Laramie Project*, 66.
71. Kaufman and Tectonic, *The Laramie Project*, 69.
72. Kaufman and Tectonic, *The Laramie Project*, 84.
73. Kaufman and Tectonic, *The Laramie Project*, 89.
74. Boone J. Hopkins, "Embodied Encounters: Ethics, Representation and Reiteration in Ten Years of *the Laramie Project*," *Performing Ethos* 2, no. 1 (2011): 14.
75. Kaufman and Tectonic Theater Project., *The Laramie Project*, 34.
76. Ibid.
77. Ibid.
78. Kaufman and Tectonic, *The Laramie Project*, 38.
79. Kaufman and Tectonic, *The Laramie Project*, 96.
80. Kaufman and Tectonic, *The Laramie Project*, 95.
81. Ibid.
82. Wangh, "Revenge," 2.
83. Wangh, "Revenge," 6.
84. Ibid.
85. Sandra Kiersky, "Revenge and Forgiveness in Psychoanalysis: Commentary on Stephen Wangh's 'Revenge and Forgiveness in Laramie, Wyoming'," ibid., no. 5: 773.
86. Dolan, *Utopia*, 120.
87. Kaufman and Tectonic, *The Laramie Project*, 46.
88. Wangh, "Revenge," 10.
89. Dolan, *Utopia*; Freeman, "Solving Laramie; Wangh, "Revenge; Alisa Solomon, "Irony and Deeper Significance: Where Are the Plays?," *Theater* 3, no. 1 (2001).
90. Solomon, "Irony and Deeper Significance: Where Are the Plays?."
91. Wangh, "Revenge," 10.
92. Wangh, "Revenge," 11.
93. Wangh, "Revenge," 13.
94. Wangh, "Revenge," 9.
95. Ibid.
96. Dolan, *Utopia*, 121.
97. Hannah Arendt, *The Human Condition* (Garden City, NY: Doubleday Anchor Books, 1959), 214–15.
98. "Religion," Gallup, http://www.gallup.com/poll/1690/religion.aspx.
99. Kaufman and Tectonic *The Laramie Project*, 30.
100. Kaufman and Tectonic, *The Laramie Project*, 31.

101. Ibid.
102. Ibid.
103. Ibid.
104. Kaufman and Tectonic, *The Laramie Project*, 58.
105. Ibid.
106. Ibid.
107. Kaufman and Tectonic, *The Laramie Project*, 59.
108. Kaufman and Tectonic, *The Laramie Project*, 91.
109. Ibid.
110. Ibid.
111. Loffreda, *Losing Matt Shepard: Life and Politics in the Aftermath of Anti-Gay Murder*, 136.
112. Sedgwick, *Epistemology of the Closet*, 19.
113. Loffreda, *Losing Matt Shepard: Life and Politics in the Aftermath of Anti-Gay Murder*, 136.
114. Kaufman and Tectonic, *The Laramie Project*, 91.
115. Clive Barnes, "Docudrama," *New York Post*, 11 June, 2000; John Heilpern, "A Vile Death in Laramie: Do Ask, Do Tell Why and How," *New York Observer*, 12 June, 2000; Charles Isherwood, "Hatred and America," *Variety*, 22 May, 2000.
116. Heilpern, "A Vile Death in Laramie: Do Ask, Do Tell Why and How."
117. Barnes, "Docudrama."
118. Ibid.
119. Isherwood, "Hatred and America."
120. Brustein, "The Staged Documentary."
121. Ben Brantley, "A Brutal Act Alters a Town," *New York Times*, May 19, 2000.
122. John Simon, "Broken Heartland," *New York*, 29 May, 2000.
123. Brustein, "The Staged Documentary; Isherwood, "Hatred and America; Brantley, "A Brutal Act Alters a Town; Linda Winer, "A High-Proile Murder in Low-Key Terms," *Newsday*, 19 May, 2000; Andrew Velez, "The Laramie Project (Review)," *HX Magazine*, 2 June, 2000; Michael Kuchwara, "The Laramie Project (Review)," *Associated Press Online*, 18 May, 2000.
124. Brustein, "The Staged Documentary; Artemis Furie, "The Laramie Project (Review)," *Show Business*, 31 May, 2000; Elysa Gardner, "Hateful Act Spurs Heartening 'Laramie'," *USA Today*, 19 May, 2000; Donald Lyons, ""The Laramie" a Project Well Worth Undertaking," *New York Post*, 19 May, 2000; Clifford Ridley, "Killing's Aftermath: Tectonic Company Indeed Says It Right," *The Philadelphia Inquirer*, 21 May, 2000; Dustin Smith, "Life after Death," *New York Blade*, 26 May, 2000; Michael Sommers, "Drama Delves into Soul of Town Struck by Tragedy," *The Star-Ledger*, 19 May, 2000.
125. Lyons, ""The Laramie" a Project Well Worth Undertaking."
126. Sy Syna, "'The Normal Hear' Offensive and Boring," *New York City Tribune*, April 22, 1985.
127. Brustein, "The Staged Documentary; Furie, "The Laramie Project (Review); Heilpern, "A Vile Death in Laramie: Do Ask, Do Tell Why and How; Kuchwara, "The Laramie Project (Review); Victor Gluck, "The Laramie Project (Review)," *Backstage*, 2 June, 2000.
128. "The Laramie Project (Review)."
129. Brantley, "A Brutal Act Alters a Town."

130. Barnes, "Docudrama."
131. Michael Feingold, "American Madness," *Village Voice*, 30 May, 2000.
132. Kaufman and Tectonic, *The Laramie Project*, 60.
133. Isherwood, "Hatred and America."
134. Heilpern, "A Vile Death in Laramie: Do Ask, Do Tell Why and How."
135. Kaufman and Tectonic, *The Laramie Project*, 59.
136. Gardner, "Hateful Act Spurs Heartening 'Laramie'."
137. Ibid.
138. Barnes, "Docudrama."
139. Jennifer Peterson, "Media as Sentimental Education: The Political Lessons of HBO's *the Laramie Project* and PBS's *Two Towns of Jasper*," *Critical Studies in Media Communication* 26, no. 3 (2009): 259.
140. Ibid.
141. Saewyc and Marshall, "Reducing Homophobia in High School: The Effects of *the Laramie Project* Play and an Integrated Curriculum," S111.
142. Mulvey and Mandell, "Using the Arts to Challenge Hate, Create Community: Laramie Lives in Lowell," 124.
143. Elsbree and Wong, "*The Laramie Project* as a Homophobic Disruption: How the Play Impacts Pre-Service Teachers' Preparation to Create Anti-Homophobic Schools," 104.

Bibliography

Anonymous. "Fatal Shooting Follows Surprise on T.V. Talk Show." *New York Times*, 1 July 1995. http://www.nytimes.com/1995/03/12/us/fatal-shooting-follows-surprise-on-tv-talk-show.html.

Arendt, Hannah. *The Human Condition*. Garden City, NY: Doubleday Anchor Books, 1959.

Austin, Diane. "Community-Based Collaborative Team Ethnography: A Community-University-Agency Partnership." *Human Organization* 62, no. 2 (2003): 143–52.

Baglia, Jay, and Elissa Foster. "Performing the 'Really' Real: Cultural Criticism, Representation, and Commodification in *the Laramie Project*." *Journal of Dramatic Theory and Criticism* 19, no. 2 (Spring 2005): 127–45.

Barnes, Clive. "Docudrama." *New York Post*, 11 June 2000, 28.

Brantley, Ben. "A Brutal Act Alters a Town." *New York Times*, 2000, E1, E4.

Brown, Rich. "Moises Kaufman: The Copulation of Form and Content." *Theatre Topics* 15, no. 1 (March 2005): 51–67.

Brustein, Robert. "The Staged Documentary." *The New Republic*, June 19 2000, 29–30.

Charles, Casey. "Panic in *the Project*: Critical Queer Studies and the Matthew Shepard Murder." *Law and Literature* 18, no. 2 (Summer 2006): 225–52.

Clinton, Bill. "Statement on the Attack on Matthew Shepard." Online from the Government Printing Office, http://www.gpo.gov.

Conquergood, Dwight. "Performing as a Moral Act: Ethical Dimensions of the Ethnography of Performance." *Text and Performance Quarterly* 5, no. 2 (1985): 1–13.

Dolan, Jill. *Utopia in Performance: Finding Hope at the Theater*. Ann Arbor: U of Michigan P, 2005.

Elsbree, Anne René, and Penelope Wong. "*The Laramie Project* as a Homophobic Disruption: How the Play Impacts Pre-Service Teachers' Preparation to Create

Anti-Homophobic Schools." *Journal of Gay & Lesbian Issues in Education* 4, no. 4 (2007): 97–117.
Feingold, Michael. "American Madness." *Village Voice*, 30 May 2000, 115.
Freeman, Roger. "Solving the *Laramie* Problem, or, Projecting onto *Laramie*." *Theatre Symposium* 15 (2007): 107–22.
Furie, Artemis. "The Laramie Project (Review)." *Show Business*, 31 May 2000, 24.
Gardner, Elysa. "Hateful Act Spurs Heartening 'Laramie'." *USA Today*, 19 May 2000, 5E.
Gluck, Victor. "The Laramie Project (Review)." *Backstage*, 2 June 2000, 56.
Heilpern, John. "A Vile Death in Laramie: Do Ask, Do Tell Why and How." *New York Observer*, 12 June, 2000.
Hopkins, Boone J. "Embodied Encounters: Ethics, Representation and Reiteration in Ten Years of *the Laramie Project*." *Performing Ethos* 2, no. 1 (2011): 5–20.
Isherwood, Charles. "Hatred and America." *Variety*, 22 May 2000, 37.
Kantor, Tadeusz. *A Journey through Other Spaces: Essays and Manifestos, 1944–1990*. Translated by Michal Kobialka. Berkeley: U of California P, 1993.
Kaufman, Moisés. "Into the West: An Exploration in Form." *American Theatre* (May/June 2000): 17–18.
Kaufman, Moisés, and Tectonic Theater Project. *The Laramie Project*. 1st Vintage Books ed. New York: Vintage Books, 2001.
Kiersky, Sandra. "Revenge and Forgiveness in Psychoanalysis: Commentary on Stephen Wangh's 'Revenge and Forgiveness in Laramie, Wyoming'." *Psychoanalytic Dialogues* 15, no. 5 (2005): 771–78.
Kuchwara, Michael. "The Laramie Project (Review)." *Associated Press Online*, 18 May, 2000.
"The Lesson of Matthew Shepard." *New York Times*, October 17, 1998.
Loffreda, Beth. *Losing Matt Shepard: Life and Politics in the Aftermath of Anti-Gay Murder*. New York: Columbia University Press, 2000.
Lyons, Donald. "'The Laramie' a Project Well Worth Undertaking." *New York Post*, 19 May, 2000, 57.
Mulvey, Anne, and Charlotte Mandell. "Using the Arts to Challenge Hate, Create Community: Laramie Lives in Lowell." *Journal of Gay & Lesbian Psychotherapy* 11, no. 3/4 (2007): 121–41.
Patterson, Romaine, and Patrick Hinds. *The Whole World Was Watching: Living in the Light of Matthew Shepard*. 1st ed. New York: Advocate Books, 2005.
Peterson, Jennifer. "Media as Sentimental Education: The Political Lessons of HBO's *the Laramie Project* and PBS's *Two Towns of Jasper*." *Critical Studies in Media Communication* 26, no. 3 (2009): 255–74.
Rapp, Linda, and Claude J. Summers. "Moisés Kaufman (B. Ca 1964) " GLBTQ: An Encyclopedia of Gay, Lesbian, Bisexual, Transgender, & Queer Culture. http://www.glbtqarchive.com/arts/kaufman_m_A.pdf
"Religion." Gallup, http://www.gallup.com/poll/1690/religion.aspx.
Rich, Frank. "Summer of Mathew Shepard." *New York Times*, July 3, 1999.
Ridley, Clifford. "Killing's Aftermath: Tectonic Company Indeed Says It Right." *The Philadelphia Inquirer*, 21 May, 2000, 104.
Saewyc, Elizabeth, and Sheila Marshall. "Reducing Homophobia in High School: The Effects of *the Laramie Project* Play and an Integrated Curriculum." *Journal of Adolescent Health* 48, no. 2 (2011): S111.
Scott, Steve. "What Moral Order?: Observations from the Trenches." *Theatre Symposium* 15 (2007): 20–28.

Sedgwick, Eve Kosofsky. *Epistemology of the Closet*. London: Harvester Wheatsheaf, 1991.
Simon, John. "Broken Heartland." *New York*, 29 May, 2000, 106.
Smith, Dustin. "Life after Death." *New York Blade*, 26 May 2000, 20.
Solomon, Alisa. "Irony and Deeper Significance: Where Are the Plays?" *Theater* 31, no. 3 (2001): 2–11.
Sommers, Michael. "Drama Delves into Soul of Town Struck by Tragedy." *The Star-Ledger*, 19 May 2000, 9.
Sullivan, Andrew. "Afterlife." *New Republic* 6 (November 22 1999).
Svich, Caridad. "Moises Kaufman: 'Reconstructing History through Theatre'—an Interview." *Contemporary Theatre Review* 13, no. 3 (2003): 67–72.
Syna, Sy. "'The Normal Hear' Offensive and Boring." *New York City Tribune*, April 22, 1985, 6B.
Thernstrom, Melanie. "The Crucifixion of Matthew Shepard." *Vanity Fair*, March 1999.
Thomas, Kendall. "Beyond the Privacy Principle." *Columbia Law Review* 92, no. 6 (1992): 1431–514.
Tigner, Amy L. "The Laramie Project: Western Pastoral." *Modern Drama* 45, no. 1 (Spring 2002): 138–56.
Velez, Andrew. "The Laramie Project (Review)." *HX Magazine*, 2 June 2000: 56.
Wangh, Stephen. "Revenge and Forgiveness in Laramie, Wyoming." *Psychoanalytic Dialogues* 15, no. 1 (2005): 1–16.
Winer, Linda. "A High-Proile Murder in Low-Key Terms." *Newsday*, 19 May, 2000, B2.

6 Conclusion
Does It Get Better?

After the Millennium

Making the Radical Palatable examines the interaction among mainstream HIV/AIDS theatre, the media, and the civil rights movement of LGBT citizens between 1985 and 2000. Because of mainstream theatre's commercialism and pride of place in the culture industry, its reach was wide and varied. Mainstream theatre's national span conveyed the culture industry's support of including LGBT citizens in the U.S. imagined community not just to theatre spectators, but to newspaper readers throughout the country via reviews. The increasing representation of LGBT people as U.S. citizens in mainstream theatre interacted with similar increased visibility in mainstream film, television, and national politics. Mainstream theatre, then, was able to be a part of a shift in the dominant ideology to include LGBT citizens in the U.S. national imaginary, taking more uncompromising views espoused as structures of feeling in radical performance, and making a more palatable, sellable product that nevertheless helped shift U.S. politics. Though it was only one actor among many, mainstream theatre worked in concert with radical performance, film, television, activism, judicial findings, and electoral politics to move LGBT citizens from social invisibility to, if not equality, at least part of the imagined community.

The book's methodology led to my fascination with reviews as archival evidence of the dominant ideology's acceptance or rejection of an emergent ideology in the contemporaneous moment. Tracing the shift in ideological reception from reviewers of all political stripes made visible ideological change over time regarding LGBT characters onstage and their status within the nation's imagined community offstage. But after the twentieth century, newspapers lost their dominance, at least in print, over consumers' understanding of current events. Instead, the Internet assumed the role of an immense polychoral and extremely ideologically diverse news outlet—though users were biased towards self-selection. While traditional newspapers still exist and still employ theatre critics in the twenty-first century, the response to plays by users of social media sites, blogs, and podcasts may count as much for archival evidence of a play's ideological reception. Does this, then, relegate the methodology of this book to the dustbin of history?

On the contrary, the increase in accessible commentary from spectators about everything from mainstream theatre to radical performance provides a correlative proliferation in data. Instead of several dozen print reviews, one now could assign oneself a seemingly endless task of gathering online responses to understand a broad spectrum of spectator responses to a single production. And, given the potential for a long string of arguments in online comments fields, a single online review and responses to it can now elucidate many varied ideological interpolations of one piece of art. Tracing ideological change over time by examining the reception of mainstream theatre—or any genre of performance, live or mediated—utilizing published receptions should be more thorough than ever.

Further, the influence of mainstream performance may be even greater 15 years into the twenty-first century than it was during the period of this study. The ability to stream most film, television, and even many theatrical performances onto any device with an Internet connection makes the penetration of the culture industry even more profound than it was at the end of the twentieth century. But the case studies of *Making the Radical Palatable* stayed primarily in twentieth century technology, even though each had a screen production by 2014. HBO produced made-for-television films of *The Laramie Project* (2002), *Angels in America* (2003), and *The Normal Heart* (2014), while *Rent* received a big-screen film release in 2005 distributed by Columbia Pictures. When released, each required paid access to a cable channel, a cinema, or, later, a DVD. This shift from the stage to television or cinema led to a wider dissemination of the work that is worth examining.

And, after examining the screen versions of this book's case studies, *Making the Radical Palatable* considers a final performance text, a use of the twenty-first century technological marvel, YouTube. This Internet site, on which anyone with a basic piece of equipment, such as a laptop or phone, can post films for public consumption, was used by journalist Dan Savage in 2010 for his groundbreaking project "It Gets Better." Originally, one video by Savage and his partner Terry Miller in response to several contemporaneous suicides by gay youth, the site now boasts over 50,000 videos that have been viewed more than 50,000,000 times. Some may suggest that Savage and Miller's original video stood as a radical DIY response to the plight of LGBT youth, but the "It Gets Better" project now boasts its own corporate sponsors, staff, social media sites, and website, separate from YouTube. If the original video was radical, which is unlikely, the culture industry nevertheless quickly coopted the project's message, shifting from advice given by an at-times controversial sex columnist to videos made by establishment figures as prominent in the dominant ideology as the President of the United States. Further, the project's corporate sponsorship, while providing videos and support without commercial interruption, places it squarely in the culture industry just like the "free" concerts of the NBC Symphony Orchestra directed by Arturo Toscanini in the 1930s alluded to in this book's first chapter. But as a finale, *Making the Radical* inspects the "It Gets Better" website in order to demonstrate ideological change over time in the U.S. culture industry between the early 1980s and 2015.

Stage to Screen(s), or A Brief History Over Time

In summer of 2014, walking around Times Square in New York City, some of the many images by which I was accosted were billboards featuring black and white photographs of the movie stars Mark Ruffalo or Julia Roberts alongside large, red text that read, "To Win a War You Have to Start One."[1] These were advertisements for HBO's then-upcoming made-for-television film of *The Normal Heart*. I was struck by the similarities between HBO's catchphrase and "War during Peacetime," the title I had been using in my writing about Larry Kramer's play for almost a decade. Then I realized that each text was utilizing ritual communication to try to (re)write history to include the story of gay men struggling against HIV/AIDS during the 1980s and using the word "war" in particular to underline the severity of the situation. Carey writes, "The archetypal case under a ritual view [of communication] is the sacred ceremony that draws persons together in fellowship and commonality."[2] By describing the 1985 premiere of *The Normal Heart* as a "war during peacetime," and by advertising the 2014 HBO film as featuring a hero that must "win a war" by starting one, each piece of discourse insisted that a war was fought in the U.S. during the 1980s, a war not recognized contemporaneously. By taking up *The Normal Heart* utilizing martial rhetoric decades after its theatrical premiere, both my writing and HBO's advertising sought to create a ritual space that drew the gay men suffering under HIV/AIDS in the early 1980s into "fellowship and commonality" with the U.S. imagined community. But HBO and I were not writing about gay men in the present. We were drawing gay men, many posthumously, into the U.S. nation's *historical* imagined community.

When each of the scripts from *Making the Radical Palatable* was adapted into films, its onscreen incarnation did similar work, highlighting and furthering the rhetoric and reception of their original theatrical productions but now as historical texts. Building on the mainstream success of the plays, the films were even more a part of the culture industry, allowing them to play a large part in defining the history of the 1980s and 1990s. The films starred big-name actors from Hollywood, employed brand-name directors, and expected a wide-reaching audience far beyond the comparably small numbers of people who see a theatrical production. This broad reception and participation of well-known figures carried the emergent ideology of LGBT civil rights and the history of the struggle for them even further into the culture industry, continuing the work of shifting LGBT citizens into the national imaginary begun by the plays, but now into the nation's memory of itself. While the plays tried to rewrite the present, the films attempted to rewrite the past.

The HBO film of *The Laramie Project* explicitly engaged in civic politics attempting to normalize gay men, and though produced in 2002 only four years after Shepard's death, it strove to keep Shepard's memory alive. Shepard works as a metonym for the many LGBT citizens killed because of their sexuality during that period, and the film's popularity only increased this commemoration. Part of the film's popularity, and the biggest difference between the play and the film, is that instead of employing a handful of actors, the film utilized a massive, star-studded cast. This showed audience members that a host of admired Hollywood actors acknowledged Shepard and other LGBT citizens, as worthy of protection under the law and found Shepard worthy of remembrance. Further, after the film aired on HBO, the network distributed DVDs of the work along with study guides to K-12 classrooms across the United States.[3] Jennifer Peterson examines these study guides and posits that they were primarily interested in shepherding students to an understanding of *The Laramie Project* through emotion and neoliberalism rather than exploring systemic oppression and structural change. This, then, suggests that the play and film both utilized compassion to address Shepard's death and citizenship, rather than the rhetoric of politics. Sympathetic to this approach yet holding strong reservations, Peterson suggests, "In doing so, [the study guide] also re-articulates the event of Matthew Shepard's death as an aberration within liberalism (and hence correctable within the system), rather than suggesting that the type of violence visited upon Matthew Shepard might have any origins in or links to the system and laws that we inhabit."[4] Thus, the film of *The Laramie Project* and its study guides, distributed to state-run education institutions, are not parts of a radical project suggesting the dismantling of state oppression. Instead, like the play, it opts for an assimilation of Shepard, and, by extension, other LGBT citizens into the extant legal system. Peterson ultimately finds that, "*The Laramie Project* aims to transform students into 'citizen-activists willing to stand up and speak out.'"[5] While not radical, this palatable message about acknowledging the citizenship of LGBT people is, nevertheless, extraordinary because of its location in public schools, one of Althusser's prime examples of a State Ideological Apparatus. Thus, the film of *The Laramie Project* continued to carry out the play's ability to "normalize" U.S. LGBT citizens and served as a reminder of violence carried out against a gay man a few years earlier.

Likewise, the film version of *Angels in America* continued the play's assimilation of gay men through its reception as canonical, that is to say "universal," art but also, as a depiction of 1985, the film, released in 2003, showed a world nearly 20 years gone and put gay men's struggles with HIV/AIDS at the center of U.S. history. *Angels in America*, like the film of *The Laramie Project*, utilized top-shelf talent, including Meryl Streep, Al Pacino, Jeffrey Wright, and Mary-Louise Parker, among others. Directed by Mike Nichols, famous for directing other canonical film adaptations of plays, such as *Who's Afraid of Virginia Woolf?*, the cast and director on their own made the case for the instant canonization of HBO's miniseries *Angels in America*. Just like the Broadway premiere production, the immediate canonization of the film came with critical acclaim in the form of reviews and prizes. *The New York Times* gushed, "There is so much to praise in Tony Kushner's Broadway masterpiece about the age of AIDS, and Mike Nichols' television version is a work of art in itself."[6] This success continued into one of the most important initial canonical gatekeepers: awards. Nichol's miniseries broke the Emmy record previously set by *Roots* (1977) with *Angels in America* earning 11 Emmys from 21 nominations. It also won five Golden Globes and was the most-watched for-cable film in 2003. All of this continued the work done by the Broadway premiere, suggesting that this massive epic about an ensemble of mainly gay men was not only mainstream but canonical and worthy of being deemed "universal" art rather than alternative or radical. The film and play have few differences, so the weaknesses—its sexism, classism, and racism—are again present, but they again make palatable the emergent ideology that gay men are worthy of citizenship. And, by depicting 1985 as a time when gay men's illness was a central, national concern, the film (re)wrote history so that gay men's contemporaneously ignored deaths were now part of the national imaginary of the United States.

The film version of *Rent* was the least successful of the four adaptations, perhaps because it tried too hard to recapture the lightning in the bottle of its premiere rather than truly create a stand-alone piece of art—perhaps also because the history it portrayed was more mythic than actual. That is, *Rent*'s 1996 East Village bohemia was a romanticized version of the starving artist life more than an historical account of HIV/AIDS. Thus, the film could add nothing to the historical imagined community, except an imprecise document of a popular Broadway play. Most of the original Broadway cast is in the film, and reviews record frequent complaints about the nine years between the premiere and the film's release making the cast too old. However, there may be an even more important failure in keeping the original cast mainly intact. Part of *Rent*'s success in 1996 was that the actors were "unknown," and thus the distance between actor and character was slight when each sang about the struggle of starving artists hoping to make it big. By 2005, many of the cast had successful careers independent of *Rent*, so seeing them as coterminous with their poor, unknown characters was difficult. Similarly, Larson's death, although still haunting at times while watching the film, did not have the dramatic immediacy that it did in 1996. The story that Larson died the night before his breakthrough play premiered is still rehashed in film reviews but no longer as a current event adding spectacle and danger to the experience. Larson's death is now more of a footnote. And, instead of praising the amalgamation of rock and musical theatre, as most reviews did in 1996, A.O. Scott, in *The New York Times*, writes, "Mr. Larson's attempt to force the marriage of rock and Broadway often sends the worst of both genres into noisy collision, as if Meat Loaf and Andrew Lloyd Webber were reworking 'Exile on Main Street.'"[7] Scott also suggests, "Precisely because some of the specific concerns of 'Rent' have become dated, the truth at its heart is clearer than ever. It is undeniably sentimental, but its sentimentality might serve as a balm to those of us, in New York and elsewhere, who sometimes find ourselves living in the long, tuneless sequel. Who would ever want to see a show called 'Mortgage'?"[8] In this sentence, Scott depicts *Rent* as "dated," perhaps because some of the medical realities of the 1990s were different in 2005—HIV/AIDS was no longer a death sentence, for example. However, *Angels in America* was not called dated, presumably because it depicted 1985 rather than a less specific "bohemian" time—*Angels in America* could be historical rather than dated. Regardless of its faults, however, *Rent* is still a "balm" for Scott who finds more interest in the "rent" of his youth than the "mortgage" of his middle-age. Scott's desire to feel young, then, relates back to the reactions related in reviews of *Rent*'s theatrical premiere that, even if one is not young and in danger, the play allowed spectators to experience those feelings. The film, though, due to a lack of excess meaning, danger, and spectacle in general, is less an experience of bohemia and danger and, instead, a documentary of one's, perhaps imagined, youth.

But *Rent* was never meant to be a documentary. *The Normal Heart* was. The first play of the book's case studies to be produced, it was the last to be turned into a film, perhaps because it was the least commercially successful of the four plays. However, once the play was turned into a film in 2014 on HBO, the network's advertising and the film's reception rehearsed the same discourse that surrounded the play in 1985: that *The Normal Heart* was historic, accurate, and more similar to activist journalism than literature or art. The *New York Times*, among other reviews, described the HBO film not as a "*j'acusse*" but as "a sort of documentary of recent history."[9] While the play—and film—have plenty of accusing to do, very quickly the advertising and reviews of the 1985 Public Theatre Production framed the play as documentary journalism. The marketing and reactions to the film version also suggested it was an historical record. Thus, *The Normal Heart* as both a play and film had a mix of art and activism beating inside it. The *New York Times* review of the film ends stating that, "Not all of these audiences are going to be comfortable with seeing a story about gay men, even three decades after AIDS first came to public consciousness. But that, perhaps, is part of the point of making this film at all. Just as those early alarm sounders warned, AIDS has turned out not to be exclusively a gay men's issue or something that the straight world could safely ignore."[10] In other words, even with the tremendous strides taken through representation of gay men in the culture industry and representational politics alike, there were still some U.S. citizens in 2014 who might "be uncomfortable" simply seeing gay men on the screen. Therefore, the film of *The Normal Heart* continued the play's work, crying out that gay men exist and cannot be ignored. But the film also works time in reverse. While the play more or less described a present-day crisis, the film stated that the gay men who struggled and, often, succumbed, to HIV/AIDS existed and could not be forgotten. *The Normal*

Heart, on stage and on screen, retained a similar message: to say that gay men were not alone, and to hope for a better future.

It Gets Better

"Motherfuckers," begins Dan Savage's hail of FOX59 News in Greensburg, Indiana, and its coverage of the suicide of 15-year-old Billy Lucas there in 2010.[11] Savage, a gay activist, media pundit, and journalist, was responding in an article for a Seattle newspaper to the bullying of Lucas that led to the young man killing himself. Lucas' peers harassed him daily with gay slurs and assaulted him mercilessly, both physically and emotionally, even though Lucas never self-identified as gay. Apparently, just being small and unpopular was enough for fellow high school students to drive Lucas to hang himself in his grandmother's barn. Shortly before his death, Lucas told his Mom, "You don't know what it's like to walk down the halls of school and be afraid of who's going to hit you, who's going to kick you."[12] Unfortunately, many people *do* understand from experience that type of societally approved high school abuse, and Dan Savage was one of them.

Nine days after Savage published his initial column about Lucas, a self-described "gay bullying survivor" wrote to Savage asking, "What the hell can we do?"[13] Before answering, Savage notes the heartless reality of America's ill-named "Heartland": "Nine out of 10 gay teenagers experience bullying and harassment at school, and gay teens are four times likelier to attempt suicide. Many LGBT kids who do kill themselves live in rural areas, exurbs, and suburban areas, places with no gay organizations or services for queer kids."[14] But Savage, a powerful voice in the U.S. mass media in 2010, had a practical suggestion for utilizing the free video sharing website YouTube.com to create an autoethnographic space to support LGBTQ[15] youth. Savage and his husband Terry Miller uploaded the first video in which the two spoke some of their bullying troubles in the Christian high schools they attended but mainly concentrated on their present lives with an adolescent son, loving extended family, and good careers. This was an illustration of both transmission and ritual communication. The video transmitted the information that, as its title suggests, "It Gets Better." The transmission of the information that life will not always be like high school was an attempt to control LGBTQ youth, to keep them from despair and self-harm. The video also created a ritual communication in which an adult life away from bullying, out of the closet, and in a loving same-sex relationship with offspring could be imagined. Thus, from a geographical distance, via the Internet, Savage and Miller attempted to utilize new technology to harness the archaic meanings inherent in communication: "'commonness,' 'communion,' 'community.'"[16] That is, Savage and Miller wanted to create a "'common faith'"[17] that life will improve for LGBTQ youth as they age. In his newspaper article introducing the "It Gets Better" YouTube.com page, Savage quoted Harvey Milk: "You gotta give 'em hope."[18] Savage also invited anyone—gay, straight, bi, young, old, whatever—to post a video encouraging those LGBTQ youth in despair to believe "It Gets Better." The response was overwhelming, creating a massive virtual community of which these heretofore isolated LGBTQ youths could now feel a part.

The sheer numbers of the videos uploaded, along with the high profiles of some of the initial posters, made the "It Gets Better" project an immediate cultural phenomenon that shifted the discourse around LGBT bullying. Within a week, 200 videos were posted, and in the second week the project hit YouTube.com's maximum number of 650 videos. The project then created its own website to house the videos, currently at about 50,000, that have been viewed more than 50 million times. The contemporaneous President of the United States, Barack Obama, Secretary of State, Hillary Clinton, and Speaker of the House of Representatives, Nancy Pelosi, all made videos. So did media personalities such as Tim Gunn, Ellen DeGeneres, Sarah Silverman, and Anne Hathaway. Even staffs of companies got involved, with ensemble-created videos made by the likes of The Gap, Google, Facebook, Pixar, and Broadway. This brings us full-circle back to the culture industry.

What made the "It Gets Better" project so successful was not just the number of videos, but the popularity of the celebrities and politicians making the videos. Also, the majority of videos from celebrities do not challenge major tenets of the U.S. dominant ideology. Savage and Miller's video, for instance, portrays them as an accomplished nuclear family, assimilating their lives into an image of recognizable success for the mainstream United States. Often a video was watched because of the personality rather than the message. For example, fans of the television show *Project Runway* might watch and share Tim Gunn's video, while fans of the film *Rachel Getting Married* could be excited about Anne Hathaway's involvement. Part of the project's message, then, was not just the medium, but the creators of the videos. Then comes the economics.

As mentioned, companies made videos, as did affiliations like Broadway, and currently the project has corporate sponsors, such as the U.S. multinational bank, Wells Fargo. While the videos were free to watch, and the stars and corporations made them without pay, remembering Horkheimer and Adorno's admonition that a concert on the radio uninterrupted by advertisements was, nevertheless, an advertisement in itself, suggests that this major media blitz was not without self-interest. The politicians, entertainers, and corporations that made the videos got publicity on the "It Gets Better" website, through social media sites on which fans could share the videos, and in these sites' comments sections. Likewise, while Wells Fargo may provide funds for the project's overhead and operating costs, the company logo emblazoned on the "It Gets Better" website provides the bank with publicity. It is important to note, however, that these people and companies in 2010 *wanted* the publicity of siding with LGBTQ youth. This is markedly different from 25 years prior. In 1985, the U.S. President felt it would be politically damaging to speak of an epidemic killing tens of thousands of gay citizens. In 2015, the U.S. President felt the need to address gay bullying that led to far fewer—though no less tragic—deaths. This variation in how U.S. presidents felt the need to address LGBT deaths demonstrates massive change in the dominant ideology over time.

The participation of national governmental figures, entertainment stars, and corporations in the "It Gets Better" project also shows the importance of the culture industry in shifting how the dominant ideology received LGBT deaths. Would the "It Gets Better" project have existed without Dan Savage's already popular, and profitable, syndicated sex-advice column? Would the videos have been viewed as many times if they did not feature beloved celebrities from the culture industry? Would companies have lent their support, either in the form of videos or sponsorship, if the videos were not part of the mainstream culture industry? Not likely. It is equally unlikely that the project would have been as successful if the videos advocated for a truly radical break with the dominant ideology. If, for instance, Savage and Miller presented themselves as a non-monogamous, non-reproductive, non-middle-class couple—or if they were classified racially or ethnically as other than "white"—would politicians, celebrities, and corporations have jumped to participate? Likely not. So was the "It Gets Better" project radical in the sense of challenging the basic structures of neo-liberal society? It was not. But it did create a new space in the U.S. national imaginary for LGBTQ youth, and likely saved children's lives. It created an amazing online community not in spite of its position in the culture industry—which, yes, probably kept it from a more radical position—but precisely because the videos were embraced by the culture industry. This position in the mainstream culture industry was *necessary* for Savage and his allies to have the chance to convince 50,000,000 viewers that their lives would get better.

But Does It Get Better, Really?

In 2013, near the birthplace of the modern LGBTQ civil rights movement, Mark Carson was called a "faggot" and "queer" and then shot and killed by Elliott Morales. Morales shot Carson dead near the Stonewall Inn in New York City. This was not an isolated incident in New York's Greenwich Village. *Slate* reports that in 2013, there were "nearly 60 reported assaults in the West Village ... nearly twice as many as occurred in the neighborhood over the same period [in 2012]. Perhaps even more troubling is that hate crimes appear to be on the upswing in New York City. According to the NYPD, there have been 22 bias-related crimes [in 2013], compared with only 13 during the same stretch in 2012."[19] How much progress, then, has really occurred since the LGBTQ uprising that took place in 1969 at the Stonewall Inn? Things did not get better for Mark Carson in his 32 years on Earth.

Inherent in the "It Gets Better" project, and in this book's structure, is a teleology of progress. In other words, both Savage's project and this book implicitly suggest that there is an onwards and upwards type of progress, a belief that, as *Angels in America* puts it, "The world only spins forward."[20] The title of the "It Gets Better" project obviously suggests an improvement over time, and the project's website also includes a "Timeline of How It's Gotten Better" citing LGBTQ activist wins throughout the world since 2010. Similarly, the chronological structure of this book suggests that over a 15-year period, LGBT citizens made strides in the U.S. culture industry, imagined community, and body politic. The victories are real, but progress is a slippery term. For every victory a loss could also be cited, especially the loss of LGBTQ citizens' lives.

One might read *Making the Radical Palatable* and feel that the final case study ends on an optimistic note: *The Laramie Project* invalidates the gay panic defense, normalizes LGBT citizens, and proves successful at creating tolerance in audiences. But hate crimes did not end after 2000. In fact, Baglia and Foster criticize *The Laramie Project*, arguing that, "Despite the widespread consumption of Shepard's fate—through multiple productions of the play as well as the HBO and NBC productions—the widespread rejection of gay rights, evidenced by the voters in the 2004 election, indicates that there has not been any awakening of the national conscience."[21] They refer, here, to the re-election of U.S. President George W. Bush whose 2004 campaign included support of the proposed Federal Marriage Amendment that would have defined marriage in the U.S. as between one man and one woman. Bush also threatened to veto the Matthew Shepard and James Byrd, Jr. Hate Crimes Act. Bush's election, clearly, was a blow to LGBT civil rights, even though the Federal Marriage Amendment did not come to fruition and the Matthew Shepard and James Byrd, Jr. Hate Crimes Act was ratified in 2009 after Bush left office. But the LGBT civil rights losses during the Bush years do not overwrite the victories. For instance, while Bush campaigned against gay marriage, the fact that it was an issue at all—that LGBT citizens were so much a part of the U.S. imagined community that they had to be commented on—was a victory in representation. How could a young man believe he was the only gay person in the U.S., as a character in *The Normal Heart* did, if the presidential campaign addressed issues relating to others with his sexuality? The move from social invisibility to social visibility was a huge victory that Bush's re-election did not dampen. However, it is more accurate to describe this success as *change* rather than *progress*.

In any society, there is radical uncertainty, and for every victory a civil rights movement has, there could be subsequent, or concurrent, failures. Returning to the Frankfurt School briefly, one day Benjamin woke up to find that he was no longer a citizen of any country, and France imprisoned him as a stateless man. Horkheimer and Adorno were lucky enough to survive the war, but the Nazi rise to power, and its subsequent defeat, destroyed the country they knew. This type of radical change could occur to any country, at any time, via natural disaster, war, or extreme political shifts. Though the human mind finds solace in stability—in believing tomorrow will be much like today with milk for sale in the grocery store and a passport that works—such feelings are false. Likewise, political beliefs based on progress or decline ignore the nuance of history. In Benjamin's magisterial, incomplete final work, *The Arcades Project*, he writes, "Overcoming the concept of 'progress' and overcoming the concept of 'period of decline' are two sides of one and the same thing."[22] Every period has contradictory elements. As Walmsley demonstrated discussing the 2015 Gay Pride celebrations in New York City, even a seemingly straightforward victory like the right for same sex couples to marry has within it a hidden failure to address the poor, marginalized members of the community whose struggles are for survival rather than for legal recognition of a stable relationship. But if history is built up of present moments of frightening uncertainty, this means that change is not only possible, but inevitable.

Therefore, as change is the one constant in history, overdetermined views on politics, whether conservative or liberal, pessimistic or optimistic, are incorrect. They are compelling because they allow a false sense of stability, a false prognosis of the future. The arc of history does not bend in any direction. There is no natural progress of material conditions. There is no innate, ideal past to which we must strive to return. There is no right conferred that cannot be revoked. There is no blessing that is not also a curse. Examining the politics within a few of the major mainstream plays to take HIV/AIDS as a topic in the 1980s and 1990s shows how they embodied contradictory politics within the culture industry that, ultimately, forwarded some aspects of an emergent ideology while simultaneously supporting elements of the dominant ideology. Despite the importance of radical performance and its contributions to structures of feeling, mainstream theatre performs the nation—or parts of the nation—before our eyes. Its spectators decode it in complex ways, which must be taken into account when attempting to understand the national imaginary. And consumers are increasingly speaking back and becoming producers of discourse in social media that is, in itself, a curious mix of the public and private spheres. Whether Internet users generate a homophobic comment under a review of *The Laramie Project* or create a video for the massive user-made "It Gets Better" project, the mainstream is increasingly dispersed and, to some degree, participatory. But, wherever the LGBTQ community is now portrayed in mainstream culture, some of its most important roots are in the mainstream HIV/AIDS theatre of the 1980s and 1990s during which its interaction with the media re-imagined the U.S. nation.

Notes

1. HBO, "Normal Heart Julia Roberts Poster," http://www.gstatic.com/tv/thumb/movieposters/9695572/p9695572_p_v7_aa.jpg.
2. James W. Carey, *Communication as Culture: Essays on Media and Society* (Boston: Unwin Hyman, 1989), 15.

3. Jennifer Peterson, "Media as Sentimental Education: The Political Lessons of HBO's *the Laramie Project* and PBS's *Two Towns of Jasper*," *Critical Studies in Media Communication* 26, no. 3 (2009): 255.
4. Peterson, "Media as Sentimental Education," 263.
5. Peterson, "Media as Sentimental Education," 258.
6. Anita Gates, "Critic's Choice; Movies," *New York Times*, 17 April, 2005.
7. A.O. Scott, "New Tenants in Tinseltown," ibid., 23 November.
8. Ibid.
9. Neil Genzlinger, "Raging Amid Tears in a Gathering Storm," ibid., 22 May, 2014.
10. Ibid.
11. Dan Savage, "Bullied Gay Teenager Commits Suicide—Will His Tormentors Face Charges?," *The Stranger*, 14 September, 2010.
12. LGBTQNation.com, "Remembering Billy Lucas, the Boy Whose Suicide Inspired a Movement," http://www.lgbtqnation.com/2013/09/remembering-billy-lucas-the-boy-whose-suicide-inspired-a-movement/.
13. Dan Savage, "Give 'Em Hope," *The Stranger*, 23 September, 2010.
14. Ibid.
15. Throughout my discussion of this book's plays I utilized LGBT because the plays mainly ignored a "queer" sexuality beyond lesbian, gay, bi-sexual, and transgender. However, the "It Gets Better" project is more comprehensive, and, hence, I have expanded the acronym for this section to LGBTQ.
16. Carey, *Communication as Culture*, 15.
17. Ibid.
18. Savage, "Give 'Em Hope."
19. Josh Voorhees, "Hate Crime in Greenwich Village: 'Do You Want to Die Right Now?'"
20. Tony Kushner, *Angels in America: A Gay Fantasia on National Themes, Part Two: Perestroika* (New York: Theatre Communications Group, 1993), 147.
21. Jay Baglia and Elissa Foster, "Performing the 'Really' Real," 141.
22. Walter Benjamin, *The Arcades Project*, trans. Howard Eiland and Kevin McLaughlin (Cambridge, MA: Belknap P of Harvard UP, 1999), 460.

Bibliography

Baglia, Jay, and Elissa Foster. "Performing the 'Really' Real: Cultural Criticism, Representation, and Commodification in *the Laramie Project*." *Journal of Dramatic Theory and Criticism* 19, no. 2 (Spring 2005): 127–45.

Benjamin, Walter. *The Arcades Project*. Translated by Howard Eiland and Kevin McLaughlin. Cambridge, MA: Belknap P of Harvard UP, 1999.

Carey, James W. *Communication as Culture: Essays on Media and Society*. Boston: Unwin Hyman, 1989.

Gates, Anita. "Critic's Choice; Movies." *New York Times*, 17 April, 2005.

Genzlinger, Neil. "Raging Amid Tears in a Gathering Storm." *New York Times*, 22 May, 2014.

HBO. "Normal Heart Julia Roberts Poster." http://www.gstatic.com/tv/thumb/movieposters/9695572/p9695572_p_v7_aa.jpg.

Kushner, Tony. *Angels in America: A Gay Fantasia on National Themes, Part Two: Perestroika*. New York: Theatre Communications Group, 1993.

LGBTQNation.com. "Remembering Billy Lucas, the Boy Whose Suicide Inspired a Movement." http://www.lgbtqnation.com/2013/09/remembering-billy-lucas-the-boy-whose-suicide-inspired-a-movement/.

Peterson, Jennifer. "Media as Sentimental Education: The Political Lessons of HBO's *the Laramie Project* and PBS's *Two Towns of Jasper*." *Critical Studies in Media Communication* 26, no. 3 (2009): 255–74.

Savage, Dan. "Bullied Gay Teenager Commits Suicide—Will His Tormentors Face Charges?" *The Stranger*, 14 September 2010.

———. "Give 'Em Hope." *The Stranger*, 23 September 2010.

Scott, A.O. "New Tenants in Tinseltown." *New York Times*, 23 November, 2005.

Voorhees, Josh. "Hate Crime in Greenwich Village: 'Do You Want to Die Right Now?'" Slate, http://www.slate.com/blogs/the_slatest/2013/05/20/mark_carson_west_village_hate_crime_elliot_morales_charged_with_hate_crime.html.

Index

absorption 45
activism 37
Activism and LGBT Psychology 154
actor, audience and 45–6
actor network theory 8, 23
Acts of Intervention (Román) 2, 37–8
Adorno, Theodor 13, 18, 170, 172; *Dialectic of Enlightenment* 6, 7, 18–21
advertising campaigns 16; *see also specific plays*
The Advocate 63, 100, 115, 117
African American civil rights movement 2–3
African American theatre 2–3
agent-network theory; *see* actor network theory
AIDS fundraisers 2
AIDS Medical Foundation 35, 38
A.I.D.S. Show Collaborators 33
Aiken, George 111, 117–18
Akalaitis, JoAnne 65
Akropolis (Growtowski) 132
alienation 40–1, 45, 46
alternative theatre 17
Althusser, Louis 6, 7, 13, 21–2, 137, 166
Amedure, Scott 125
American Spectator 84–6
Anderson, Benedict 7–8, 13, 18, 25, 60–1, 81; *Imagined Communities* 23–4
And the Band Played On (Shilts) 32, 33, 52, 53n6
angels, symbolism of 78–80
Angels in America: A Gay Fantasia on National Themes (Kushner) 4–5, 133, 139, 151, 167; academia and 80–1; activism and 86–7; advertising campaigns 60, 65, 66–8; alienation and 69; angels in 80–1, 140; artistic and economic expectations of 64–5, 83; artistic merit of 64, 82–6; as art rather than propaganda 60, 65, 82, 86–7; assimilationist vision of 60–96, 90n62, 167; awards 62, 64, 65, 67, 84, 86, 88n18, 167; as beacon for gay civil rights 60, 62, 63, 64, 65–70, 83; Benjamin and 80–1; Brechtian elements of 69, 86–7; Broadway premiere of 60–3; Broadway production of 9, 65, 66–7, 68, 69, 70, 81; canonization of 80–1, 82, 86; change of venue 64–5; in Charlotte, North Carolina 116–17; as "classical" art 82–3; class in 61; Clinton campaign and 61–2, 65, 70–3, 76, 80; commercial success of 64, 86; compared to opera 82–3; conservative aspects of 61; consumerism and 66, 70; conversion of horror into maternal comfort 67–8; criticism of Reagan Administration 65; cross-casting in 75; cultural milieu of 65–70; culture industry and 60–1, 64, 65, 67, 80, 87; design of 80; dominant ideology and 60–1, 80; drag in 75–6; economics in 72; as embodiment of Benjamin's theory of history 80–1; epilogue of 87n13; femininity in 75–8; gay civil rights and 5, 83; gender in 61, 75–8; hailed by the press as mainstream 81–2; HBO film production of 164, 166–7, 168; HBO miniseries 81; historical context of 60–1, 63; ideological fluctuation in 71; institutional support for 81; LGBT citizenship and 78–86; LGBT citizenship in 63–4; location of 65, 66–7; London production of 62, 65; Los Angeles production of 61–2, 65;

mainstream status of 60, 66–7; Mark Taper Forum premiere of 61–2; the media and 64, 80–2, 86, 118; merchandising and 65, 70, 80, 86; "minority" characters in 68; *mise-en-scène* 65; mixed reactions to 86; NEA grant and 68; New Democrat movement and 70–3; *The New York Times* and 67, 82–3, 167; "old values" in 72; opening monologue of 72; optimism of 4–5, 78–80; path to Broadway 81; political implications of 83, 84–6; pre-Broadway honors of 64; production costs of 64; production schedule 64–5; program note 66, 67–8, 68, 80; progress and 78–81; race in 61, 72, 80; reception of 60–5, 86, 88n18, 88n19; reviews of 9, 60, 62, 64, 67, 69, 81–6, 88n19, 116, 118; reviews of film version 167, 168; rewriting of history in film version 167; San Francisco production of 65; scholarship on 80–1; spectators of 62, 83; split screens and 69; subtitle of 72; success of 64–5, 86; symbolism of angels and 78–80; textual content of 66; ticket prices 62, 64, 86; Tony Award nominations 67; as transition between structure of feeling and emergent ideology 61; as "universal" 81, 84–5, 86, 87, 167; U.S. government financial support and 68; utopianism of 4–5, 62, 72–3, 80; as vehicle of socialization 4–5; women in 75–8, 80, 87; Yale Kramer's artistic and political rejection of 84–6
anti-gay violence 127–37, 147–54, 172
Approaching the Millennium (Geis and Kruger) 81
appropriation 99–100, 105
The Arcades Project (Benjamin) 173
architecture 16
Arendt, Hannah 147
art: ideologies and 21–2; mainstream 18; self-definition in 15
Arts and Science Council 116
As Is (Hoffman) 2, 34
assimilation process 3–5, 14–15, 24–5, 26, 90n62
audience, actor and 45–6
Auslander, Philip 12n13
Austin, Diane E., "Community-Based Collaborative Team Ethnography: A Community-University-Agency Partnership" 136
authority, obedience to 19, 28n16
awards: local 16; national 16

Baglia, Jay 134, 135, 172
Baptist Church 142, 143, 144
Barnes, Clive 49
Bash 128
Beirn, Terry 35
Bell, John 102
Benjamin, Walter 13, 18, 19, 26, 172; *The Arcades Project* 173; "Theses on the Philosophy of History" 80–1
Bennett, Susan 7–8, 12n13
Bergman, David 12n13, 42
Bernstein, Leonard 34
Birmingham School 6, 7–8, 18, 19–20
Black Arts Movement 3
Blau, Herbert 12n13
blogs 163
Blumenthal Center for the Performing Arts 116
La Bohème 98, 111, 119
Botcharova, Olga 147
Botnick, Victor 48
Bourdieu, Pierre, *Distinction* 83
Boys Don't Cry 128–9
Brantley, Ben 103–4, 152
Brecht, Berthold 44, 45
Broadway 68, 170; *see also specific productions*
Brody, Jennifer Devere 12n13
Brook, Peter 131
Browning, Christopher 19
Brustein, Robert 64, 65, 82, 135
Buck-Morss, Susan 13
Bull, John 12n13
bullying 169–70
Bush, George H.W. 63, 87n13
Bush, George W. 172
Bush Administration (George H.W.) 60, 61, 71, 87n13, 136–7
Business Improvement Districts (BIDs) 102, 133
Butler, Judith 75–6

Cadden, Michael 12n13, 90n62
California 51
Callen, Michael, *How To Have Sex in an Epidemic: One Approach* 44
canonization 81
Cantway, Dr. 144–5
capitalism 4, 15, 17, 18–19, 26

Caracas, Venezuela 131–2
Carey, James 6, 7, 13, 18, 23, 25, 26, 165; *Communication and Culture* 24–5
Carlson, Marvin 12n13, 108
Carson, Mark 171
case studies 5–6, 8, 22, 23, 164; *see also specific plays*
Catholic Church 141–4
Causy, Matthew 17
CBS 36
celebrities 170; *see also specific celebrities*
Centers for Disease Control (CDC) 33, 35, 36, 38, 41
Central Park 35
Charles, Casey, *Law and Literature* 126
Charlotte, North Carolina 98, 113, 115–17, 119; Chamber of Commerce in 116–17
Charlotte Magazine 117
Chesley, Robert 33
Chicago, Illinois 16
The Christian Science Monitor 49–50, 56–7n90, 83–4, 86
Citibank 36
citizenship 19, 24; *see also* LGBT citizens; LGBT civil rights
classical music 100
Clay, Paul 103
Clinton, Bill 21, 64, 70–3, 79; 1991 keynote address at Democratic Leadership Council (DLC) conference 71–2; assimilationist campaign promises 61, 71–2; "Don't Ask, Don't Tell" policy 63; economics and 72; election as symbolic of dominant ideology's increased support for LGBT rights 63; election of 60, 63, 65, 73; hate crimes legislation and 126, 127–8; inclusiveness and 72; increase of HIV/AIDS funding by 80; presidential campaign of 61–2, 65, 70–3, 76; promise to overturn military ban on military service by LGBT citizens 72–3; race and 72; speech at Macomb County Community College 72; speech at Pleasant Grove Baptist Church 72; utopianism of 72–3
Clinton, Hillary 76, 170
Clinton Administration (Bill) 10, 73, 79
Clum, John 12n13, 42, 43, 44

Cohn, Roy 63, 66, 69, 73–4, 87–8n14, 90n62
Cold War, end of 72
Columbia Law Review 127
Columbia Pictures 164, 167–8
commercialism 7, 11, 26, 32, 97–124, 163
communication: mass communication 18, 23; *see also* mass media; ritual communication 10–11, 24–5, 52; transmission view of 6
Communication and Culture (Carey) 24–5
conditions of production 16
condom use 44
Conquergood, Dwight 12n13, 136
consumerism 4, 39–40, 66
corporations 170–1
counterculture 98
Cox, J. Robert 46, 61
cultural appropriation 99–100, 105
cultural politics, performance and 17
cultural studies 12n13
culture industry 3–5, 10–11, 15–21, 26, 163, 170, 173; *Angels in America* (Kushner) and 60–1, 64, 65, 67, 80, 87; as changeable 26; conservative 4; dominant ideology and 18–21, 171; film adaptations and 165; liberal potential of 32; mainstream theatre and 26; *The Normal Heart* (Kramer) and 50; penetration of 164; prejudice towards 6–7
Curran, James 38

Daily News 114
Davis, Tracy C. 12n13
Davy, Kate 12n13
Dead Class (Kantor) 134
DeGeneres, Ellen 170
De Jongh, Nicholas 12n13
Denver, Colorado, production of *The Laramie Project* in 133
Dialectic of Enlightenment (Horkheimer and Adorno) 6, 7, 18–21
Diamond, Elin 12n13, 17
Distinction (Bourdieu) 83
Dolan, Jill 12n13, 62, 80, 146, 147
Doll's House (Ibsen) 77
Donahue 36
"Don't Ask, Don't Tell" policy 63
drag 75–6
Drescher, Jack 154

Durkheim, Emile, *Elementary Forms of Religious Life* 24

Eagleton, Terry 13, 18–19, 21; *Ideology: An Introduction* 21–2
Edelstein, Gordon 104
Eichmann, Adolf, trial of 28n16
Elementary Forms of Religious Life (Durkheim) 24
Ellen 128
Elsbree, Anne René 154–5
An Enemy of the People (Ibsen) 48–9
Enlightenment 15
Equity theatre 16
Eureka Theatre 65
Eustis, Oskar 65, 68

Facebook 170
Federal Marriage Amendment (proposed) 172
Feingold, Michael 48–9
Feldstein, Mark 56–7n90
Fettner, Anne Giudici 45
film adaptations 11, 165–9; *see also specific plays*
Finley, Karen 89n36
the Fireside 147–8
Fischer-Lichte, Erika 13
Fisher, James 12n13
Fleck, John 89n36
Fluty, Reggie 138–9, 151
Fondakowski, Leigh 144, 146
formalism 19–20
Foster, Elissa 134, 135, 172
Foster, Emmett 34–5
FOX59 News 169
Frankfurt School 6, 7, 15, 17–21, 24, 32, 172
Frantzen, Allen J. 12n13
Freeman, Roger 135, 137
From Caligari to Hitler 19

The Gap 170
Gardner, Elysa 153
gay civil rights; *see* LGBT civil rights
"gay lifestyle" 23, 34, 37, 43–4, 50, 106, 140, 143, 151
gay marriage; *see* marriage equality
gay men; *see* LGBT citizens
Gay Men's Health Crisis (GMHC) 9, 34–5, 37, 38, 47
"gay panic defense" 10, 125, 126, 147–9, 154, 172
Gay Pride 2015 14, 173

Geertz, Clifford 13, 15, 86
Geffen Records 115
Geis, Deborah 12n13; *Approaching the Millennium* 81
Gelb, Arthur 36–7
gender 75–8, 80, 87
Gerard, Jeremy 82
Glassgold, Judith M. 154
Goodman, Lizbeth 12n13
Google 170
Gottlieb, Michael 51
Gray, Carroll 116–17
Greensburg, Indiana 169
Greenwich Village 39, 40, 85, 98, 99, 102, 103, 171
Grey, Joel 45
Gronich, Amanda 142, 143
Gross, Gregory 40, 41, 45
Gross Indecency: The Three Trials of Oscar Wilde 132–3
Grotowski, Jerzy 131; *Akropolis* 132
Guillory, John 81
Gunn, Tim 170
Gussow, Mel 48

Habermas, Jürgen 23, 24–5, 26
Hagedorn, Jeff 33
Hair 103, 112
Hall, Stuart 6, 13, 19–20, 23
Hamburg, Victoria 35
Hanks, Tom 130
Hansberry, Lorraine, *Raisin in the Sun* 3
Harlem Renaissance theatre 2–3
Hart, Bill 46
hate crimes; *see* anti-gay violence
hate crimes legislation 10, 125, 126, 127–8, 172
"Hate Crimes Prevention Act" 127
Hathaway, Anne 170
HBO 81, 155, 157n36, 164, 165, 166–7, 168–9, 172
Health Department 36
Heilpern, John 60, 150, 152–3
Helms, Jesse 68
Henderson, Russell 125, 130, 140, 141, 143, 144, 147–8
Herbst, Susan 13
Heredia, Wilson Jermaine 109
Heyman, Steve 129
historical change 172–4
Hitler, Adolf 18–20
HIV/AIDS epidemic 1–3, 19, 21, 23–6, 60, 147, 165, 170–1; *see also Angels*

in America: A Gay Fantasia on National Themes (Kushner); *see also The Normal Heart* (Kramer); Clinton Administration's increase of funding for 80; commercialization of 3, 5, 9, 105; condom use and 44; declaration of HIV as epidemic 8, 35; dominant ideology and 36; dominant ideology's blindness to 33–4, 46; government inaction during Reagan and Bush Administrations 136–7; historical change and 168; hysteria about 50; knowledge of 54n28; *The Laramie Project* (Kaufman) and 130, 136–7, 151; media coverage of 32, 51–2; media response to 33–5; mismanagement of 34; portrayal of heterosexual characters with HIV/AIDS in *Rent* 118; public recognition of 32; Reagan Administration and 71; Reagan's acknowledgment of 33; *Rent* (Larson) and 9–10, 106, 109–11, 118; representation of 3; rhetoric of "murder" of gay men by Reagan and Bush Administrations and 136; Shepard's murder and 128; shift in ideology and 21; silence about 33–7, 61; war metaphors and 52; writing on 52

HIV/AIDs epidemic, *Rent* (Larson) and 9–10, 105, 106, 109–11, 118

HIV/AIDS theatre 2, 6, 163; the media and 173; as negotiating force between emergent and dominant ideologies 173; in New York 5; popularity of 3; role in transforming dominant ideology 173; studies of 12n13

Hoffman, William, *As Is* 34

Holderness, Graham 12n13

Holdsworth, Nadine 13, 25; *Theatre and National Identity: Re-Imagining Conceptions of Nation* 24

Holland, Bernard 114

Horkheimer, Max 13, 170, 172; *Dialectic of Enlightenment* 6, 7, 18–21

How To Have Sex in an Epidemic: One Approach (Callen) 44

Hudson, Rock 37, 51–2

Huffington Post 14

Hughes, Amy E. 12n13, 105, 107, 108, 109, 117

Hughes, Holly 89n36

Hughes, Langston, 1935 production of *Mulatto* 2–3

Human Rights Campaign (HRC) 127

Ibsen, Henrik: *Doll's House* 77; *An Enemy of the People* 48–9

ideologies 7, 15, 21–2; in *Angels in America* 71; art and 21–2; changes in 5; competing 6; contestation of 26; definition of 18; definitions of 21–2; dominant 2–6, 9, 11, 16–22, 26, 32, 163–4; emergent 2–4, 6, 9, 16, 22, 26, 32, 61, 163–4; explanations of usage in this book 21–2; ideological positions 22; ideological reception 163–4; as lens 21; mainstream theatre as negotiating force between 32; radical 3–4; residual 6, 22; spectatorship and 15–16; transformation of 5–6, 11, 16; transmission of 19–20; venues and 2; Williams' three aspects of 22; in World War II 19

Ideology: An Introduction (Eagleton) 21–2

imagined communities 23–4, 64, 69–70, 72, 163, 172; *see also* U.S. national imaginary

Imagined Communities (Anderson) 23–4

inclusion 60–1, 72

the Internet 163, 173

interpellation 6, 9, 21–2, 39

Isherwood, Charles 115, 150

"It Gets Better" campaign 11, 164, 169–73

Ivosky, Fernando 131

Jenkins, Speight 82–3

The Jenny Jones Show 125

Joel, Billy 100

John, Elton 100

Johnson, Richard 13

journalism 7, 25

Journal of American Culture 78

Journal of Gay & Lesbian Psychotherapy 154

A Journey through Other Spaces (Kantor) 138

Jujamcyn Theatres 65, 67, 70

juxtaposition 132, 138

Kantor, Tadeusz 131–2; *Dead Class* 134; *A Journey through Other Spaces* 138

Kaufman, Moisés 125–62; background of 131–2; decision to write about Shepard's murder 130–1; *The Laramie Project* 5, 10–11; membership in multiple communities 131–2, 136; use of juxtaposition 132
Keaton, Buster, *Steamboat Willie* 105
Keebler, Hiram 36
Kershaw, Baz 4, 12n13, 15, 16, 39, 70, 105
Kiersky, Sandra 145–6
Kinzer, Craig 45
Kirkpatrick, Jeane 63
Kirshenblatt-Gimblett, Barbara 12n13
Kissel, Howard 40
Knowles, Ric 12n13
Koch, Ed 34–6, 41, 47–8
Kracauer, Siegfried 19
Kramer, Larry 136; *The Normal Heart* 5, 8–9, 23, 32–59
Kramer, Yale 84–6, 116
Kroll, Jack 50
Kruger, Steven F. 12n13; *Approaching the Millennium* 81
Kushner, Tony 136; *Angels in America* 4–5, 9, 60–96, 133, 139, 151

La Mama 102
Laramie, Wyoming 10, 127–37; Baptist and Mormon leaders of 142–4; earlier murders of gay men in 129; imagined community of 138; interviews of townspeople in 132–3, 134, 136, 150; as protagonist 133, 135–6, 138, 147; as synecdoche for the nation 137, 138, 150, 151–3
The Laramie Project (Kaufman) 5, 10–11, 125–62, 173; allusion to Jesus' crucifixion of 144; angels in 133, 140; *Angels in America* (Kushner) and 139–40, 151; assimilationism of 155; Brechtian devices in 134; Christian imagery in 138–47, 150–1; claims to objective documentary status 133–7; combination of documentary and spectacle in 133–7; compassion in 144–5; connection to earlier AIDS plays 151; criticism of 135, 172; demonstrated effect of reducing homophobic attitudes among audiences 154–5; Denver production of 133; as documentary 133–7; dramatic structure of 135; as ethnography 134; forgiveness and 137–8, 145–7; "gay panic defense" and 125, 126, 147–9, 154, 172; grounding in Christian compassion and mercy rather than in LGBT politics 133–4, 137–47, 149, 150–1, 154; HBO film production of 155, 157n36, 164, 166, 172; HIV/AIDs epidemic and 136–7, 151; horizon of expectations for spectators in 134–5, 151; juxtaposition in 134–5, 138–47; LGBT citizenship and 137; as mainstream rather than avant-garde 133; the media and 150–4; moral order in 137–8; move away from anger in 146–7; NBC production of 172; New York premiere of 146, 150; *The New York Times* and 152; normalization of LGBT civil rights issues in 154, 155, 166, 172; polychoral protagonist of 135–6; premiere of 128; reception of 150–4; reviews of 131, 150–4; spectacle in 133–7; study guides for 166; symbolism of fence in 144; at Union Square Theater 133; use of religion as basis for ideological work 138; U.S. imagined community in 153–4
LaRoche, Lyndon 51
Larson, Jonathan: death of 97–8, 104–8, 117, 167; life of 100; *Rent* 5, 9–10, 97–124
Latour, Bruno 8, 13, 23; *Reassembling the Social* 25–6
Law and Literature (Charles) 126
Lawson, D.S. 12n13, 44
Lee, Eugene 40
Leoncavallo, Rugerro, *La Bohème* 98, 111, 119
LGBT activists 33
LGBT characters 1–3, 6, 15, 26, 163–4; *see also specific plays*; acceptance of 64; canonization of 81; received as "universal" 81
LGBT citizens 86, 126, 163, 172; assimilation process and 14–15, 23, 24–5, 26, 60–5, 69–70, 73, 79–83, 86, 163, 167; comparison to Jews in Nazi Germany 19, 23; of color 2; compassion for 155; deaths of 147, 170–1; homeless 14; inclusion of 3, 72; invisibility of 128; legal protection of 126, 128, 147–50, 154; legal representation of 1; marginalized 14; move

from invisibility to visibility 172; normalization of 3, 5, 147–50; representation of 1–2, 3, 5, 9, 10; Shepard as martyr for 130; symbolic death faced by 127; in the U.S. national imaginary 3–7, 9, 15, 23, 26, 60–1, 63–5, 69–70, 72, 79–83, 86, 137, 167, 172; violence against 127–37, 147–54, 172; visibility of 1–5, 11, 23, 86, 127, 149–50, 154; white 2

LGBT civil rights 1, 3, 6, 14, 16–18, 22, 26, 50–1, 65–71, 78–86, 126–7, 137, 150, 163, 166; *Angels in America* (Kushner) and 5, 60, 62, 63–4, 66, 78–86; Bush Administration (George W.) and 172; commercialization of 9; *The Laramie Project* (Kaufman) and 166; *Rent* (Larson) and 9, 98, 112–19

LGBT communities, inclusion of 60–1

LGBTQ community 170–1, 174n15; activism and 172; assimilation of 173; legal protection of 125; suicide and 169; in U.S. national imaginary 171

LGBT theatre; *see also specific plays*: research on 6–7; studies of 12n13

Life magazine 37

Lindsey-Hogg, Michael 40

Loffredda, Beth 129

London 62, 65

Long, Thomas L. 12n13

Los Angeles 61–2, 65

Lucas, Billy 169

The Lucifer Effect: Understanding How Good People Turn Evil (Zimbardo) 27–8n15

Madison Square Garden 34

Madonna 101

Madsen, Christine 56–7n90

mainstream theatre 2–3, 18, 163; *see also specific plays*; activism and 3–4; capitalism and 5; conformity and 5, 8; culture industry and 26; definition of 16–17; influence of 164; Marxist critique of 7; the media and 7–8; political potential of 8, 32; prejudice towards 15–16; role in transforming dominant ideology 3–4, 5–6, 11, 21, 22, 26, 32, 52, 163, 173; supposedly conservative nature of 3–4

Mandell, Charlotte 154

marketing 21
Mark Taper Forum 61–2, 65
marriage equality 1, 14, 172
Martin, Hoyle 116
Marxist critique 7, 18
Massachusetts 56–7n90
mass communication 18, 23
mass media 24, 32
materialist melodrama 111–12
materialist semiotics 16
Matthew Shepard and James Byrd, Jr. Hate Crimes Act 172
McAdams, John 131
McCarthy, Joseph 87–8n14
McClintock, Anne 12n13
McConachie, Bruce 104, 111
McKinney, Aaron 125, 126, 130, 140, 143–9
McNulty, Charles, *Modern Drama* 80–1
Mead, George Herbert 24
Mecklenburg County Commission 116–17
the media 10–11, 21, 23, 33, 163; *see also* mass media; reviews; *specific media; specific writers and outlets*; *Angels in America* (Kushner) and 81–2, 118; coverage of HIV/AIDS epidemic 32; HIV/AIDS theatre and 173; *The Laramie Project* (Kaufman) and 150–4; local 16; mainstream theatre and 7–8; national 16; *The Normal Heart* (Kramer) and 118–19; *Rent* (Larson) and 98, 101–5, 113–14, 118–19; Rock Hudson announcement and 51–2; Shepard's murder and 128; sparked by *Angels in America* 64; sparked by Clinton's election and promises 64
media theory 23
Meese, Ed 63
melodrama 104, 111–12
The Melting Pot (Zangwill) 73
merchandise 11, 16; *see also specific plays*
Merrill, Lisa 12n13
methodology 163–4
Milgram, Stanley 19; *Obedience to Authority: An Experimental View* 28n16
military service, ban on LGBT service in 61, 63, 72–3
Milk, Harvey 169
Millenials 1
Millenium 72

Miller, Terry 164, 169, 170, 171
Miller, Tim 89n36
minority art, cultural appropriation of 99–100
Min Tian 45
mise-en-scène 16; *see also specific plays*
Modern Drama (McNulty and Tigner) 80–1, 129
Morales, Elliott 171
moral order, narrative structure and 137
Morissette, Alanis 101
Mormon Church 143, 144
Moses, Robert 34
mourning, ritual of 45–6
Mulatto 2–3
Mulvey, Anne 154
Munt, Sally 12n13
Murdoch, Rupert 49
Murger, Henri, *Scènes de la Vie de Bohème* 98
Murray, Marge 139

narrative structure, moral order and 137
nation 23–6; *see also* U.S. national imaginary
National Institutes of Health (NIH) 36
The Native 36
Nazi Germany 18–19, 20, 23, 172
NBC 172
NBC Symphony Orchestra 20, 164
NEA Four 89n36
NEA grants 68
Nederlander Theatre 102, 103, 104, 105
Nelson, Emmanuel S. 12n13
New Democrat movement 70–3
New England Journal of Medicine 36
The New Republic 82
news broadcasting 24
Newsday 84–6, 102
newspapers 6, 7–8, 23, 25, 163; performative aspect of 25–6; reading of 25; theories of 18
Newsweek 36, 50, 82
New York City 33, 35–6, 66, 98, 102, 165; 2015 Gay Pride celebrations 173; *Angels in America* (Kushner) production in 62–3; Broadway 68, 170; *see also specific productions*; Greenwich Village 39, 40, 85, 98, 99, 102, 103, 171; Times Square 66, 98, 102, 165
The New York City Tribune 43

New York magazine 41, 49
The New York Native 41, 45, 51, 52
The New York Observer 60, 150, 152–3
The New York Post 49, 150, 152, 153
The New York Review of Books 44
New York Shakespeare Festival/Public Theater 34–6
New York Theatre Workshop 97, 101–2, 103, 104–5, 107, 113, 115, 132
The New York Times 3, 23; *Angels in America* (Kushner) and 60, 67, 69, 82–3, 167; culture section 113; *The Laramie Project* (Kaufman) and 152; *The Normal Heart* (Kramer) and 36–8, 41, 43, 47–8, 168; *Rent* (Larson) and 100, 103–4, 106, 107, 112, 113–14, 167–8; Shepard's murder and 128; Sunday arts section 67; theatre section 38
Nichols, Mike 166–7
The Normal Heart (Kramer) 2, 5, 8–9, 32–59, 172; absense of concept of safe sex in 44; absorption in 45; acting in 44–5; activism of 38–40, 46, 50, 52; advertising campaigns 38; alienation in 44–5, 46; Brechtian elements of 40, 44, 45; collision of fictional and non-fictional time in 45–6; compared to Ibsen's *An Enemy of the People* 48–9; condemnations of promiscuity in 43–4; content of 38; culture industry and 50; direction of 40–1, 44–5; as educational rather than artistic 38–40, 43, 44, 46, 50, 52, 70; emphasis on affinities between gay and straight communities 42–3; HBO film production of 164, 165, 168–9; interpellation of spectators as activists 39–40, 44, 46; libel issues 36; marketing strategy 38; marriage in 43; material aspects of production 38–40, 44, 46; the media and 46, 118–19; merchandise plan 39–40; mise-en-scène 40–1; *The New York Times* and 168; opening of 3; political effects after opening day 47; at the Public Theatre 32, 37–40, 44, 46, 52, 168; realism of 40, 42, 44–5; reception of 33, 37–8; revelation of social boundaries in 46; reviews of 9, 23, 26, 34, 38, 42–5, 47–50, 49–50, 118–19; reviews of

film version 168; ritual of mourning in 45–6; scholarship on 37; self-consciousness of living history in 45–6; set design 40; spectators of 40–1, 42, 45–6; status as "first" play dealing with AIDS 33–4; success of 37–8, 42, 50; symbolism in 41–2; writing on the walls in 40–1, 45
normalization 5, 125–62, 172

Obama, Barack 11, 164, 170
Obedience to Authority: An Experimental View (Milgram) 28n16
Obergefell v. Hodges 1, 14
off-Broadway productions 2, 9, 10, 16, 97, 102–4; *see also specific plays and venues*
opening nights 17
oppositional readings 23
Orion, Michigan 125
Our Town (Wilder) 151–3

Pacino, Al 166
pamphlets 38–40
Papp, Gail Merrifield 34, 35
Papp, Joseph 34–6, 37, 38, 47–8, 52
parades 4
Parker, Mary-Louise 166
Patterson, Romaine 129, 139–41, 144, 148
Pelosi, Nancy 170
People in Trouble (Schulman) 99
People magazine 113, 114
Perestroika 72
performance: cultural politics and 17; "performance beyond the theatre" 4; political performance 6–7; politics of 26
Performance, Identity, and the Neo-Political Subject (Causy and Walsh) 17
Peterson, Jennifer 166
Phelan, Peggy 12n13
Phelps 158n62
Phelps, Fred 140, 141, 142, 144, 146
Philadelphia 130
Pierotti, Greg 144
pinklisting 73–4, 90n62
Pixar 170
Playbill 114
podcasts 163
Poitier, Sidney 3
political performance studies 12n13
political theatre, theory of 6–7

politics, spectatorship and 15–16
Poole, Mary 45
the press; *see* the media
Price, Kristen 147
production; *see also specific plays*: conditions of 16; location of 16–17; peripherals of 8; production text 16
program notes 16; *see also specific plays*
propaganda 19, 20
Proposition 64 (California) 51
protests 4
providential melodrama 111–12
Public Theatre 168; *Angels in America* (Kushner) and 64, 65, 67; architecture of 38, 39; *La Bohème* 119; location of 39, 40; *The Normal Heart* (Kramer) and 9, 32, 34–6, 37–40, 44, 46, 52, 168
Puccini, Giacomo, *La Bohème* 98, 111

Queer Nation, manifesto of 64
queer scholarship 6–7

radical performance 4, 15–16, 17, 26
Raisin in the Sun (Hansberry) 3
Ranson, Rebecca 33
Rather, Dan 36
Raywood, Keith 40
reader response theories 7–8
readers: ideologies of 25; of newspapers 25–6, 163
Reagan, Ronald 21, 63, 68, 71; acknowledgment of HIV/AIDS epidemic 33
Reagan Administration 32, 33, 60, 61, 63, 65, 71, 136–7, 170–1
Reassembling the Social (Latour) 25–6
reception 8, 16; *see also* reviews; *specific plays*; conditions of 16; ideological 163–4
Redford, Robert 132
Reinelt, Janelle 12n13, 69
Rent (Larson) 97–124, 130; appropriation of 1990s counterculture 98, 105; assimilation of LGBT citizens into U.S. national imaginary 112; authenticity and 98–104, 108, 112; breaking of the fourth wall in 108; Broadway production of 97–8, 102, 103, 104, 113; in Charlotte, North Carolina 98, 113, 115–17, 119; classical music and 100–1, 114; class in 109; Columbia

186 *Index*

Pictures film version of 164, 167–8; commercialization and 97–124; commercial potential beyond Broadway 115–17; commercial success of 9–10, 98, 113–14, 117–19; conditions of reception 118; conflation of author, cast, and characters in 106–8; conservative aspects of 9–10; copyright questions and 99; costumes of 102–3; cultural appropriation and 99–100, 105; danger and 106–8; depictions of poverty and counterculture 98–104, 112, 114–15, 118; emergent ideology of gay civil rights and 98; failings of film version 167–8; fashion spreads based on 114–15; faux bohemianism of 114–15; gay civil rights and 98; heterogeneity in 109–10; heterosexual characters with HIV/AIDS 118; HIV/AIDs epidemic and 9–10, 105, 106, 109–11, 118; horizon of expectations and 98; inclusivity of 113; influence of 113; intensity and excess of 107, 108; interviews about 104–5; jarring of norms in 109–10; Larson, Jonathan 5, 9–10; Larson's death and 97–8, 104–8, 117, 167; LGBT characters in 9–10; LGBT civil rights and 9; location of 98; lyrics of 101; mainstream popularity of 112; materialist melodrama and 111–12; the media and 98, 101–5, 113–14, 118–19; as melding rock and musical theatre 100–1; melodrama and 104–12, 119; minority cast and 106; *mise-en-scène* 98; *The New York Times* and 100, 103–4, 106, 107, 112, 113–14, 167–8; normalization of LGBT civil rights issues in 112–19; off-Broadway productions 97, 102–4; opera and 100–1, 114, 119; peripheral sales and 113; plot of 98–9, 100; politics as secondary in 115; popularity of 118–19; premiere of 98, 101, 104, 105, 113, 115; providential melodrama and 112; race in 109–10, 112; reception of 97, 99, 100; reviews of 98–101, 103–9, 113, 117, 118–19; reviews of film version 167–8; as rock opera 98, 100–1; same-sex love in 118; score of 100–1, 103, 107–8, 109–10, 114, 117; set of 102–3; setting of 112; sexuality in 109–11, 112; soundtrack of 113, 115; spectacle of 105–9, 114–15; ticket prices 105; ticket sales 113; timeless aspect of 112; touring productions and 113, 115, 117; transgender characters in 117–18
Republicans 71–2
reviews 4, 9, 16, 17, 23, 26; *see also specific productions*; as archival evidence of 8, 163–4; shift from newspapers to the Internet 163–4
Rich, Frank 3, 47–8, 67, 69, 100, 104, 112, 128–9
ritual communication 10–11, 24–5, 52
Roach, Joseph 46, 61
Roberts, Julia 165
Rolling Stone magazine 113, 114
Román, David 3, 4–5, 9, 12n13, 44, 61; *Acts of Intervention* 2, 37–8
Rosenberg, Ethel 87–8n14
Rosenberg, Julius 87–8n14
Rubin-Vega, Daphne 114
Ruffalo, Mark 165

safe sex 44
Salvato, Nick 12n13
same-sex marriage; *see* marriage equality
San Francisco 7, 32, 65
The San Francisco Chronicle 32, 33
Savage, Dan 11, 164, 169–72
Savran, David 4, 8, 12n13, 105
Schanke, Robert 12n13
Schindler, Amy 78
Schmit, Father Roger 141–6, 150–1
Schmitz, Jonathan T. 125
Schneider, Rebecca 12n13, 98
Schulman, Sarah 100; *People in Trouble* 99; *Stagestruck: Theater, AIDS, and the Marketing of Gay America* 99
Schultz, Jedadiah 139–41, 148
Scott, A.O. 167–8
Scott, Steve 142; "What Moral Order? A Report from the Trenches" 137
Sedgwick, Eve Kosofsky 12n13, 70, 126, 149
Seeger, Pete 100
Seller, Jeffrey 115
Sencer, David 48
Shatzky, Joel 41
Shepard, Dennis 145, 146, 147, 154
Shepard, Matthew 10, 125, 147, 158n62; appearance of 129; compared to Jesus Christ 129, 130, 144–5, 150–1; death of 172; HIV-positive status of

127, 130, 136, 151; "marketing" of 129–30; as martyr for LGBT civil rights 130, 150–1; memory of 166; murder of 125–6, 127–37, 138, 147–9; national media coverage of 129–30, 132; stature of 129; three factors making him face of hate crimes legislation 129–30
Shilts, Randy, *And the Band Played On* 32, 33, 52, 53n6
Shklovsky, Viktor 45
Silverman, Sarah 170
Silvernail, Warren D. 56–7n90
Simon, John 41, 49
Six Degrees of Separation 116
Slate 171
social boundaries 46
social media 11, 163, 173
social theory 23
Solomon, Alisa 12n13, 84, 146
Sommers, Michael 41
Sondheim, Steven 100
Southern Poverty Law Center 128
spectators: as activists in *The Normal Heart* 39–40, 44, 46; as analogous to voters 62; of *Angels in America* 83; commentary from 163–4; horizon of expectations and 83; of *The Normal Heart* (Kramer) 40–1, 42; positionality of 19–20; as *tabula rasa* 19–20
spectatorship 7–8, 15–16, 19–20, 26; *see also* spectators
Stagestruck: Theater, AIDS, and the Marketing of Gay America (Schulman) 99
Stanford Prison Experiment 27–8n15
State Ideological Apparatus 166
Steamboat Willie (Keaton) 105
Stonewall Inn 171
Streep, Meryl 166
"structure of feeling" concept (Williams) 22, 61
suicides 169
Sullivan, Andrew 63, 129–30
Summer of Sam 128
Sundance Theatre Institute 132
Sussman, Mark 102
Svich, Caridad 131
Szajna, Józef 132

TDR 102
Tectonic Theater Project 10, 126–7, 131–2, 134, 136, 142, 145–6, 150, 152–3

texts, decoding of 19–20, 26
theatre; *see also* performance; *specific kinds of theatre*: in non-typical environments 4; radical potential of 4; role in transformation to social visibility 2; theatre research 12n13
Theatre and National Identity: Re-Imagining Conceptions of Nation (Holdsworth) 24
Theatre Symposium 137
"Theses on the Philosophy of History" (Benjamin) 80–1
Thespis 131
Thomson, Lynn 99, 100
ticket sales 17
Tigner, Amy I., *Modern Drama* 129
Time magazine 36, 50, 63–4
TimeOut New York 113, 114
Times Square 66, 98, 102, 165
Today Show 36
Toscanini, Arturo 20, 164
transmission view of communication 24–5
Triumph of the Will 19
Tylenol scare of 1982 36, 40

Uncle Tom's Cabin (Aikin) 111, 117–18
Union Square Theater 133
Unitarian Church 143
United States 1; as "melting pot" 73
University of Wyoming 136
USA Today 82, 153
U.S. federal government 33; *see also specific administrations*
U.S. national imaginary 3, 5, 6–7, 18, 23, 60–1, 112, 137, 163; LGBTQ youth in 171
U.S. Supreme Court 14
utopian performatives 62

Vanity Fair 129–30
Variety magazine 82, 150, 152
venues 2, 17; *see also specific venues*
Viagas, Robert 114
victimhood 147
The Village Voice 36, 48–9, 84, 152
visibility 1–5, 11, 17, 23, 86, 127, 128, 149–50, 154, 172

The Wall Street Journal 83–4, 86, 113
Walmsley, Colin 14
Walsh, Finton 17
Walter Kerr Theatre 62, 65, 66–7, 70

Index

Wangh, Stephen 141, 145, 146
Warner, Sara 12n13
The Washington Post 36
Weixlmann, Joe 81
Wells Fargo 170
Wendt, Angela 103
West, Michael 56–7n90
Westboro Baptist Church 158n62
"What Moral Order? A Report from the Trenches," Scott, Steve 137
Wilde, Oscar 132
Wilder, Thornton, *Our Town* 151–3
Williams, Raymond 6, 7, 13, 22
Wilson, Edwin 83
Wing-Davey, Mark 69

Wolf, Stacy 12n13
Wolfe, George C. 65, 69–70
women 75–8, 80, 87
Wong, Penelope 154–5
World War II 18, 19
Wright, Jeffrey 166

Young, Harvey 12n13
YouTube 164, 169–71

Zangwill, Israel, *The Melting Pot* 73
Zimbardo, Philip G. 19; 27–8n15; *The Lucifer Effect: Understanding How Good People Turn Evil* 27–8n15
Zuidervaart, Lambert 13

Printed in Great Britain
by Amazon